Destination .NET: Migrating to Visual Basic .NET

PUBLISHED BY
Microsoft Press
A Division of Microsoft Corporation
One Microsoft Way
Redmond, Washington 98052-6399

Printed and bound in the United States of America.

1 2 3 4 5 6 7 8 9   QWT   8 7 6 5 4 3

Microsoft Press books are available through booksellers and distributors worldwide. For further information about international editions, contact your local Microsoft Corporation office or contact Microsoft Press International directly at fax (425) 936-7329. Visit our Web site at www.microsoft.com/mspress.

Acquisitions Editor: Rob Linsky
Project Editor: Barbara Moreland

SubAssy Part No. X09-48685
Body Part No. X09-48686

The readings in this book are taken from the following Microsoft Press publications. You can find complete descriptions of each title at the end of this book.

Upgrading Microsoft Visual Basic 6 to Microsoft Visual Basic .NET

Ed Robinson, Mike Bond, Robert Ian Oliver

Programming Microsoft Visual Basic .NET

Francesco Balena

Practical Standards for Microsoft Visual Basic .NET

James Foxall

Coding Techniques for Microsoft Visual Basic .NET

John Connell

Developing Windows-Based Applications with Microsoft Visual Basic .NET and Microsoft Visual C# .NET (Training Kit)

Table of Contents

Introduction   xi

Part I   **Visual Basic .NET**

1   **Visual Basic .NET Is More Than Visual Basic 6 + 1**   **3**

Why Break Compatibility?   6
   Adding New Features   6
   Fixing the Language   7
   Modernizing the Language   8
It Is Still Visual Basic   8
   Expect Subtle Differences   8
   Plan for a 95 Percent Automated Upgrade   9
Why Should I Upgrade?   10
   New Language Features   10
   Windows Forms   15
   New Web Development Features   16
   Better Development Environment   16
   Is Visual Basic Still the Best Choice for Visual Basic Developers?   17

2   **Visual Basic 6 and Visual Basic .NET: Differences**   **21**

.NET Framework vs. ActiveX   21
   .NET Framework   23
   Memory Management   24
   Type Identity   27
   Threading Model   30
Differences in the Development Environment   31
   Menu Editor   32
   Toolbox   33
   Property Browser   34
   Tab Layout Editor   35
Forms Packages   36
   A Single Standard for Windows Forms   36
   Two Forms Packages for the Price of One   37

Language Differences   37
        All Subroutine Calls Must Have Parentheses   39
        ByVal or *ByRef* Is Required   40
        Is That My Event?   40
        Arrays Must Have a Zero-Bound Lower Dimension   41
        Fixed-Length Strings Are Not Supported   42
        Variant Data Type Is Eliminated   42
        Visibility of Variables Declared in Nested Scopes Is Limited 43
    Changes in the Debugger   44
        No Edit and Continue   44
        Cannot Continue After an Error   44
        No Repainting in Break Mode   45
    The .NET Framework Class Library   45
    Structures   50

3   Exception Handing   53
    The Exception Object   54
    Types of Exception Handlers   55
    Writing an Exception Handler by Using *Try...Catch...Finally*   56
        Catching Exceptions   58
        Exception Handlers and the Call Stack   61
    Central Exception Handlers   64
        Logging Exceptions to a Text File   67
    Directives   70
        3.1 Use *Try...Catch...Finally* to handle unexpected as well as
        anticipated exceptions.   70
        3.2 Use a consistent format when dealing with
        unanticipated exceptions.   71
        3.3 Never blame the user.   72

4   Arrays, Lists, and Collections   75
    The Array Class   75
        Creating Nonzero-Based Arrays   77
        Copying Arrays   78
        Sorting Elements   79
        Clearing, Copying, and Moving Elements   81
        Searching Values   83
        Arrays of Arrays   85

The System.Collections Namespace	86
The ICollection, IList, and IDictionary Interfaces	86
The BitArray Class	88
The Stack Class	90
The Queue Class	91
The ArrayList Class	92
The Hashtable Class	95
The SortedList Class	98
The StringCollection and StringDictionary Classes	101
Custom Collection and Dictionary Classes	103
The ReadOnlyCollectionBase Abstract Class 1	103
The CollectionBase Abstract Class	105
The DictionaryBase Abstract Class	107
5 Windows Forms Applications	**109**
Form Basics	109
The Form Designer	110
The Windows Forms Class Hierarchy	113
Using Menus	126
Creating Menus at Design Time	126
Using the MainMenu Component	126
Separating Menu Items	128
Modifying Menus at Run Time	130
Enabling and Disabling Menu Commands	130
Displaying Check Marks on Menu Items	131
Displaying Radio Buttons on Menu Items	131
Making Menu Items Invisible	131
Cloning Menus	132
Merging Menus at Run Time	132
Adding Menu Items at Run Time	133
Part II Object-Oriented Programming	
6 Object-Oriented Programming in Visual Basic .NET	**137**
An Object Lesson	137
Starting Out with Objects	138
A Class Is Really Only a Blueprint	138

Let's Talk Objects   139
Our Form as an Object   140
Reading, Writing, Invoking   142
Inheritance   144
Understanding Namespaces   146
Polymorphism   150

7   Inheritance   **151**

Inheritance in Previous Visual Basic Versions   151
Inheritance by Delegation   152
Inheritance and Late-Bound Polymorphic Code   152
Early-Bound Polymorphic Code   153
Inheritance in Visual Basic .NET   154
Extending the Derived Class   155
Using the Derived Class   155
Inheriting Events   157
Inheriting Shared Members   157
Polymorphic Behavior   158
Overriding Members in the Base Class   159
Override Variations   161
The MyBase Keyword   162
Constructors in Derived Classes   163
Finalizers in Derived Classes   165
The MyClass Keyword   166
Member Shadowing   169
Redefining Shared Members   173
Sealed and Virtual Classes   174
The NotInheritable Keyword   174
The MustInherit Keyword   175
The MustOverride Keyword   176
Scope   178
Nested Classes   178
Public, Private, and Friend Scope Qualifiers   181
The Protected Scope Qualifier   182
The Protected Friend Scope Qualifier   185
Using Scope Qualifiers with Constructors   186
Redefining Events   189

Part III   ADO.NET

8   ADO.NET   195

Introducing ADO.NET   195
Major Changes from ADO   195
.NET Data Providers   196
Database Independence with ADO.NET   197
The Connection Object   199
    Setting the ConnectionString Property   200
    Opening and Closing the Connection   203
    Working with Transactions   209
The Command Object   213
    Creating a Command Object   215
    Issuing Database Commands   216
    Reading Data   216
    Working with Parameters and Stored Procedures   219
The DataReader Object   226
    Iterating over Individual Rows   226
    Reading Column Values   228
    Using Specific SQL Server Types   231
    Reading Multiple Resultsets   232
The DataSet Object   234
    Exploring the DataSet Object Model   234
The DataAdapter Class   239
    Introducing the DataAdapter   240
    Reading Data from a Database   242
Adding a DataAdapter Object to Our Program   243
Finishing the User Interface   247
A Sneak Preview of Our Data from the DataAdapter   248

Part IV   ASP.NET

9   ASP.NET and Web Services   253

A Look Back at ASP   253
Why ASP.NET?   254
Our First Web Form   256
    New Server Controls   259

The HTML Presentation Template 261
Viewing the Code-Behind File 264
Setting the Properties on Our Web Page 265
Adding the Calendar Control Code 266
Running the Web Form 267
Examining the HTML Sent to the Browser 268
Building a Loan Payment Calculator 270
Building Our Loan Application Project 273
Adding Code to the Code-Behind Form 275
The Life of a Web Form 276
How Our Program Works 277
Taking a Closer Look at Our Drop-Down List 279
Adding the Payment Schedule Page 280
Adding Our Class Code 282
How the Calculator Works 285
Tracing Our Program 288
Web Services: The New Marketplace 289
What Are Web Services? 289
OK, Now How Do We Communicate? 290
Finding Out Who Is Offering What in the Global Marketplace 291
Where Are Web Services Going? 293
Building a Web Service 294
Run the Program 296
Consuming the MagicEightBall Web Service 299
Building Our Web Services Client Program 301
Adding a Proxy Class to Our Program 302
Adding Code to Get Our Magic Eight Ball Answers 303

Index 305

Introduction

When Microsoft started to design their .NET Framework, they decided that it would be valuable for their primary developer source languages—Visual Basic, C++, and C#—to generate executable code (through the common language runtime, or CLR) that would be compatible regardless of the original source language. To achieve this goal, the languages would need to standardize on data types, parameter passing, and a common set of support classes.

This design goal lead to some modifications to the original source languages, with Visual Basic most affected. These included changes to language syntax, data types, and the underlying database model; more object orientation; and a number of new and exciting features including support for Web applications and XML technologies. In the long run, these modifications will have a positive impact on the ability of Visual Basic .NET programmers to create solutions using state-of-the-art technologies. However, in the short run, the changes from Visual Basic 6.0 will present some challenges to faculty who teach programming in Visual Basic.

Microsoft professionals recognized these challenges and assembled a team of college faculty members to advise them on helping other faculty move from Visual Basic 6.0 to Visual Basic .NET. Together they have designed a transitional course and identified material from a variety of Microsoft Press publications that would help support the course. This book is the result of that effort.

This book does not cover the entire Visual Basic .NET language nor does it cover the entire .NET Framework. Other books provide that complete coverage. Instead, the main goal for this book is to identify and document those language features that have changed in the move from Visual Basic 6.0 to Visual Basic .NET and to highlight new features such as the way errors are handled, the ADO.NET database model, new and expanded object-oriented features, and Web Forms. Along with your course material, the book will provide you with information that should help in your transition to Microsoft Visual Basic .NET.

Many of us have been involved with teaching programming using Basic since the original Dartmouth Basic (circa 1964). We have seen Basic evolve over the years and have found its evolution to be valuable and exciting. We believe that the latest incarnation of the language, Visual Basic .NET, continues the evolution in a very positive way. Combined with the Microsoft Visual Studio

IDE, Visual Basic .NET provides an awesome set of features while still maintaining its ease of use for the beginner. As faculty, we have to "unlearn" some things that we were comfortable with as we transition to Visual Basic .NET. We must remember, however, that a student new to the language will not have to "unlearn" anything. Thus, what we consider odd compared to the way we used to do things will not seem that way to a student learning Visual Basic .NET for the first time.

We hope you find this text helpful as you move from Visual Basic 6.0 to your new destination, Visual Basic .NET.

William Burrows, Professor Emeritus
University of Washington

Part I

Visual Basic .NET

Reading 1

Visual Basic .NET Is More Than Visual Basic 6 + 1

If you're familiar with Visual Basic but aren't familiar with Visual Basic .NET, you may be wondering why we have written a book on upgrading. Surely Visual Basic .NET will open Visual Basic 6 projects as effortlessly as Visual Basic 6 opens Visual Basic 5 projects. "How different can Visual Basic .NET be?" you might ask. So before we start discussing the details of upgrading, let's clear up any confusion: Visual Basic .NET, the latest version of Visual Basic, is not merely Visual Basic 6 with a few new features added on. Instead, Visual Basic has been thoroughly redesigned and restructured. The language has been modernized, with new, richer object models for data, forms, transactions, and almost everything else. The file formats have also changed.

Unfortunately, these changes mean that Visual Basic .NET is not entirely backward compatible with Visual Basic 6. Projects from previous versions need to be upgraded before they will compile and run in Visual Basic .NET. The Upgrade Wizard handles much of this work for you, but most real-world projects will require additional modifications before they can be run. Some people consider moving applications from Visual Basic 6 to .NET to be a migration rather than an upgrade, but the changes in the language are a logical step, and they make Visual Basic more powerful than ever before.

This is an exciting time for Visual Basic developers. Sure, upgrading applications takes some effort, but on the other hand Visual Basic .NET is incredibly capable, extending Visual Basic's Rapid Application Development

(RAD) model to the server and to the Web. Visual Basic .NET adds more features to Visual Basic than did Visual Basic 2, 3, 4, 5, and 6 combined. Microsoft made the changes because the focus of the language has shifted from previous versions. Whereas Visual Basic 6 was primarily a Windows development tool, Visual Basic .NET is designed to leverage the .NET platform, enabling the user to create Windows applications, console applications, class libraries, NT services, Web Forms applications, and XML Web services—all while allowing seamless integration with other programming languages.

Let's look a little deeper at Visual Basic .NET to see where it differs from Visual Basic 6. We will look at the following three issues:

- The development environment
- The syntax of the language and object models of the classes
- The run-time behavior of the compiled components

In each of these three areas, Visual Basic .NET departs from the conventions of Visual Basic 6. First, the integrated development environment (IDE) has been redesigned to house all of the Visual Studio languages: Visual Basic, C#, and Visual C++. Second, the language itself has been modernized, removing some keywords, such as *GoSub*; adding new keywords, like *Inherits*; and changing the meaning of other keywords, like *Return* and *Integer*. Finally, the run-time behavior of the compiled components is different. .NET applications are free-threaded; Visual Basic .NET projects are compiled to "assemblies" rather than to familiar Win32 applications, and variables and objects are garbage-collected, meaning that they lack a deterministic lifetime. A noticeable effect of this last change is that the class *Finalize* event is not triggered until sometime after the object is actually destroyed. Let's continue to look at what these changes mean to the Visual Basic developer.

With so much that is new, how familiar will it all be to traditional Visual Basic users? To what extent can you leverage your existing Visual Basic skills when you move to Visual Basic .NET? To answer these questions, let's take a quick look at the history of Visual Basic.

In 1991, Microsoft released Visual Basic 1, which opened the doors to Windows RAD. Visual Basic 1 was an instant success, and it's easy to see why. Before Visual Basic, developers had to write *WndProc* handlers, work with pointers, and know when to apply the Pascal calling convention to methods. Visual Basic took over the handling of all of these details, allowing developers to concentrate on building business objects instead of writing the basic plumbing in every program.

In Visual Basic versions 2 though 6, Microsoft kept the underlying architecture of the product the same and simply added new features. Visual Basic 2 and 3 introduced the property grid, Data Access Objects (DAO) database programming, and object linking and embedding (OLE), resulting in a great set of features for Windows 3.1 programming. In 1995, Microsoft released Visual Basic 4, which enabled developers to write 32-bit EXEs, ActiveX controls, and class libraries. The year 1995 also saw the explosion of the Internet, and people began wanting to build Web sites. With versions 5 and 6, Visual Basic added its own flavor of Web development—WebClasses, ActiveX documents, and Dynamic HTML (DHTML) pages—yet for the most part, it still remained a Windows development tool.

It's interesting to compare Visual Basic 1 with Visual Basic 6 to see how far the language has come. Visual Basic 1 had no IntelliSense, no support for open database connectivity (ODBC), no classes, limited debugging, no support for COM components, no Property Browser, no Web development features, and it created only EXEs. Visual Basic 6 had come a long way from the basic forms and modules development of version 1, yet it still had the spirit of Visual Basic. Visual Basic .NET also has that spirit: It has the same human-readable language, case insensitivity, support for late binding, automatic coercions, and familiar Visual Basic keywords, functions, and constructs, like *Left$*, *MsgBox*, and *On...Error...GoTo*. If you're a Visual Basic 6 programmer, it's a comfortable step to Visual Basic .NET. Yes, there are new concepts to learn, but your existing knowledge of Visual Basic is a great foundation.

After the release of Visual Basic 6, Microsoft was faced with a challenge. Developer needs were changing. More and more programmers were developing for the Web, and the Web development capabilities built into Visual Basic 6 were not addressing their needs. Visual Basic's DHTML pages and ActiveX documents were client-side technologies, meaning that both the component and the Visual Basic runtime had to be installed on client machines. Visual Basic's WebClasses, a server-based technology, stored state on the server and wasn't scalable. In addition, the design experience for both WebClasses and DHTML pages could only be described as rudimentary! In short, the technologies were too limiting. Internet developers wanted "thin" clients, not Visual Basic downloads. They wanted code that ran on the server. They wanted security, and they needed scalability, since the more successful a Web site was, the more people would use it concurrently, and therefore the more capacity it had to have.

Clearly, a better architecture was needed. Programmers had also been asking for some significant new language features: inheritance, easier access to the underlying platform, and a solution for the many different component versioning problems that had collectively been labeled "DLL hell." When looking for a solution to these problems, Microsoft also saw the opportunity to create a unified framework for developing applications. To understand why such a framework was desirable, consider that developers wanting to create forms for

Windows in Visual Basic 6, Visual C++, and Microsoft Office Visual Basic for Applications (VBA) had to learn a different forms package for each language. If only there were a common forms package for all these products, life would be so much simpler! This objective and others led Microsoft to develop a common framework available to all .NET languages.

One side effect of giving all languages access to a common framework is that each language must support the same data types. This support prevents the sort of headaches familiar to anyone who has tried to use Windows APIs from Visual Basic 6. Once all languages support the same data types, it's simple to add cross-language interoperability: inheritance, debugging, security access, and an integrated compilation process. As you can see, the benefits of such a system would be amazing—and that system is exactly what the .NET platform is: a multiple-language system with a common forms package, set of base classes, and data types. For Visual Basic to be part of this revolution meant more than just changing the language—it meant reconceptualizing it from the ground up for the .NET platform.

Why Break Compatibility?

Why did Microsoft redesign and restructure the language? Why couldn't it add these new features and still keep compatibility with Visual Basic 6? There are several reasons for this, as we discuss in the sections that follow.

Adding New Features

Some of the new features in Visual Basic .NET could not have been added without out a redesign. Adding visual inheritance and accessibility support to the forms package required redesigning the forms object model. Adding *Interface* statements and attributes to the language made the language more powerful by enabling a greater degree of fine-tuning but required changing the language and file formats. Fixing "DLL hell" meant that versioning and deployment had to be redesigned.

By far the biggest reason for the changes, however, was the need to integrate Visual Basic with the .NET platform. Cross-language inheritance, debugging, and unfettered access to the underlying APIs required the standardization of data types across languages, which meant changing arrays to be zero based and removing fixed-length strings from the language. Redesigning the Web and data access classes to be more scalable meant even more changes from Visual Basic 6.

Fixing the Language

Visual Basic has grown over time, and as the language has been extended, some areas have become inconsistent and problematic. A good example of such an area is default properties. The rules for when an assignment is to be a default property and when it is to be an object have become inconsistent. Consider the following Visual Basic 6 example, where *Form1* is a form in the current project:

```
Dim v As Variant
v = Form1
```

This code causes an error because Visual Basic 6 tries to assign the default property of the form (the controls collection) to the variable *v*. Contrast this behavior with the following Visual Basic 6 code:

```
Dim v As Variant
Set v = Form1
```

In this example, *v* is assigned the value *Form1*. In both examples, the right side of the expression is exactly the same, yet the value changes depending on the context. To anyone who didn't write the code, it's unclear from looking at the code what is being assigned: the object or the default property of the object. In Visual Basic .NET, parameterless default properties are not supported and must be resolved.

Another example of an inconsistent feature is the *New* statement. Consider the following Visual Basic 6 code:

```
Dim c1 As New Class1
Dim c2 As Class1: Set c2 = New Class1
```

At first glance, the two lines seem to do exactly the same thing. Both *c1* and *c2* are being set to new instances of *Class1*. Yet the two lines have quite different behavior. The statement

```
Dim c1 As New Class1
```

means that the variable will be re-created if it is set to *Nothing* and subsequently reused, whereas the effect of

```
Dim c2 As Class1: Set c2 = New Class1
```

is that *c2* is created once. If *c2* is set to *Nothing*, it will not be re-created automatically if it is referenced again. This subtle difference in behavior can lead to hard-to-find bugs. In Visual Basic .NET, both statements cause one instance of the class to be created. If the class is destroyed, it is not automatically re-created if it is referenced again.

Modernizing the Language

Another reason for breaking compatibility is to modernize the language. For example, the meaning of *Long* is now 64 bits, *Integer* is 32 bits, and the keyword *Type* has been changed to *Structure*. Some of these changes we can probably attribute to the "floodgate effect." Once Microsoft opened the floodgates to new features and changes to fix the language, it became more acceptable to make other changes that were not quite as critical.

It Is Still Visual Basic

Despite the changes, programmers will still recognize the Visual Basic they know and love. Let's now look at what changes you will expect to see moving to Visual Basic .NET.

Expect Subtle Differences

Visual Basic .NET has been rebuilt for the .NET platform. What does this statement mean? It means that the product has been rewritten from the ground up. One of the side effects of rewriting Visual Basic is that any similarities with previous versions of the language had to be added intentionally—you don't get them for free, as you do when you simply add new features to an existing code base. A programming language is composed of a million subtle nuances: the behavior of the *Format* function, the order of events on a form, and the undocumented hacks that are possible, like subclassing a form's message loop. Some of these subtleties are not exactly the same in Visual Basic .NET, and after upgrading an application, you may find small differences in the way the application works.

A good example is the *Currency* data type. In Visual Basic 6, the *Currency* data type has 4 digits of precision. In Visual Basic .NET, the *Currency* data type is renamed *Decimal* and has 12 digits of precision. If you run the following line of code in Visual Basic 6:

```
MsgBox( CCur(10/3) )
```

it produces 3.3333. If you run the equivalent line of code in Visual Basic .NET,

```
MsgBox( CDec(10 / 3) )
```

the result is 3.333333333333. This is not a huge change, but it underlies a principle of upgrading: Visual Basic .NET is subtly different from Visual Basic 6, and therefore upgraded applications will be different from their Visual Basic 6 counterparts in subtle ways. In most cases you will not notice the difference, yet it's important to be aware of the changes and to test your applications thoroughly after upgrading them. Now, let's turn our attention to upgrading.

The Decision to Break Compatibility

When did Microsoft decide to break compatibility with Visual Basic 6? It was actually in early December 1999, during the development of Visual Basic .NET. Until that time, Visual Basic .NET was being developed to support the notion of "Visual Basic 6 sourced" projects that allowed you to edit and compile Visual Basic 6 projects in Visual Basic .NET. These projects would have a compatibility switch turned on, meaning that the language would be backward compatible with Visual Basic 6 and would even have access to the old Visual Basic 6 forms package.

By the end of 1999, it was obvious that this strategy wasn't working. Little differences were slipping through: The old forms package could not be fully integrated into .NET, and the Visual Basic 6 sourced projects could not use some of the new features of the .NET platform. At that point Microsoft made the decision to break compatibility and instead concentrate on ensuring that people could upgrade their projects from Visual Basic 6 to Visual Basic .NET.

Plan for a 95 Percent Automated Upgrade

The effect of the changes and subtle differences in Visual Basic .NET is that, unlike previous versions of Visual Basic, most real-world projects cannot be upgraded 100 percent automatically. To understand why, consider that for a 100 percent upgrade there has to be a one-to-one correlation between every element of Visual Basic 6 and a corresponding element in Visual Basic .NET. Unfortunately, this correlation does not exist. The upgrade process is closer to 95 percent, meaning that the Visual Basic .NET Upgrade Wizard upgrades 95 percent of your application, and you modify 5 percent of the application to get it working. What does 5 percent mean? If it took you 100 days to write the original Visual Basic 6 application, you might expect to take 5 days to upgrade it. This number is not set in stone—some applications are easier to upgrade than others, and the experience of the person doing the upgrade is an important factor.

Once you've gotten your application working, Visual Basic .NET has a bunch of exciting new features that you can use to add value to your application straight away. We encourage you to think of the upgrade as occurring in three steps:

1.   Use the Upgrade Wizard to bring your application into Visual Basic .NET.

2.   Make the modifications to get your application working.

3.   Start adding value with the great new features of Visual Basic .NET.

Why Should I Upgrade?

If it requires work to upgrade your applications from Visual Basic 6 to Visual Basic .NET, you may wonder, "Is upgrading worth the trouble? Why should I bother to upgrade an application that requires modifications when it works in Visual Basic 6 today?" The main reason for upgrading is to take advantage of the new features of Visual Basic .NET. What are these new features? Listing them all would be a book in itself. The following sections discuss some of the features that people commonly add to their upgraded applications.

New Language Features

Visual Basic .NET adds a number of new language features that make the language more powerful and will forever dispel the myth that Visual Basic is a "toy" programming language.

Inheritance

For years we developers had been asking Microsoft to add "real" inheritance to Visual Basic. Sure, Visual Basic 6 supports interface inheritance, but we wanted more; we wanted implementation inheritance. We wanted to benefit from code reuse and to truly implement object-oriented designs. Visual Basic .NET fully supports inheritance, via the new *Inherits* keyword. You can inherit classes from within your own application, from other applications, and from .NET components written in other languages. You can even use inheritance in forms to inherit the layout, controls, and code of another form. This is called *visual inheritance*. The following code illustrates the use of the *Inherits* keyword:

```
Public Class BaseClass
End Class
```

```
Public Class InheritedClass : Inherits BaseClass
End Class
```

Interfaces in Code

Along with "real" inheritance, Visual Basic .NET still supports interface inheritance and improves on it by providing the *Interface* keyword. The *Interface*
keyword defines the interfaces in code. Your classes then implement the interfaces, as in the following example:

```
Interface myInterface
    Function myFunction()
End Interface
Public Class myImplementedClass
    Implements myInterface
    Function myFunction() _
    Implements myInterface.myFunction
        'Some Code
    End Function
End Class
```

Structured Exception Handling

In addition to supporting the familiar *On...Error...GoTo* error catching, Visual
Basic .NET provides a *Try...Catch...End Try* exception-handling block that adds
error handling. This construct allows you to embed code within an error-handling
block. A great use for this type of block is to create a global error handler for your
application by including a *Try...Catch* block in the startup object such as Sub
Main. In the following example, *Sub Main* opens a new instance of *Form1* and
will catch and report any errors that are thrown anywhere in the application:

```
Sub Main()
    Try
        Windows.Forms.Application.Run( _
        New Form1())
    Catch ex As Exception
        MsgBox(ex.Message)
    End Try
End Sub
```

Arithmetic Operator Shortcuts

All arithmetic operators in Visual Basic .NET now have shortcuts that let you operate on and assign the result back to a variable. For example, in Visual Basic 6, you
might write

```
Dim myString As String
myString = myString & "SomeText"
```

In Visual Basic .NET, you can write this in a much more elegant format:

```
Dim myString As String
myString &= "SomeText"
```

These expression shortcuts apply to &=, *=, +=, -=, /=, \=, and ^=. Note that you can also use the old Visual Basic 6–style expressions.

Overloaded Functions

Visual Basic .NET introduces function overloading. With overloading, you can declare multiple functions with the same name, each accepting a different number of parameters or accepting parameters of different types. For example, suppose that you have a method that deletes a customer from a database. You might want to create two versions of the *deleteCustomer* method, one to delete a customer based on ID and one to delete a customer by name. You can do so in Visual Basic .NET as follows:

```
Sub deleteCustomer(ByVal custName As String)
    'Code that accepts a String parameter

End Sub
Sub deleteCustomer(ByVal custID As Integer)
    'Code that accepts an Integer parameter
End Sub
```

Attributes

Visual Basic .NET also now includes attributes. Attributes give one the ability to fine-tune how an application behaves. They modify the behavior of code elements and can be applied to methods, classes, interfaces, and the application itself. You can use attributes to explicitly declare the GUID for a class or to define how a variable should be marshaled when it is passed to a COM object. Suppose, for example, that you have written a common utility function that you want the debugger always to step over, rather than step into. The *DebuggerHidden* attribute allows you to do this:

```
<DebuggerHidden()> _
Function nToz(ByVal input) As Integer
    If Not IsNumeric(input) Then input = 0
    Return Input
End Function
```

Multithreading

By default, your Visual Basic .NET applications are single threaded, but the language has new keywords that allow you to spawn new threads. This ability can be very useful if you have processes that take a long time to complete and that can run in the background. The following example creates a new thread and uses it to run the subroutine *loadResultsFromDatabase*:

```
Sub Main()
    Dim myThread As New Threading.Thread( _

    AddressOf loadResultsFromDatabase)
    mythread.Start()
End Sub
Sub loadResultsFromDatabase()
    'Some Code
End Sub
```

Reduced Programming Errors

Visual Basic .NET helps you reduce programming errors by supporting stronger type checking. For example, if you use the wrong *enum* value for a property or you assign a variable type to an incompatible type, the compiler will detect and report it at design time. With ADO.NET, you can add strongly typed datasets to your application, and if you refer to an invalid field name, it will be picked up as a compile error instead of a run-time error. These features allow you to catch errors as you write your program. For the ultimate in strong type checking, you can use *Option Strict On* in your application, which prohibits late binding and ensures that you use conversion functions whenever you assign a variable from one type to another. This feature can be useful in applications that don't use late binding, but it enforces a stricter and more verbose coding standard than many developers are used to.

The .NET Framework

In addition to the familiar VBA library of functions, such as *Left$*, *Right$*, *Command$*, and the Win32 APIs, Visual Basic .NET has access to the .NET Framework, which is designed specifically for Visual Basic, C#, and the other .NET languages. The .NET Framework is a collection of more than 3800 classes and 28,000 methods for forms, graphics, XML, Internet development, file access, transactions, and almost everything else you can think of. The set of .NET classes you will most likely become familiar with first is the new forms package—Windows Forms—which looks a lot like the familiar Visual Basic 6 forms package but which is implemented as a set of .NET classes available to all languages. The next section describes the features of this package.

✳✳✳

Data Types Are Upgraded to Fit

The storage size for Visual Basic intrinsic types such as *Integer* and *Long* has changed in Visual Basic .NET. In Visual Basic 6 an *Integer* is 16 bits and a *Long* is 32 bits. In Visual Basic .NET an *Integer* is 32 bits and a *Long* is 64 bits. Most of the time it doesn't matter whether you use an *Integer* instead of a *Long*. If you have a loop index that goes from 0 to 10, you can nitpick over the performance implications of using one size or another, but generally it makes no difference. The program works the same way.

Sometimes, however, the size difference matters. For example, if you're calling Windows API functions that require a 32-bit integer argument, you had better use a *Declare* statement that declares the argument as 32 bits.

To keep your application running smoothly after upgrade, the Upgrade Wizard declares all of your numeric types to use the correct Visual Basic .NET equivalent based on size. This means that an *Integer* variable is upgraded to *Short*. A variable of type *Long* is upgraded to type *Integer*. In the case of the *Variant* type, the Upgrade Wizard maps to the closest equivalent type found in Visual Basic .NET: *Object*. Table 7-4 gives a mapping of types between Visual Basic 6 and Visual Basic .NET. The table provides mappings where the name of the type is different between Visual Basic 6 and Visual Basic .NET. All other types, such as *Byte*, *Single*, *Double*, and *String,* map as is.

Table 7-4   Mapping of Types Between Visual Basic 6 and Visual Basic .NET

Visual Basic 6 Type	Upgrades to Visual Basic .NET Type
Integer	Short
Long	Integer
Variant	Object
Currency	Decimal

✳✳✳

From *Updating Microsoft Visual Basic 6.0 to Microsoft Visual Basic .NET* by Ed Robinson, Mike Bond, and Ian Oliver. pp. 143-144. (Redmond: Microsoft Press. 2002.) Copyright © 2002 by Microsoft Corporation.

Windows Forms

Windows Forms is a new forms development system that replaces the old Visual Basic forms. Along with features that make it powerful and easy to use, Windows Forms is available to all Visual Studio .NET languages.

Faster Development

Windows Forms in Visual Basic .NET has several features that speed up development. An in-place menu editor and visual editing of tab orders make form design easier. Control anchoring allows you to remove all your old resizing code and instead visually anchor the controls so that they remain a fixed length from the edge of the form and resize whenever the form resizes. Visual inheritance allows you to inherit the controls, properties, layout, and code of a base form. A good use for this feature is to define a standard form layout for an application, with a standard size, header, footer, and close button. You can then inherit all forms from this standard form.

GDI+

GDI+ allows you to add rich visual effects to your application. For example, to make a form semitransparent, you would place the following line of code in the form load event:

```
Me.Opacity = 0.5
```

Figure 1-1 shows the effects of visual inheritance and GDI+ semitransparency in a Windows application.

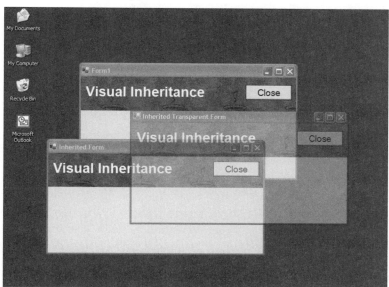

Figure 1-1   Visual inheritance and GDI+ semitransparency.

Internationalization

Windows Forms has built-in support for internationalization. To add support for other languages, you set the *Localizable* property of the form to *True*, set the *Language* property to the desired language, and then change the *Font* and *Size* properties of the form and controls. Every change that you make is saved as specific to the current locale. For example, you can have different-sized controls with different text for both Spanish and English.

New Web Development Features

Visual Basic .NET offers many enhancements to Web development. Two of the most significant involve XML and Web Forms.

Better Support for XML

Visual Basic .NET has designers that allow visual editing of HTML documents, XML documents, and XML schemas. In addition, there are .NET Framework classes that support serializing and deserializing any .NET class to and from XML. Visual Basic .NET can create XML Web services that use HTTP to pass XML backward and forward to other applications. If your application uses XML, Visual Basic .NET has great support for it. If you're looking to add XML support to your application (or to learn how to use XML), Visual Basic .NET is a great tool for doing so.

Web Services and Web Forms

Visual Basic .NET allows you to add Web services to your application. As you will see later in this book, in many cases you can actually convert your business objects to Web services. You can also easily add a Web Forms presentation layer that leverages your Visual Basic 6 or upgraded business objects. Visual Basic .NET makes Web development as easy as Windows development.

Better Development Environment

Along with language, form, and Web development enhancements, the IDE in Visual Basic .NET has a number of new features.

Cross-Language Interoperability

Visual Basic .NET is designed for cross-language interoperability. Because .NET unifies types, controls and components written in one language can easily be used in another. Anyone who has struggled to get a Visual Basic 6 user control to work in a Visual C++ project will immediately recognize the benefits of this. You can inherit from a class written in any other language built on the .NET platform or create components in other languages that inherit from your Visual Basic classes. Visual Studio .NET provides a single environment for developing and compiling multilanguage applications. Using the unified debugger, you can step from a component written in one language into another written in a different language. You can also debug COM+ services and step into SQL Server stored procedures.

Background Compiler and Task List

Visual Basic .NET has a compiler that continually works in the background. Compilation errors are flagged in code in real time with blue squiggle underlines. The Task List updates in real time with the list of compilation errors, and it also shows any ToDo comments you add to your code. ToDo comments are a great way to keep track of what you still need to do. For example, if you add a button to a form, and plan to finish the click code later, you can add a comment like

```
'TODO: Finish the code later
```

and the statement appears in the Task List. You can filter the Task List by task type and even choose what sort of comments are shown using the Task List pane. Figure 1-2 shows the Visual Basic .NET Task List.

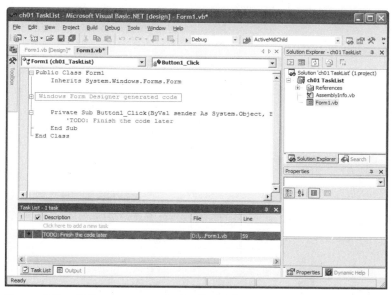

Figure 1-2   ToDo comments in the Task List.

Is Visual Basic Still the Best Choice for Visual Basic Developers?

If you are faced with learning the new features of Visual Basic .NET, you may ask yourself, "Why should I stick with Visual Basic? Why don't I choose another language instead? Why not move to C# (a new language in Visual Studio .NET derived from C++)?" Although the choice is yours, we should point out that Visual Basic .NET is now as powerful as C#, Visual C++, or any other language. All the .NET languages have access to the same .NET Framework classes. These classes are powerful, and they allow Visual Basic .NET to smash through the "glass ceiling" of previous versions.

Visual Basic .NET also keeps the spirit of Visual Basic alive. It is designed by Visual Basic developers for Visual Basic developers, whereas a language like C# is designed for C developers. Each language has some unique features that are not available in other languages. Let's compare C# with Visual Basic to see what makes each language unique.

Features Found in C# but Not in Visual Basic .NET

The C# language supports pointers. Pointers allow you to write "unsafe" code that modifies memory locations directly. The following code shows how to use pointers in C#:

```
unsafe static void Main(string[] args)
{
    int myInt = 5;
    int * myptr =  & myInt;
    * myptr = 55;
    Console.WriteLine(myInt.ToString() );
}
```

Although Visual Basic .NET doesn't support pointers in the language itself, you can still access memory locations using methods of the .NET *Garbage Collector* class. C# also supports document comments that allow you to embed self-documenting comments in your source code. These comments are compiled into the metadata of the component and can be extracted and built into help files.

Features Found in Visual Basic .NET but Not in C#

Visual Basic .NET's most appealing feature is the human-readable Visual Basic language, which is case insensitive with great IntelliSense. If you declare a variable as *MyVariable* and then later change the case to *myVariable*, Visual Basic .NET automatically changes the case of all occurrences in the code. C# and Visual C++ don't do this. In fact, C# treats *MYVariable* and *myVariable* as two separate variables. Most Visual Basic programmers have grown to know and become comfortable with case-insensitive behavior and will find Visual Basic .NET the most natural language to use.

Visual Basic .NET also supports late binding and optional parameters. C# supports neither of these. In addition, Visual Basic supports automatic coercions between types. For example, in C#, you cannot assign a *Long* to an *Integer* without using a conversion method (since it may cause an overflow). Visual

Basic allows narrowing conversions like this one, since in most cases overflows don't occur. If you want to prevent automatic coercions, you can use a new compiler option, *Option Strict On*, that enforces C-like strict type coercion.

Visual Basic has richer IntelliSense and better automatic formatting than any other language. It automatically indents code, corrects casing, and adds parentheses to functions when you press Enter.

The result is a true Visual Basic experience, enhanced by background compilation as you type. For example, if you misspell the keyword *Function*, as in

```
Funtion myFunction
```

as soon as you move off the line, the compiler parses it and puts a compiler error in the Task List. It also underlines the word "Funtion" with a blue squiggle indicating the location of the compile error. As soon as you correct the line, the compiler removes the Task List item and erases the underline. Background compilation helps you write better code and is unique to Visual Basic—no other language has a background compiler.

The language you use is a matter of choice. However, if you enjoy programming in Visual Basic, you will find Visual Basic .NET a great experience and the best upgrade ever.

Conclusion

Whew—it's time to breathe. We've covered a lot of ground in this chapter. First we established that Visual Basic .NET is not 100 percent backward compatible with Visual Basic 6. We then took a lightning tour of the history of Visual Basic and saw that, although it is redesigned and restructured, Visual Basic .NET is part of the natural progression of Visual Basic. We looked at some of the differences between Visual Basic 6 and Visual Basic .NET and discussed some of the new features you can add to your upgraded applications. We also covered how you can add value to your upgraded applications and why you should continue to use Visual Basic.

The next reading takes a deeper look at what the .NET platform is and outlines the significant differences in Visual Basic .NET. Later chapters go further into the upgrading options and describe what you can do to prepare your application for the upgrade to Visual Basic .NET. Welcome to Visual Basic .NET, the future of Visual Basic.

Reading 2

Visual Basic 6 and Visual Basic .NET: Differences

More than three years ago, the Microsoft Visual Basic team set out to create Visual Basic .NET. At that time managers would kid the development team by saying that they were making only three "simple" changes to Visual Basic 6: a new runtime system, a new development environment, and a new compiler. The Visual Basic development team spent the next three years working on one of these changes: the new compiler. Two other teams provided the development environment and runtime. As we pointed out in earlier, the end result is not a new version of Visual Basic 6 but an entirely new product: *Microsoft Visual Basic .NET*. The name is important for two reasons. First, Visual Basic is still Visual Basic. Second, Visual Basic .NET is not Visual Basic 7.

This chapter describes the three "simple" changes made to create Visual Basic .NET, including changes to the runtime, the development environment, and the compiler. Microsoft also added other features to Visual Basic .NET along the way, including a new forms package and a new debugger, and these are also discussed in this chapter.

.NET Framework vs. ActiveX

As a Visual Basic developer, you will normally not be concerned with the runtime systems that underlie your Visual Basic applications. Visual Basic 6, for example, makes the details of how ActiveX works largely transparent. The

From *Updating Microsoft Visual Basic 6.0 to Microsoft Visual Basic .NET* by Ed Robinson, Mike Bond, and Ian Oliver. pp. 19-43. (Redmond: Microsoft Press. 2002.) Copyright © 2002 by Microsoft Corporation.

Visual Basic 6 runtime handles all of the messy details that come with implementing an ActiveX-compliant component or application. Licensing, persistable objects, Microsoft Transaction Server (MTS) transaction awareness, and binary compatibility are exposed as simple settings that you can turn on or off. In the same vein, Visual Basic .NET does a good job of hiding the details of what happens under the hood. For example, you do not need to know that you are creating or using a .NET component. A .NET component is just like any other component. It has properties, methods, and events just as an ActiveX component does. Why should you care about the differences between ActiveX and .NET if everything basically looks the same?

On the surface, it doesn't matter whether you're using ActiveX, .NET, or your best friend's component model—they all look about the same. When you dig into the details, however, you need to understand the machine that lies beneath.

If you have ever created an ActiveX control in Visual Basic 6, you may have found that it behaves slightly differently from other ActiveX controls that you bought off the shelf. For example, if you add a *BackColor* property to your control, you'll notice when you test it that the color picker is not associated with your control. Digging deeper, you'll find that you need to change the type of the property to *OLE_COLOR* and set the *Property ID* attribute on the property to *BackColor*. Only then will the property behave like a *BackColor* property. In solving this problem, you needed to cross over from pure Visual Basic into the world of ActiveX. Although Visual Basic attaches different terminology to options and language statements, you end up being directly or indirectly exposed to ActiveX concepts such as dispatch IDs (DISPIDs), what Visual Basic refers to as property IDs, and OLE types such as *OLE_COLOR*. Visual Basic, as much as it tries, cannot hide this from you. The more properties, events, methods, and property pages you add to your Visual Basic 6 ActiveX control, the more problems you encounter that require an ActiveX-related solution.

Visual Basic .NET works in much the same way. Most of the time, you are just dealing with Visual Basic. However, when you need your application or component to behave consistently with other types of applications, whether they be standard Windows applications or Web service server objects, you will need a detailed understanding of the environment in which you want your application to run. In the case of .NET applications, you will need to understand how .NET works. The more you know about the target environment, the better equipped you are to create a component or application that behaves well in that environment. So let's dig a bit and uncover the machine that will run your upgraded Visual Basic .NET application: the .NET Framework.

.NET Framework

The .NET Framework is composed of two general parts: the common language runtime and the Framework class library. The runtime is the foundation upon which the .NET Framework is based. It provides the basic services on which all .NET applications depend: code execution, memory management, thread management, and code security. The Framework class library provides building blocks for creating a variety of .NET applications, components, and services. For example, the Framework class library contains the base classes for creating ASP.NET Web applications, ASP.NET XML Web services, and Windows Forms. It defines all of the value types, known as *System* types, such as *Byte*, *Integer*, *Long*, and *String*. It gives you complex structure classes such as *Collection* and *Hashtable*, as well as interfaces such as *ICollection* and *IDictionary* so you can define your own custom implementation of a standard *Collection* or *Hashtable* class.

The .NET Framework as a whole, since it works across all .NET languages, can be thought of as an expanded version of the Visual Basic 6 runtime. The common language runtime corresponds to the Visual Basic Language Runtime in Visual Basic 6, which includes the byte code interpreter and memory manager. The counterparts of the .NET Framework class library in Visual Basic 6 include the Visual Basic forms package, the *Collection* object, and global objects such as *App*, *Screen*, *Printer*, and *Clipboard*.

The main difference between the two environments is that Visual Basic 6 is a closed environment, meaning that none of the intrinsic Visual Basic types, such as *Collection*, *App*, *Screen*, and so on, can be shared with other language environments, such as C++. Likewise, Microsoft Visual C++ is largely a self-contained language environment that includes its own runtime and class libraries, such as MFC and ATL. The MFC *CString* class, for example, is contained within the MFC runtime and is not shared with other environments such as Visual Basic.

In closed environments such as these, you can share components between environments only when you create them as ActiveX components, and even then there are a number of limitations. ActiveX components need to be designed and tested to work in each target environment. For example, an ActiveX control hosted on a Visual Basic 6 form may work wonderfully, but the same control may not work at all when hosted on an MFC window. You then need to add or modify the interfaces or implementation of your ActiveX component to make it work with both the Visual Basic 6 and MFC environments. As a result, you end up duplicating your effort by writing specialized routines to make your ActiveX component work in all target environments.

The .NET Framework eliminates this duplication by creating an environment in which all languages have equal access to the same broad set of .NET types, base classes, and services. Each language built on the .NET Framework shares this common base. No matter what your language of choice is—Visual Basic .NET , C#, or COBOL (for .NET)—the compiler for that language generates exactly the same set of .NET runtime instructions, called Microsoft Intermediate Language (MSIL). With each language distilled down to one base instruction set (MSIL), running against the same runtime (the .NET common language runtime), and using one set of .NET Framework classes, sharing and consistency become the norm. The .NET components you create using any .NET language work together seamlessly without any additional effort on your part.

Now that you have seen some of the differences between the Visual Basic 6 ActiveX-based environment and the Visual Basic .NET environment, let's focus on various elements of the .NET Framework and see how each element manifests itself in Visual Basic .NET. The elements we will be looking at are memory management, type identity, and the threading model. Each of these areas will have a profound impact on the way you both create new Visual Basic .NET applications and revise upgraded Visual Basic 6 applications to work with Visual Basic .NET.

Memory Management

Visual Basic .NET relies on the .NET runtime for memory management. This means that the .NET runtime takes care of reserving memory for all Visual Basic strings, arrays, structures, and objects. Likewise, the .NET runtime decides when to free the memory associated with the objects or variables you have allocated. This is not much different from Visual Basic 6, which was also responsible for managing the memory on your behalf. The most significant difference between Visual Basic 6 and Visual Basic .NET in terms of memory management involves determining when an object or variable is freed.

In Visual Basic 6, the memory associated with a variable or object is freed as soon as you set the variable to *Nothing* or the variable falls out of scope. This is not true in Visual Basic .NET. When a variable or object is set to *Nothing* or falls out of scope, Visual Basic .NET tells the .NET runtime that the variable or object is no longer used. The .NET runtime marks the variable or object as needing deletion and relegates the object to the Garbage Collector (GC). The Garbage Collector then deletes the object at some arbitrary time in the future.

Because we can predict when Visual Basic 6 will delete the memory associated with a variable, we refer to the lifespan of a variable in that language as being **deterministic**. In other words, you know the exact moment that a variable comes into existence and the exact moment that it becomes nonexistent. The lifespan of a Visual Basic .NET variable, on the other hand, is **indeterministic**, since you cannot predict exactly when it will become nonexistent. You can tell Visual Basic .NET to stop using the variable, but you cannot tell it when to make the variable nonexistent. The variable could be left dangling for a few nanoseconds, or it could take minutes for the .NET Framework to decide to make it nonexistent. In the meantime, an indeterminate amount of your Visual Basic code will execute.

In many cases it does not matter whether or not you can predict when a variable or object is going to be nonexistent. For example, a simple variable such as a string or an array that you are no longer using can be cleaned up at any time. It is when you are dealing with objects that things get interesting.

Take, for example, a *File* object that opens a file and locks the file when the *File* object is created. The object closes the file handle and allows the file to be opened by other applications when the object is destroyed. Consider the following Visual Basic .NET code:

```
Dim f As New File
Dim FileContents As String
f.Open("MyFile.dat")
FileContents = f.Read("MyFile.dat")
f = Nothing
FileContents = FileContents & " This better be appended to my file! "
f.Open("MyFile.dat")
f.Write(FileContents)
f = Nothing
```

If you run this application in Visual Basic 6, it will run without error. However, if you run this application in Visual Basic .NET, you will encounter an exception when you attempt to open the file the second time. Why? The file handle associated with MyFile.dat will likely still be open. Setting *f* to *Nothing* tells the .NET Framework that the *File* object needs to be deleted. The runtime relegates the object to the garbage bin, where it will wait until the Garbage Collector comes along to clean it up. The *File* object in effect remains alive and well in the garbage bin. As a result, the MyFile.dat file handle is still open, and the second attempt to open the locked file will lead to an error.

The only way to prevent this type of problem is to call a method on the object to force its handle to be closed. In this example, if the *File* object had a *Close* method, you could use it here before setting the variable to *Nothing*. For example,

```
f.Close
f = Nothing
```

Dispose: Determinism in the Face of Chaos

Despite all of the benefits that a garbage-collected model has to offer, it has one haunting side effect: the lack of determinism. Objects can be allocated and deleted by the hundreds, but you never really know when or in what order they will actually terminate. Nor do you know what resources are being consumed or locked at any given moment. It's confusing, even chaotic. To add some semblance of order to this system, the .NET Framework offers a mechanism called *Dispose* to ensure that an object releases all its resources exactly when you want it to. Any object that locks resources you need or that otherwise needs to be told to let go should implement the *IDisposable* interface. The *IDisposable* interface has a single method, *Dispose*, that takes no parameters. Any client using the object should call the *Dispose* method when it is finished with the object.

One More Thing to Worry About

If you've been using Visual Basic 6, you're not accustomed to calling *Dispose* explicitly on an object when you write code. Unfortunately, when it comes to Visual Basic .NET, you will have to get accustomed to doing so. Get in the habit now of calling *Dispose* on any object when you are done using it or when the variable referencing it is about to go out of scope. If we change the *File* object shown earlier to use *Dispose*, we end up with the following code:

```
Dim f As New File
Dim FileContents As String
f.Open("MyFile.dat")
FileContents = f.Read("MyFile.dat")
f.Dispose
f = Nothing
FileContents = FileContents & " This better be appended to my file! "
f.Open("MyFile.dat")
f.Write(FileContents)
f.Dispose
f = Nothing
```

> **Note** The Visual Basic Upgrade Wizard does not alert you to cases in which you may need to call *Dispose*. We advise you to review your code after you upgrade to determine when an object reference is no longer used. Add calls to the object's *Dispose* method to force the object to release its resources. If the object—notably ActiveX objects that do not implement *IDisposable*—does not support the *Dispose* method, look for another suitable method to call, such as *Close*. For example, review your code for the use of ActiveX Data Objects (ADO) such as *Recordset* and *Connection*. When you are finished with a *Recordset* object, be sure to call *Close*.

When You Just Want It All to Go Away

While your application runs, objects that have been created and destroyed may wait for the Garbage Collector to come and take them away. At certain points in your application, you may need to ensure that no objects are hanging around locking or consuming a needed resource. To clean up objects that are pending collection, you can call on the Garbage Collector to collect all of the waiting objects immediately. You can force garbage collection with the following two calls:

```
GC.Collect
GC.WaitForPendingFinalizers
```

> **Note**   The two calls to *Collect* and to *WaitForPendingFinalizers* are required in the order shown above. The first call to *Collect* kicks off the garbage collection process asynchronously and immediately returns. The call to *WaitForPendingFinalizers* waits for the collection process to complete.

Depending on how many (or few) objects need to be collected, running the Garbage Collector in this manner may not be efficient. Force garbage collection sparingly and only in cases where it's critical that all recently freed objects get collected. Otherwise, opt for using *Dispose* or *Close* on individual objects to free up needed resources as you go.

Type Identity

Mike once played on a volleyball team where everyone on his side of the net, including himself, was named Mike. What a disaster. All the other team had to do was hit the ball somewhere in the middle. Someone would yell, "Get it, Mike!" and they would all go crashing into a big pile. To sort things out, they adopted nicknames, involving some derivation of their full names. After that, the game went much better.

Like names in the real world, types in Visual Basic can have the same name. Instead of giving them nicknames, however, you distinguish them by using their full name. For example, Visual Basic has offered a variety of data access models over the years. Many of these data access models contain objects with the same names. Data Access Objects (DAO) and ActiveX Data Objects (ADO), for instance, both contain types called *Connection* and *Recordset*.

Suppose that, for whatever reason, you decided to reference both DAO and ADO in your Visual Basic 6 project. If you declared a *Recordset* variable, the variable would be either a DAO or an ADO *Recordset* type:

```
Dim rs As Recordset
```

How do you know which type of *Recordset* you are using? One way to tell is to look at the properties, methods, and events that IntelliSense or the event drop-down menu gives you. If the object has an *Open* method, it is an ADO *Recordset*. If instead it has an *OpenRecordset* method, it is a DAO *Recordset*. In Visual Basic 6, the *Recordset* you end up with depends on the order of the references. The reference that appears higher in the list wins. In Figure 2-1, for example, the Microsoft ActiveX Data Objects 2.6 Library reference occurs before the reference to the Microsoft DAO 3.6 Object Library, so ADO wins and the *Recordset* is an ADO *Recordset* type.

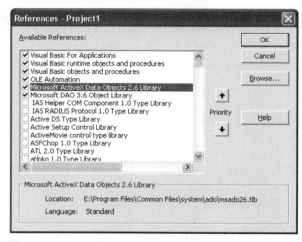

Figure 2-1   ADO 2.6 reference takes precedence over DAO 3.6.

If you change the priority of the ADO reference by selecting it and clicking the down arrow under Priority, the DAO reference will take precedence. Clicking OK to apply the change transforms your *Recordset* type to a DAO *Recordset*.

Suppose you want to use both types of *Recordset* objects in your application. To do so, you need to fully qualify the type name as follows:

```
Dim rsADO As ADODB.Recordset
Dim rsDAO As DAO.Recordset
```

As you can see, Visual Basic 6 is quite flexible when it comes to using types. Indeed, you could argue that it is too flexible, since you could mistakenly change the type for variables in your code simply by changing the order of a reference.

Visual Basic .NET is stricter about the use of the same types in an application. The general rule is that you need to fully qualify every ambiguous type that you are using. If you are referencing both ADO and DAO, for example, you are forced to fully qualify your use of the types just as you would in Visual Basic 6:

```
Dim rsADO As ADODB.Recordset
Dim rsDAO As DAO.Recordset
```

Using Imports

To help you cut down on the number of words and dots that you need to type for each reference, Visual Basic .NET allows you to import a namespace. You can think of it as a global *With* statement that is applied to the namespace. (A namespace is similar to a library or project name in Visual Basic 6.) For example, type references can become quite bothersome when you are dealing with .NET types such as *System.Runtime.Interopservices.UnmanagedType*. To simplify the qualification of this type, you can add an *Imports* statement to the beginning of the file in which it is used:

```
Imports System.Runtime
```

This statement allows you to reference the type as *Interopservices.UnmanagedType*. You can also expand the *Imports* clause to

```
Imports System.Runtime.Interopservices.
```

and then simply refer to *Unmanaged Type* in your code.

Managing Conflicts

Imports works great until there is a conflict. As we indicated earlier, in Visual Basic 6, the rule is that the type library that is higher in the precedence list takes priority. Visual Basic .NET is different in that all conflicts are irreconcilable. You have to either change your *Imports* clause to avoid the conflict or fully qualify each type when it is used. Suppose that you add *Imports* statements for ADO and DAO as follows:

```
Imports ADO
Imports DAO
```

Now suppose that you want to declare a variable of type *Recordset*. As in the volleyball game described earlier, it's as if you yelled out, "Recordset!" Both ADO and DAO jump in. Crash! Big pile. Any attempt to use the unqualified type *Recordset* will lead to an error that states, "The name 'Recordset' is ambiguous, imported from Namespace ADO, DAO." To resolve the problem, you need to either fully qualify the type or remove one of the *Imports* statements.

No More GUIDs

Each ActiveX type, whether it is a class, an interface, an enumerator, or a structure, generally has a unique identifier associated with it. The identifier is a 128-bit, or 16-byte, numeric value referred to as UUID, GUID, LIBID, CLSID, IID, or <whatever>ID. No matter what you call it, it is a 128-bit number.

Rather than make you think in 128-bit numbers, Visual Basic (and other languages) associates human-readable names with each of these types. For example, if you create a Visual Basic 6 class called *Customer*, its type identifier will be something like {456EC035-17C9-433c-B5F2-9F22C29D775D}. You can assign *Customer* to other types, such as *LoyalCustomer*, if *LoyalCustomer* implements the *Customer* type with the same ID value. If the *LoyalCustomer* type instead implements a *Customer* type with a different ID value, the assignment would fail with a "Type Mismatch" error. In ActiveX, at run time, the number is everything; the name means little to nothing.

In .NET, on the other hand, the name is everything. Two types are considered the same if they meet all of the following conditions:

- The types have the same name.
- The types are contained in the same namespace.
- The types are contained in assemblies with the same name.
- The assemblies containing the types are weak named.

Note that the types can be in assemblies that have the same name but a different version number. For example, two types called *Recordset* contained in the namespace ADODB are considered the same type if they live in an assembly such as Microsoft.ADODB.dll with the same name. There could be two Microsoft.ADODB.dll assemblies on your machine with different version numbers, but the *ADODB.Recordset* types would still be considered compatible. If, however, the *Recordset* types lived in different assemblies, such as Microsoft.ADODB_2_6.dll and Microsoft.ADODB_2_7.dll, the types would be considered different. You cannot assign two variables of type *Recordset* to each other if each declaration of *Recordset* comes from an assembly with a different name.

Threading Model

Visual Basic 6 ActiveX DLLs and controls can be either single threaded or apartment threaded; they are apartment threaded by default. **Apartment threading** means that only one thread can access an instance of your Visual Basic 6

ActiveX component at any given time. In fact, the same thread always accesses your component, so other threads never disturb your data, including global data. Visual Basic .NET components, on the other hand, are **multithreaded** by default, meaning that two or more threads can be executing code within your component simultaneously. Each thread has access to your shared data, such as class member and global variables, and the threads can change any data that is shared.

Visual Basic .NET multithreaded components are great news if you want to take advantage of MTS pooling, which requires multithreaded components. They are bad news if your component is not multithread safe and you wind up trying to figure out why member variables are being set to unexpected or random values in your upgraded component.

Differences in the Development Environment

Although Visual Basic 6 shipped as part of Microsoft Visual Studio 6, it did not share a common infrastructure with its siblings C++, Visual InterDev, and Visual FoxPro. The only sharing came in the form of ActiveX components and in designers such as the DataEnvironment. Although Visual Studio 6 shipped with a common integrated development environment (IDE) called MSDev, Visual Basic 6 did not participate in MSDev and instead came with its own IDE called VB6.exe.

Visual Studio .NET ships with a single IDE that all languages built on the .NET Framework share called Devenv.exe. The Visual Studio .NET IDE is a host for common elements such as the Windows and Web Forms packages, the Property Browser, Solution Explorer (also known as the project system), Server Explorer, Toolbox, Build Manager, add-ins, and wizards. All languages, including Visual Basic .NET and C#, share these common elements.

Although the Visual Studio .NET IDE provides a common environment for different languages, the various languages are not identical or redundant. Each language maintains its own identity in the syntax, expressions, attributes, and runtime functions you use. When you write code behind a form in a common forms package such as Windows Forms or Web Forms, the code behind the form is represented by the language you are using. If you use Visual Basic, the events for the form are represented using Visual Basic syntax and have event signatures almost identical to those you are accustomed to using in Visual Basic 6. If you use C#, all of the Windows Forms event signatures appear in the syntax of the C# language.

What happened to the common tools that you have grown to love or hate in Visual Basic 6? They have all been rewritten for Visual Studio. NET, as you'll see next.

Menu Editor

Do you really want to keep using the same clunky Menu Editor that has been around since Visual Basic 1, shown in Figure 2-2? We doubt it. So you'll probably be pleased to know that you won't find it in the Visual Studio .NET environment. Instead, you create menus by inserting and editing the menu items directly on a Windows form.

Figure 2-2 Visual Basic 6 Menu Editor.

To insert a new menu in the .NET environment, you drag a *MainMenu* component from the Toolbox and drop it on the form. Then you select the *MainMenu1* component in the component tray, below the form, and type your menu text in the edit box that says "Type Here" just below the title bar for your form. Figure 2-3 shows the Visual Basic .NET menu editor in action.

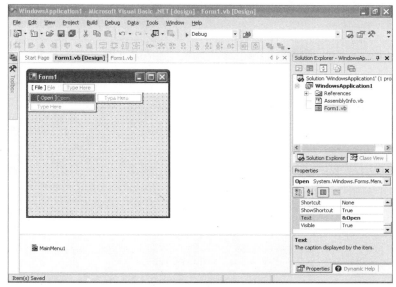

Figure 2-3   Visual Basic .NET's in-place menu editor.

Toolbox

The Visual Studio .NET Toolbox is similar to the Visual Basic 6 Toolbox in appearance and use. A difference you will notice right away is that the Visual Studio .NET Toolbox contains the name of each Toolbox item in addition to the icon. Also, depending on the type of project selected, the Toolbox displays a variety of tabs containing different categories of controls and components that you can add to a form or designer. For example, when you are editing a Windows Forms project, the Toolbox will contain categories titled Data, Components Windows Forms, Clipboard Ring, and General. Each tab contains ADO .NET data components such as *DataSet* and *OleDBAdaptor*; system components such as *MessageQueue* and *EventLog*; and Windows Forms controls and components such as *Button*, *TextBox*, *Label*, and *TreeView*.

A subtle difference between the Visual Basic 6 Toolbox and the Visual Basic .NET Toolbox relates to references. In Visual Basic 6, any ActiveX control you add to the Toolbox is also added as a reference within your project. The reference exists whether you use the ActiveX control on a form or not. In Visual Basic .NET, the items you add to the Toolbox are not referenced by default. It is not until you place the control on a Windows form or designer that a reference to that component is added to your project.

Because a reference to an ActiveX control automatically exists when you place the control on the Toolbox in Visual Basic 6, you can use the reference in code. For example, suppose you add the Masked Edit ActiveX control to the Toolbox but don't add an instance of the control to the form. You can write code to add an instance of the Masked Edit ActiveX control to a form at runtime, as follows:

```
Dim MyMSMaskCtl1 As MSMask.MaskEdBox
Set MyMSMaskCtl1 = Controls.Add("MSMask.MaskEdBox", "MyMSMaskCtl1")
MyMSMaskCtl1.Visible = True
```

If you attempt to place a Masked Edit ActiveX control on a Visual Basic .NET Toolbar, you will find that if you declare a variable of the ActiveX control type, the statement will not compile. For example, if you attempt to declare the Masked Edit control, using Visual Basic .NET equivalent syntax, the statement won't compile, as follows:

```
Dim MyMSMaskCtl1 As AxMSMask.AxMaskEdBox
```

To declare a variable of the ActiveX control type, you need to place the ActiveX control on a form. You will then be able to dimension variables of the ActiveX control type.

Note After you place an ActiveX control on a Visual Basic .NET form, you will find that you can declare variables of the control type. However, you will not be able to use *Controls.Add*, as demonstrated in the Visual Basic 6 code above. *Controls.Add* is not supported in Visual Basic .NET.

Property Browser

The Visual Studio .NET Property Browser is, for the most part, identical in terms of appearance and use to the Visual Basic 6 Property Browser. One minor difference is that the default view for the Property Browser in Visual Studio .NET is Category view, meaning that related properties are grouped under a descriptive category. Alphabetical view is also supported. The Visual Basic 6 Property Browser, on the other hand, defaults to listing properties alphabetically, although it supports a categorized view.

The Visual Studio .NET Property Browser can list all of the properties associated with a control or component. This is not the case when you are using the Visual Basic 6 Property Browser. For example, the Visual Basic 6

Property Browser cannot list object or variant-based properties. It can display properties for a limited number of objects, such as *Picture* or *Font*, but it cannot represent an object property such as the ColumnHeaders collection of a List-View control. Instead the Visual Basic 6 Property Browser relies on an ActiveX control property page to provide editing for object properties such as collections.

The Visual Studio .NET Property Browser allows direct editing of an object property if a custom editor is associated with the property or the property type. For example, the Visual Studio .NET Property Browser provides a standard Collection Editor for any property that implements *ICollection*. In the case of the ColumnHeaders collection for a ListView control, a ColumnHeader Collection Editor, based on the standard Collection Editor, is provided for you to edit the ColumnHeaders collection for the ListView. Figure 2-4 shows an example of editing the *ListView Columns* property.

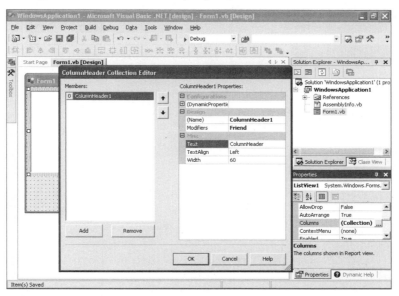

Figure 2-4   Visual Basic .NET ColumnHeader Collection Editor in action.

Tab Layout Editor

Your days of clicking a control, setting the *TabIndex* property, and then repeating the process for the several dozen controls on your form are over. Welcome to the Visual Studio .NET Tab Layout Editor. The Tab Layout Editor allows you to view and edit the tab ordering for all elements on the form at once. To view your tab layout for the current form, select Tab Order from the View menu. A tab index number displays for each control on the form. You can start with the control that you want to be first in the tab order, and then click the remaining controls in the tab order that you want. The tab index numbers will correspond to the order in which you click the controls. Figure 2-5 illustrates the Tab Layout Editor.

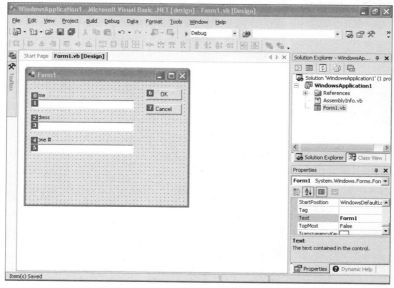

Figure 2-5   Visual Studio .NET Tab Layout Editor in action.

Forms Packages

The forms package that you use in Visual Basic 6 to create standard .exe projects or ActiveX control projects is essentially the same package that has been in existence since Visual Basic 1. Visual Basic .NET offers a brand new forms package called Windows Forms. In addition, Visual Basic .NET gives you a second forms package to help in creating Web applications: the Web Forms package.

A Single Standard for Windows Forms

A significant difference between Visual Basic .NET and Visual Basic 6 is that the forms you use with Visual Basic .NET can be used in any type of .NET project. For example, you can use the same forms with both a Visual Basic application and a C# application.

The forms package found in Visual Basic 6 is local to that environment. You can use Visual Basic 6 forms only in Visual Basic 6. Microsoft has tried in the past to create a single, standard forms package that could be shared across multiple products such as Visual Basic, C++, and Microsoft Office. The initiative, called Forms3 (pronounced Forms Cubed), never realized this goal. Forms3 is alive and well in Office but was never made fully compatible with the Visual Basic forms package.

The Windows Forms package reignites some hope of having a single forms standard applied across various Microsoft products—at least for client applications based on the .NET platform. The ideal of having a single, universal forms package, however, will have to wait; Visual Studio .NET also introduces a separate forms package for Web applications.

Two Forms Packages for the Price of One

One of the appealing features of Visual Studio .NET is that you can create a Web application more quickly and easily than you ever have before. This ease stems from the marriage between the Web Forms package and Visual Basic .NET. For the first time, you can create a Web application in the same manner that you create a Windows client application. You drag and drop controls onto a Web form and then write code to handle the form and control events. All of the skills that you use to create Visual Basic Windows applications can now be used to create Web applications.

> **Note**   The Upgrade Wizard will upgrade your client-based applications to use Windows Forms and will upgrade your WebClasses-based applications to use Web Forms.

Language Differences

With each new version of Visual Basic, Microsoft has expanded the language by offering new keywords, new syntactical elements, new conditional statements or modifiers, new attributes, and so on. Visual Basic .NET is no exception. It makes the same types of additions to the language as previous versions have, but on a much grander scale than before. Table 2-1 gives a complete list of keywords that have been added to the Visual Basic .NET language.

Table 2-1   New Keywords in Visual Basic .NET

Visual Basic .NET Keyword	Description
AddHandler and *RemoveHandler*	Dynamically adds or removes event handlers at runtime, respectively
AndAlso and *OrElse*	Short-circuited logical expressions that complement *And* and *Or*, respectively
Ansi, Auto, and *Unicode*	Declare statement attributes
CChar, CObj, CShort, CType, and *DirectCast*	Coercion functions
Class, Interface, Module, and *Structure*	Type declaration statements
Default	Attribute for indexed property declarations
Delegate	Declare pointer to instance method or shared method
GetType	Returns *Type* class for a given type
Handles	Specifies event handled by a subroutine
Imports	Includes given namespace in current code file
Inherits	Optional statement used with a class to declare classes that inherit from another class
MustInherit	Optional statement used with a class to declare the class as an abstract base class
MustOverride	Optional subroutine attribute that specifies an inherited class must implement the subroutine
MyBase	Refers to base class instance
MyClass	Refers to the current class instance. Ignores a derived class.
Namespace	Defines a namespace block
NotInheritable	Optional statement used with *Class* to indicate the class cannot be inherited
NotOverridable	Optional subroutine attribute which specifies that a subroutine cannot be overridden in a derived class
Option Strict	Allows you to turn strict type conversion checking on or off. Default is off.
Overloads	Optional subroutine attribute that indicates the subroutine overloads a subroutine with the same name, but different parameters
Overridable	Optional subroutine attribute which specifies that a subroutine can be overridden in a derived class

Table 2-1   New Keywords in Visual Basic .NET *(continued)*

Visual Basic .NET Keyword	Description
Overrides	Optional subroutine attribute that indicates the subroutine overrides a subroutine in the base class
Protected	Class member attribute that limits member access to the class and any derived class
Protected Friend	Same as *Protected*, but expands the scope to include access by any other class in the same assembly
ReadOnly and *WriteOnly*	Attribute on a *Property* declaration to specify the property is read-only or write-only
*Return**	Statement used to return, possibly with a value from a subroutine
Shadows	Attribute on class members to specify that a class member is distinct from a same-named base class member
Short	16-bit type known as *Integer* in Visual Basic 6
SyncLock	Specifies the start of a thread synchronization block
Try, *Catch*, *Finally*, and *When*	Keywords related to structured error handling
Throw	Keyword to throw an exception

* Existing keyword with different behavior.

Because the Upgrade Wizard generally does not modify or update your code to take advantage of new Visual Basic .NET features, only a subset of the new features come into play after an upgrade. Therefore, we will focus here on some of the general language differences that affect your upgraded Visual Basic 6 application.

All Subroutine Calls Must Have Parentheses

Parentheses are required on all subroutine calls. If you write code that does not use the *Call* keyword, as follows:

```
MsgBox "Hello World"
```

you are required to use parentheses in your Visual Basic .NET code, as follows:

```
MsgBox("Hello World")
```

ByVal or *ByRef* Is Required

In Visual Basic .NET, all subroutine parameters must be qualified with *ByVal* or *ByRef*. For example, instead of this Visual Basic 6 code:

```
Sub UpdateCustomerInfo(CustomerName As String)
End Sub
```

you will see the following Visual Basic .NET code:

```
Sub UpdateCustomerInfo(ByRef CustomerName As String)
End Sub
```

In this case, an unqualified Visual Basic 6 parameter has been upgraded to use the *ByRef* calling convention. In Visual Basic .NET, the default calling convention is *ByRef*.

Is That My Event?

Visual Basic 6 associates events by name, using the pattern <Object-Name>_<EventName>. For example, the click event associated with a command *CommandButton* is

```
Private Sub Command1_Click()
```

If you change the name of the Visual Basic 6 event to the name of a subroutine that does not match any other event, it becomes a simple subroutine. The name pattern, therefore, determines whether a subroutine is an event or not.

Handles Clause

Visual Basic .NET does not associate events by name. Instead, a subroutine is associated with an event if it includes the *Handles* clause. The name of the subroutine can be any name you want. The event that fires the subroutine is given in the *Handles* clause. For example, the click event associated with a Visual Basic .NET button has the following signature:

```
Private Sub Button1_Click(ByVal sender As System.Object, _
    ByVal e As System.EventArgs) _
    Handles Button1.Click
```

Because the event hookup is an explicit part of the event declaration, you can use unique names for your events. For example, you can change the name of your *Button1_Click* event to *YouClickedMyButton* as follows:

```
Private Sub YouClickedMyButton(ByVal sender As System.Object, _
    ByVal e As System.EventArgs) _
    Handles Button1.Click
```

Event Parameters

Another interesting change related to events is that event parameters are different between Visual Basic 6 and Visual Basic .NET. In Visual Basic 6, the event subroutine contains the name and type of each parameter. In Visual Basic .NET, the parameters are bundled up in an *EventArgs* object and passed in as a reference to that object. Also, the event subroutine for a Visual Basic .NET event includes a reference to the object that fired the event.

As an example of the different handling of event parameters in the two versions of Visual Basic, consider a form with a Listbox control on it, for which you need to write code to show the checked item.

In Visual Basic 6, you would write the following code:

```
Private Sub List1_ItemCheck(Item As Integer)
    MsgBox "You checked item: " & Item
End Sub
```

The equivalent code in Visual Basic .NET is as follows:

```
Private Sub CheckedListBox1_ItemCheck(ByVal sender As Object, _
    ByVal e As System.Windows.Forms.ItemCheckEventArgs) _
    Handles CheckedListBox1.ItemCheck
    MsgBox("You checked item: " & e.Index)
End Sub
```

Observe how the item that is checked is passed directly as a parameter in Visual Basic 6. In Visual Basic .NET, it is passed as a member of the passed-in *Item-CheckEventArgs* object *e*.

Arrays Must Have a Zero-Bound Lower Dimension

You cannot declare an array in Visual Basic .NET to have a nonzero-bound lower dimension. This requirement also means that you cannot use Option Base 1. In fact, you cannot specify a lower dimension in an array declaration, since it must always be zero. The following types of declarations are no longer supported:

```
Dim MyIntArray(-10 To 10) As Integer    '21 elements
Dim  MyStringArray(1 To 100) As String    '100 elements

Option Base 1
Dim MyOptionBase1Array(5) As Long     '5 elements (1-5)
```

Instead, you must use zero-based lower bound arrays, and you need to adjust the bounds to create an array with the same number of elements, such as

```
Dim MyIntArray(20) As Integer    '21 elements (0-20)
Dim  MyStringArray(99) As String    '100 elements (0-99)

'Option Base 1        'Not supported by VB .NET
Dim MyOptionBase1Array(4) As Long        '5 elements (0-4)
```

Fixed-Length Strings Are Not Supported

Visual Basic .NET does not support fixed-length strings. For example, the following type of declaration is not supported:

```
Dim MyString As String * 32
```

Instead, you can dimension the string as a fixed-length array of characters, as follows:

```
Dim MyString(32) As Char
```

Or you can use a special class, *VBFixedLengthString*, defined in the Visual Basic .NET compatibility library. If you use the *VBFixedLengthString* class the declaration will be:

```
Imports VB6 = Microsoft.VisualBasic.Compatibility.VB6
...
Dim MyFixedLenString As New VB6.FixedLengthString(32)
```

To set the value of a *FixedLengthString* variable you need to use the *Value* property as follows:

```
MyFixedLenString.Value = "This is my fixed length string"
```

Variant Data Type Is Eliminated

Visual Basic .NET eliminates the *Variant* data type. The main reason is that the underlying .NET Framework does not natively support the *Variant* type or anything like it. The closest approximation that the .NET Framework offers is the *Object* type. The *Object* type works somewhat like the *Variant* type because the *Object* type is the base type for all other types, such as *Integer* and *String*. Just as you can with a *Variant*, you can assign any type to an *Object*. However, in Visual Basic .NET, to get a strong type back out of a *Variant* to assign, for example, to an *Integer* or a *String*, you need to use a type-casting function, such as *CInt* or *CString*. With Visual Basic 6, you can write code such as the following:

```
Dim v As Variant
Dim s As String
v = "My variant contains a string"
s = v
```

When using Visual Basic .NET, however, you need to use type conversion functions such as *CStr*, as follows:

```
Dim v As Variant
Dim s As String
v = "My variant contains a string"
s = CStr(v)
```

Visibility of Variables Declared in Nested Scopes Is Limited

Variables that are declared in a nested scope, such as those occurring within an *If...Then* or *For...Next* block, are automatically moved to the beginning of the function. The Upgrade Wizard does this for compatibility reasons. In Visual Basic 6, a variable declared in any subscope is visible to the entire function. In Visual Basic .NET, this is not the case. A variable declared within a subscope is visible only within that subscope and any scope nested beneath it.

Take, for example, the following Visual Basic code:

```
Dim OuterScope As Long

If OuterScope = False Then
    Dim InnerScope As Long
End If

InnerScope = 3
```

This code works fine in Visual Basic 6, but it will lead to a compiler error in Visual Basic .NET. The compiler error will occur on the last line, *InnerScope = 3*, and will indicate that the name *InnerScope* is not declared.

> **Note**   The Upgrade Wizard will upgrade your code so that no compiler error occurs. It does this by moving the declaration for *InnerScope* to the top of the function along with all other top-level declarations. Moving the variable declaration to the top-level scope allows the variable to be used from any scope within the function. This move makes the behavior compatible with Visual Basic 6. It is one of the few cases in which the Upgrade Wizard changes the order of code during upgrade.

Changes in the Debugger

Visual Basic .NET shares the same debugger with all .NET languages in Visual Studio .NET. This debugger works much the same as the one in Visual Basic 6 in that you can step through code and set breakpoints in the same way. However, there are some differences that you should be aware of. These are discussed in the following sections.

No Edit and Continue

What percentage of your Visual Basic 6 application would you say is developed when you are debugging your application in what is commonly referred to as break mode? Ten percent? Forty percent? Ninety percent? Whatever your answer, the number is likely above zero. Any problems you encounter while debugging your Visual Basic 6 application are quite easy to fix while in break mode. This is a great feature that allows you to create applications more quickly. You will miss this ability in Visual Basic .NET.

The Visual Studio .NET common debugger does not allow you to edit your code while in break mode. Any time you encounter code that you want to change or fix, you need to stop debugging, make the change, and then start the application again. Doing so can be a real pain.

The Visual Basic .NET team recognizes that this is not what you would call a RAD debugging experience. The team hopes to offer an updated debugger that supports edit and continue in a future release of Visual Studio .NET. Until then, prepare to break, stop, edit, and rerun your application.

Cannot Continue After an Error

If an error or exception occurs while you are running your application, the Visual Basic .NET debugger will stop at the point where the exception occurred. However, unlike Visual Basic 6, in the Visual Basic .NET debugger you cannot fix your code or step around the code that is causing the error. If you attempt to step to another line, the application will terminate and switch to Design view. You will need to determine the source of the exception, fix your code, and then rerun the application.

No Repainting in Break Mode

In Visual Basic 6, the form and all controls on it continue to display even when you are in break mode. This happens because the Visual Basic 6 debugger lets certain events occur and allows certain code to execute when you are in break mode. For example, painting is allowed to occur.

When debugging your application using Visual Basic .NET, you will find that your form does not repaint. In fact, if you place another window over it while you are in break mode, you will find that the form image does not update at all. The Visual Basic .NET debugger does not allow any events or code to run while you are in break mode.

One benefit of the Visual Basic .NET debugger is that you can debug your paint code and watch your form update as each statement that paints the form executes. It allows you to pinpoint the exact statement in your code that is causing a problem with the display. Because the Visual Basic 6 debugger allows the form to repaint constantly, it is difficult to pinpoint painting problems using the Visual Basic 6 debugger.

✳✳✳

The .NET Framework Class Library

The .NET Framework class library is a collection of classes that managed applications use to access the operating system, the file system, databases, and any other resource. In this section, let's look at the most interesting portions of the .NET class library.

To better organize the hundreds of classes in the library, the .NET Framework supports the concept of namespaces. Namespaces are similar to directories on disk: just as a directory can contain files and other directories, a namespace can contain classes and other (nested) namespaces. For example, all the classes that have to do with database programming are grouped in the *System.Data* namespace. The *System* namespace is arguably the most important namespace because all the basic types are defined there, including numeric, data, and string types.

Tthe most interesting namespaces in are summarized Table 2-2, sorted in alphabetical order. Note that a namespace can be split into more DLLs; in fact, the logical organization of the types in an assembly is distinct from its physical organization. For example, you can put types that are used less frequently into a separate DLL so that they aren't loaded if they aren't used.

Table 2-2 The Most Important Namespaces in the .NET Framework

Namespace	DLL Name	Sample Classes	Description
System	MSCorLib.dll	*Double, String, Array, Exception, Math*	The core .NET classes and all the basic data types
System. CodeDom	System.dll	*CodeExpression, CodeNamespace*	Types for program-matically creating code
System. Collections	MSCorLib.dll	*ArrayList, Hash-table, SortedList, BitArray*	Collectionlike data types
System. Component-Model	System.dll	*Component, PropertyDescriptor*	Types for control-ling components
System. Component-Model.Design	System.dll and System. Design.dll	*DesignerCollection, DesignerVerb*	Types for imple-menting design-time features of components
System.Data	System. Data.dll	*DataSet, DataTable, DataRow*	Types for client-side processing of database data
System. Data.OleDb	System. Data.dll	*OleDbConnection, OleDbCommand*	Types for working with OLE DB data-bases
System. Data.SqlClient	System. Data.dll	*SqlConnection, SqlCommand*	Types for working with SQL Server databases
System. Diagnostics	MSCorLib.dll and System.dll	*Debug, EventLog*	Types for aiding testing and debugging
System. Directory-Services	System. DirectorySer-vices.dll	*DirectoryEntry, SearchResult*	Types for working with Active Directory
System. Drawing	System. Drawing.dll	*Brush, Pen, Font*	Types for creating graphics in Windows Forms applications
System. Drawing. Drawing2D	System. Drawing.dll	*HatchBrush, Matrix*	Additional types for more sophisticated 2-D graphics

Table 2-2   The Most Important Namespaces in the .NET Framework *(continued)*

Namespace	DLL Name	Sample Classes	Description
System. Drawing. Imaging	System. Drawing.dll	*BitmapData, Metafile*	Types for working with image files
System. Drawing. Printing	System. Drawing.dll	*PageSettings, PrintController*	Types for outputting to a printer device
System. Drawing.Text	System. Drawing.dll	*FontCollection, InstalledFont-Collection*	Types for enumerating and installing fonts
System.Globalization	MSCorLib.dll	*CultureInfo, Calendar*	Types for authoring multi-language applications
System.IO	MSCorLib.dll	*Path, File, Stream, FileStream, StreamReader*	Types that provide access to files' attributes and contents
System. Messaging	System. Messaging.dll	*Message, MessageQueue*	Types for working with Microsoft Message Queue Server (MSMQ)
System.Net	System.dll	*HttpWebRequest, Dns, WebResponse*	Types for sending HTTP Web requests
System. Net.Sockets	System.dll	*Socket, UdpClient*	Types for working with sockets
System. Reflection	MSCorLib.dll	*Assembly, Property-Info, MethodInfo*	Types for reflecting over existing assemblies and types
System. Reflection. Emit	MSCorLib.dll	*AssemblyBuilder, MethodBuilder*	Types for programmatically creating new assemblies
System. Resources	MSCorLib.dll	*ResourceReader, ResourceWriter*	Types for working with resource files
System. Runtime. Interop-Services	MSCorLib.dll	*Marshal, COMException*	Types for working with unmanaged COM components

(continued)

Table 2-2   The Most Important Namespaces in the .NET Framework (continued)

Namespace	DLL Name	Sample Classes	Description
System. Runtime. Remoting	MSCorLib.dll	ObjHandle, SoapServices	Types for enabling remote execution
System. Runtime. Serialization. Formatters. Binary	MSCorLib.dll	BinaryFormatter	Type for serialization in binary format
System. Runtime. Serialization. Formatters. Soap	System. Runtime. Serialization. Formatters. Soap.dll	SoapFormatter	Type for serialization in SOAP format
System. Security	MSCorLib.dll	PermissionSet, Code- AccessPermission	Types for security support
System. Security. Cryptography	MSCorLib.dll	DES, RSA	Types for cryptographic services
System. Security. Permissions	MSCorLib.dll	FileIOPermission, RegistryPermission	Types for querying for security permissions
System. ServiceProcess	System. ServicePro- cess.dll	ServiceController, ServiceBase	Types for creating and controlling Windows services
System. Text.Regular- Expressions	System.dll	Regex, Match	Types for working with regular expressions
System. Threading	MSCorLib.dll and System.dll	Thread, Monitor, ThreadPool	Types for controlling multithreading capabilities
System.Timers	System.dll	Timer	Timer class for server-side applications
System.Web	System. Web.dll	HttpApplication, HttpCookie	Types for working with generic HTTP applications

Table 2-2   The Most Important Namespaces in the .NET Framework *(continued)*

Namespace	DLL Name	Sample Classes	Description
System. Web.UI	System. Web.dll	*Page, DataBinding*	Basic types for working with ASP.NET applications
System. Web.UI. HtmlControls	System. Web.dll	*HtmlButton, HtmlTable*	ASP.NET controls that parallel old-style HTML controls
System. Web.UI. WebControls	System. Web.dll	*Button, CheckBox, Table*	ASP.NET controls with rich user-interface capabilities
System. Web.Services	System. Web. Services.dll	*WebService, WebMethodAttribute*	Types for creating XML Web services
System. Web.Services. Protocols	System. Web. Services.dll	*SoapHeader, SoapExtension*	Types for low-level work with Web Services
System. Windows. Forms	System. Windows. Forms.dll	*Form, TextBox, ListBox*	Types for creating Windows Forms applications
System.Xml	System.Xml.dll	*XmlDataDocument, XmlNode*	Types for working with XML documents
System. Xml.Schema	System.Xml.dll	*XmlSchema, XmlSchemaElement*	Types for working with XML schemas
System. Xml.XPath	System.Xml.dll	*XPathDocument, XPathExpression*	Types for working with XML XPath queries
System. Xml.Xsl	System.Xml.dll	*XslTransform, XslContent*	Types for working with XSL transformations

✳✳✳

Structures

The *Type...End Type* block isn't supported in Visual Basic .NET and has been replaced by the *Structure...End Structure* block, which offers many additional features and is actually more similar to classes than to the old user-defined types (or UDTs) allowed in previous language versions. You can have a structure at the namespace level, inside a *Class* or *Module* block, or even inside another structure.

Members inside a structure must be prefixed with an accessibility (visibility) qualifier, as in this code:

```
Structure PersonStruct
    Dim FirstName As String           ' Dim means Public here.
    Dim LastName As String
    Public Address As String
    Private SSN As String
End Structure
```

The declaration of the structure's data members can neither include initializers nor use the As New declaration syntax. As comments in the preceding example suggest, the default accessibility level for structures—that is, the visibility level implied by a Dim keyword—is Public (unlike classes, where the default level is Private). Visual Basic .NET unifies the syntax of classes and structures, and structures support most of the functionality of classes, including methods:

```
Structure PersonStruct
    Dim FirstName As String
    Dim LastName As String
    Public Address As String
    Private SSN As String

    Function CompleteName() As String
        CompleteName = FirstName & " " & LastName
    End Function
End Structure
```

Like classes, structures can also embed properties. Unlike classes, however, structures are value types rather than reference types. Among other things, this means that Visual Basic .NET automatically initializes a structure when you declare a variable of that type; in other words, this line:

```
Dim p As PersonStruct
```

is equivalent to one of the following statements:

```
Dim p As PersonStruct = New PersonStruct()   ' Verbose initializer
Dim p As New PersonStruct                     ' Shortened syntax
```

Each structure implicitly defines a parameterless constructor, which initializes each member of the structure to its default value (0 for numeric members, null string for *String* members, and *Nothing* for object members). It's illegal to define an explicit parameterless constructor or a destructor for the structure. But you can define a *New* constructor method with arguments, as follows:

```
Structure PersonStruct
    Dim FirstName As String
    Dim LastName As String
    Public Address As String
    Private SSN As String

    ' A constructor for this structure
    Sub New(ByVal FirstName As String, ByVal LastName As String)
        ' Note how you can use the Me keyword.
        Me.FirstName = FirstName
        Me.LastName = LastName
    End Function
    ⋮
End Structure
```

The constructor method is especially important because it lets you initialize the structure's members correctly. That you manage this task is vital, for example, when the structure contains fixed-length strings or, more precisely, their closest approximation under the .NET Framework:

```
' A structure with a fixed-length string

Structure PersonStruct
    Dim FirstName As String
    Dim LastName As String
    ' Simulate a fixed-length string.
    Dim ZipCode As Microsoft.VisualBasic.Compatibility.VB6.FixedLengthString

    Sub New(ByVal firstName As String, ByVal lastName As String)
        Me.FirstName = firstName
        Me.LastName = lastName
        ' Initialize the fixed-length string.
        ZipCode = New _
            Microsoft.VisualBasic.Compatibility.VB6.FixedLengthString(10)
    End Sub

    ' ...(The remainder of the code as in preceding code snippet)...
    ⋮
End Structure
```

That said, consider fixed-length strings your last resort because it's far preferable to convert them to regular strings when you're porting an application from
previous versions of the language.

A consequence of the value type nature of *Structure* variables is that the
actual data is copied when you assign a structure variable to another variable,
whereas only a pointer to data is copied when you assign a reference value to
a variable. Also note that the equality operator isn't supported for structures.
This code summarizes the differences between classes and structures:

```
' This code assumes you have a PersonClass class, with the same structure
' as the PersonStruct structure.

Sub TestCompareStructuresAndClasses()
    ' Creation is similar, but structures don't require New.
    Dim aPersonObject As New Person()
    Dim aPersonStruct As PersonStruct          ' New is optional.

    ' Assignment to members is identical.
    aPersonObject.FirstName = "Joe"
    aPersonObject.LastName = "Doe"
    aPersonStruct.FirstName = "Joe"
    aPersonStruct.LastName = "Doe"

    ' Method and property invocation is also identical.
    Console.WriteLine(aPersonObject.CompleteName())        ' => Joe Doe
    Console.WriteLine(aPersonStruct.CompleteName())        ' => Joe Doe

    ' Assignment to a variable of the same type has different effects.

    Dim aPersonObject2 As Person = aPersonObject
    ' Classes are reference types; hence, the new variable receives
    ' a pointer to the original object.
    aPersonObject2.FirstName = "Ann"
    ' The original object has been affected.
    Console.WriteLine(aPersonObject.FirstName)     ' => Ann
    '
    Dim aPersonStruct2 As PersonStruct = aPersonStruct
    ' Structures are value types; hence, the new variable receives
    ' a copy of the original structure.
    aPersonStruct2.FirstName = "Ann"
    ' The original structure hasn't been affected.
    Console.WriteLine(aPersonStruct.FirstName)     ' => Joe
End Sub
```

A few other features of classes aren't supported by structures in Visual
Basic .NET. For example, structures implicitly inherit all the methods of the
Object class, but they can't explicitly inherit from another structure, nor can they
be inherited from.

Reading 3

Exception Handling

The grandest of intentions and the most thorough planning can't eliminate errors in code. Errors can be programmer errors (usually caused by bad assumptions, such as that a denominator will never be 0) or environmental errors (such as an attempt to save a file that is too large for the amount of free space on a disk). You should strive for error-free code, but you should also create every procedure with the assumption that an error might occur. This means that every procedure must contain an error handler.

There are practically an infinite number of possible program errors, but they basically fall into two types: compile (build) errors and run-time errors (called *exceptions*). A *build error* is an error that prevents Microsoft Visual Basic's compiler from compiling the code; Visual Basic won't execute a procedure that has a compile error in it, and you can't distribute a run-time version of an application that has a compile error. Most compile errors are a result of erroneous syntax.

For example, if you attempt to call a procedure defined as

```
Public Sub MyProcedure(ByVal intMyVariable As Integer)
```

by using the statement below, a compile error occurs because of the added argument in the *Call* statement.

```
Call MyProcedure(intVariable1, intVariable2)
```

Run-time errors occur while a program is running and are usually the result of trying to perform an invalid operation on a variable. For instance, the following code doesn't generate a compile error.

From *Practical Standards for Microsoft Visual Basic .NET* by James Foxall. pp. 179-199. (Redmond: Microsoft Press. 2003.) Copyright © 2003 by James Foxall.

```
Dim intNumerator As Integer
Dim intDenominator As Integer
Dim intResult As Integer

' Modify variables here
⋮

intResult = intNumerator / intDenominator
```

Under most circumstances, this code won't even generate a run-time error. However, if the value of *intDenominator* is 0, Visual Basic throws an exception because the result of 10 divided by 0 (which Visual Basic treats as infinity) can't be placed into an Integer. If a run-time error occurs when you run a project in the integrated development environment (IDE), code execution stops at the offending line and an error message appears. In a compiled program, an unhandled exception is fatal, causing the entire application to crash to the desktop (without calling any necessary clean-up code, I might add). You can prevent execution from stopping when run-time exceptions occur by creating exception handlers.

The Exception Object

Before you can write effective exception-handling code, you must understand Visual Basic .NET's Exception class. Objects derived from the Exception class contain information about an exception that has occurred. The properties of an Exception object are populated when an exception is encountered at run time or when you deliberately throw an exception using the *Throw* statement. Table 3-1 lists the most useful properties of the Exception object.

Table 3-1   Useful Properties of the Exception Object

Property	Description
Source	The name of the application that caused the exception. *Source* is most useful when catching exceptions thrown by other components.
Message	A string describing the exception.
StackTrace	A string representation of the frames on the call stack at the time the exception was thrown.
TargetSite	A string describing the method that caused the exception.

Types of Exception Handlers

When you run a project as a compiled program or component, untrapped exceptions are fatal—they cause your program to terminate. You must make every effort to prevent this from happening. To prevent exceptions from stopping code execution (and terminating compiled programs), you create exception handlers to trap the exceptions. When an exception is trapped, Visual Basic doesn't display an error message or terminate the application. Instead, code that you've written to specifically handle the exception is executed.

> **Note**   In previous editions of Visual Basic, error handlers were created using *On Error* statements. This method of handling errors was considered an unstructured approach. Although Visual Basic .NET still supports this method, it has been replaced with the new structured exception-handling construct *Try...Catch...Finally*. It might not make sense to attempt to convert all of the error handlers of existing code to use *Try...Catch...Finally* (although you can choose to do so), but you *should* use the new structured exception-handling mechanism for all new code. I do not discuss *On Error* in this book because it is considered an outdated methodology.

Microsoft Knowledge Base article Q301283 states, "A *try-catch-finally* block is a 'wrapper' that you put around any code where the possibility of an exception exists." This statement is misleading. Every single statement you write has a "possibility" of encountering an error. Therefore, all procedures should have an exception handler, regardless of the amount of code they contain.

It's best to place a *Try* statement as the first line of code, immediately after the procedure header and just after the variable declarations. If your variable declarations use other variables as initializers (for example, *Dim intMyVariable As Integer = intAnotherVariable + 2*), you should place these declarations within the *Try* structure. Be aware that exceptions can "bubble up" the call stack to exception handlers in procedures higher in the stack (as I'll discuss later in this chapter). If a procedure's exceptions are allowed to bubble up in this manner, you should clearly explain this behavior in a prominent comment at the top of the procedure.

> **Important**   Variables declared within the *Try* block of an exception handler have block scope—they aren't available to any *Catch* or *Finally* blocks, and they aren't available outside of the *Try...End Try* construct. For this reason, it's best to leave declarations outside of the *Try* block unless the declaration has an inherent risk of throwing an exception.

You can create multiple exception handlers in a procedure by nesting *Try...Catch...Finally* blocks, but no more than one exception handler is active at a time. Visual Basic treats the handler identified by the most recent *Try* statement (discussed in the next section) as the enabled exception handler. It's often advantageous to switch exception handlers at different points within a procedure, as I'll also discuss in this chapter.

Writing an Exception Handler by Using *Try...Catch...Finally*

Exception handlers allow you to determine how an exception is treated, rather than rely on Visual Basic's default behavior, which is to display the exception and terminate the application. As I mentioned earlier, Visual Basic .NET supports structured exception handling in the form of a *Try...Catch...Finally* structure. This structure has the following syntax—see Table 3-2 for a description of each component.

```
Try
    ' Statements to try.
Catch [exception As type] [When expression]
    ' Statements to run when an exception is thrown.
Finally
    ' Statements to run when execution leaves any other block in the
    ' structure, such as Try or Catch. These statements run regardless
    ' of whether an exception occurred.
End Try
```

Table 3-2   Components of the *Try...Catch...Finally* Structure

Part	Description
Try	The *Try* section is where you place code that might cause an exception (i.e., all code other than exception-handling code). You can place all of a procedure's code within the *Try* section or just a few lines.
Catch	Code within the *Catch* section executes only when an exception occurs. This is where you place code to deal with an exception.
Finally	Code within the *Finally* section occurs when the code within the *Try* section and/or code within the *Catch* section completes. This section is where you place your "cleanup" code—code that you want always executed regardless of whether an exception occurs.

Consider the following code:

```
Try
    Debug.WriteLine("Try")
Catch
    Debug.WriteLine("Catch")
Finally
    Debug.WriteLine("Finally")
End Try

Debug.WriteLine("Done Trying")
```

If you were to run this code, here's what would happen:

1.   The *Try* block would begin, and code within the *Try* section would execute.

2.   The code contains no errors, so no exception would be thrown. Therefore, the code within the *Catch* section wouldn't execute.

3.   When all statements within the *Try* section finished executing, the code within the *Finally* section would execute.

4.   When all statements within the *Finally* section finished executing, execution would jump to the statement immediately following *End Try* statement.

The following would print to the Output window:

```
Try
Finally
Done Trying
```

Now consider this code:

```
Dim intNumerator As Integer = 10
Dim intDenominator As Integer = 0
Dim intResult As Integer

Try
    Debug.WriteLine("Try")
    intResult = intNumerator / intDenominator
Catch
    Debug.WriteLine("Catch")
Finally
    Debug.WriteLine("Finally")
End Try

Debug.WriteLine("Done Trying")
```

If you were to run this code, the following would be printed to the Output window:

```
Try
Catch
Finally
Done Trying
```

Notice that this time the code within the *Catch* section would execute. This happens because the statement that sets *intResult* causes an Overflow exception. Had this statement not been placed in within a *Try* block, Visual Basic would have raised the exception and an error dialog box would have appeared. However, because the statement is placed within the *Try* block, the exception would be "caught." This means that when the exception occurs, Visual Basic directs execution to the *Catch* section. Notice also how the code within the *Finally* section executes after the code within the *Catch* section. Remember, code within the *Finally* section always executes, regardless of whether an exception occurs.

Catching Exceptions

The *Catch* section is where you deal with an exception. Technically, you don't *have* to include a *Catch* section, but leaving it out is a *very bad idea!* Ignoring an exception (by not including a *Catch* section) is worse than not including exception trapping to begin with because exceptions will occur and neither you nor your customers will know about them.

> **Important**   You should always include a *Catch* section to deal with exceptions.

Dealing with Exceptions

Catching exceptions so that they don't crash your application is a noble thing to do, but it's only part of the exception-handling process. Usually, you'll want to tell the user (in a friendly way) that an exception has occurred. Not only do you want to tell them an exception occurred, but you'll probably also want to tell them what type of exception occurred. To do this, you have to have a way of knowing what exception was thrown. This is also important if you intend to write code to deal with specific exceptions. The *Catch* statement allows you to specify a variable to hold a reference to an Exception object. Using this Exception object, you can get information about the exception. Here's the syntax used to place the exception in an Exception object:

```
Catch variablename As Exception
```

If an exception occurs, you can manipulate the properties of the variable—see Table 3-1—as you see fit. For instance, to simply inform the user of an error, you could use code such as this:

```
Try
    ' Try something here.

Catch ex As Exception
    MessageBox.Show("Error: " & ex.Message, "Error!", _
                    MessageBoxButtons.OK, MessageBoxIcon.Exclamation)

End Try
```

Recall from Table 3-1 that the *Message* property of the Exception object contains the text that describes the specific exception that occurs. As with other code structures, Visual Basic has a statement that can be used to exit a *Try...End Try* structure at any time: *Exit Try*. Note, however, that if you use *Exit Try*, the *Finally* block *will* execute. When writing clean-up code in a *Finally* block for an exception handler that uses *Exit Try*, be sure that no problems arise from the *Exit Try* diverting code to the *Finally* block.

Handling a Specific Anticipated Exception

There may be times that you'll anticipate a specific exception being thrown. For example, you might write code that attempts to open a file when the file might not exist. In such an instance, you'll probably want to perform specific actions when the anticipated exception is thrown. When you anticipate a specific exception, you can create a *Catch* section designed specifically to deal with that one exception.

In the previous section, I showed how you could catch an exception using a *Catch* statement such as *Catch e As Exception*. By creating a generic Exception variable, such a *Catch* statement would catch any and all exceptions thrown by statements within the *Try* section. To catch a specific exception, change the data type of the exception variable to a specific exception type. For example:

```
Dim lngAnswer As Long
Try
    lngAnswer = 100 / CLng(txtInput.Text)
    MessageBox.Show("100/" & txtInput.Text & " is " & lngAnswer)

Catch objException As System.OverflowException
    MessageBox.Show("You must enter something in the text box.")

Catch objException As Exception
    MessageBox.Show("Caught an exception that wasn't an overflow.")

End Try
```

Notice that there are two *Catch* statements in this structure. The first *Catch* statement is designed to catch only an Overflow exception—it won't catch exceptions of any other type. The second *Catch* statement doesn't care what type of exception is thrown. *Catch* sections are evaluated from top to bottom, much like *Case* statements in *Select...Case* structure. This means the general *Catch* section shown here would never catch an Overflow exception.

You could add as many *Catch* sections as you need to catch other specific exceptions. However, if you are anticipating specific exceptions, it might be best to wrap that code in its own *Try...End Try* structure, like this:

```
Try
    ' Do stuff here.

    ' The following code might generate an anticipated error
    Try
        ' Code that might generate an anticipated error.
    Catch ex As AnticipatedError
        ' Code to deal with anticipated error.
    Catch
        ' Code to deal with an unexpected error.
```

```
    End Try
Catch
    ' Code to deal with an unexpected error.
End Try
```

> **Important**   When specifying multiple Catch blocks for an exception handler, order them from most specific to least specific. This ensures that exceptions are handled correctly.

Exception Handlers and the Call Stack

It's extremely important to understand how exceptions are passed up the call stack. Although *Try…Catch…Finally* structures can be nested—even across procedures, as shown in the following code—only one *Try* block is active at any given point in time. Consider the following two procedures:

```
Private Sub cmdCreateErrorHandler_Click(ByVal sender As _
            System.Object, ByVal e As System.EventArgs) _
            Handles cmdCreateErrorHandler.Click
    ' Purpose    :   Create an error handler.

    Try
        Call TestSub()
    Catch
        MessageBox.Show("Error caught in Click event.")

    End Try
End Sub

Private Sub TestSub()
    ' Purpose    :   Demonstrate error handlers and the call stack.
    Dim intNumerator As Integer = 100
    Dim intDenominator As Integer = 0

    Try
        ' This next statement throws an exception.
        Dim intResult As Integer = intNumerator / intDenominator

    Catch
        Messagebox.Show("Error caught in TestSub().")
    End Try

End Sub
```

When the *cmdCreateErrorHandler* button is clicked, the *Try* statement creates an exception handler. When the *TestSub* method is invoked, its exception handler becomes enabled when its *Try* statement is encountered; any exceptions encountered within the *Try* structure in the *TestSub* method (such as the divide-by-zero error deliberately created here) are handled by the current exception handler. When the *Try...End Try* structure *is* completed, the *Try* structure of the *Click* event becomes active once more.

Next consider these two procedures:

```
Private Sub cmdCreateErrorHandler_Click(ByVal sender As _
            System.Object, ByVal e As System.EventArgs) _
            Handles cmdCreateErrorHandler.Click
  ' Purpose   :  Create an error handler.

  Try
     Call TestSub()
  Catch
     MessageBox.Show("Error caught in Click event.")
  End Try

End Sub

Private Sub TestSub()
  ' Purpose   :  Demonstrate error handlers and the call stack.
  Dim intNumerator As Integer = 100
  Dim intDenominator As Integer = 0

  ' This next statement throws an exception.
  Dim intResult As Integer = intNumerator / intDenominator

End Sub
```

When the button is clicked, the *Try* statement creates an active exception handler. When the *TestSub* method is invoked, code is still executing within the *Try* structure of the *Click* event. When the exception occurs, Visual Basic looks back through the thread of execution to determine whether the code is executing within a *Try* block. In this case, it would determine that the code was indeed within a *Try* block, so the exception would be handled in the *Click* event, as illustrated by the following two procedures:

```
Private Sub cmdCreateErrorHandler_Click(ByVal sender As _
            System.Object, ByVal e As System.EventArgs) _
            Handles cmdCreateErrorHandler.Click
  ' Purpose   :  Create an error handler.

  Try
     Call TestSub()
```

```
            MessageBox.Show("Statement in Click event.")
        Catch
            MessageBox.Show("An exception has been caught!")
        End Try

End Sub

Private Sub TestSub()
    ' Purpose   :  Demonstrate error handlers and the call stack.
    Dim intNumerator As Integer = 100
    Dim intDenominator As Integer = 0

    ' This next statement throws an exception.
    Dim intResult As Integer = intNumerator / intDenominator
    MessageBox.Show("Statement in TestSub() method.")

End Sub
```

When the *Click* event is fired, an exception handler is enabled by the *Try* statement. When execution transfers to the *TestSub* procedure, the exception handler remains enabled because no *Catch*, *Finally*, or *End Try* statement has been reached. When the exception occurs, what's printed? Because the exception isn't part of a *Try* block within the same procedure, Visual Basic looks deeper in the call stack to see whether execution is occurring within a *Try* block higher up the stack. Because the code is within a *Try* block higher up the call stack, the exception is handled and the following text gets printed:

```
An exception has been caught!
```

This concept is true for multiple nested procedures as well. If an exception occurs within a procedure and the code isn't contained in a *Try* block, Visual Basic looks up the call stack to see whether execution is occurring in a *Try* block somewhere deeper in the stack. If the top of the call stack is reached and code execution is found *not* to be running within a *Try* block, the exception is treated as untrapped (and rightly so). Such an error will cause a message to be displayed to the user, and your application will crash to the desktop.

Note   If an exception is encountered in a *Catch* block, one of two things happened. If an exception handler is wrapped around the current exception handler (or one higher up the call stack), the *Finally* block of the current exception handler is called, and execution then jumps to the *Catch* block of the next active exception handler. If no other exception handler is active, the program will crash.

Central Exception Handlers

It's tedious to add exception handling to all procedures in a project, but it's a *necessity*. Every unexpected exception must be displayed to the user in the same format, and this can take a considerable amount of code. Adding a central exception handler can help tremendously.

A *central exception handler* is a procedure that you call when an exception occurs. At a minimum, a central exception handler displays a consistent error message to the user. However, you can add capabilities to the central exception handler as you see fit. For instance, you can have your central exception handler send an e-mail message to a support specialist whenever an unexpected exception occurs, or you can actually include code to take a snapshot of the state of the machine and log the loaded applications and loaded DLLs along with their versions.

The following is a typical central exception handler:

```
Friend Sub HandleException(ByVal strModule As String, ByVal e As Exception)
    ' Purpose   :  Provide a central exception-handling mechanism.
    ' Accepts   :  strModule - the module in which the error was
    '                 encountered (form, class, standard, and so on.)
    '              e - the exception that occurred.
    Dim strMessage As String
    Dim strCaption As String

    Try
        ' Build the error message.
        strMessage = "Exception: " & e.Message & ControlChars.CrLf & _
                    ControlChars.CrLf & _
                    "Module: " & strModule & ControlChars.CrLf & _
                    "Method: " & e.TargetSite.Name & ControlChars.CrLf & _
                    ControlChars.CrLf & _
                    "Please notify My Software's tech support " & _
                    "at 555-1213 about this issue." & ControlChars.CrLf & _
                    "Please provide the support technician with " & _
                    "information shown in " & ControlChars.CrLf & _
                    "this dialog box as well as an explanation of what " & _
                    "you were" & ControlChars.CrLf & "doing when this " & _
                    "error occurred."

        ' Build the title bar text for the message box. The text includes
        ' the version number of the program.
        With System.Reflection.Assembly.GetExecutingAssembly.GetName.Version
            strCaption = "Unexpected Exception! Version: " & _
                        .Major & "." & _
```

```
                         .Minor & "." & _
                         Format(.Revision, "0000")
            End With

            ' Show the error to the user.
            MessageBox.Show(strMessage, strCaption, _
                        MessageBoxButtons.OK, MessageBoxIcon.Exclamation)
        Finally

        End Try

End Sub
```

To use this central exception handler, you simply call the procedure in an exception handler like this:

```
Private Sub Button1_Click(ByVal sender As System.Object, _
                        ByVal e As System.EventArgs) _
                        Handles Button1.Click

    Dim intNumerator As Integer = 100
    Dim intDenominator As Integer = 0
    Dim lngResult As Long

    Try

        ' This next statement throws an exception.
        lngResult = CLng(intNumerator / intDenominator)

    Catch objE As Exception
        Call HandleException(Me.Name, objE)

    End Try

End Sub
```

When the exception illustrated in the previous example occurs, the central exception handler is called and it displays the dialog box shown in Figure 3-1. Imagine trying to display such a comprehensive error message from every exception handler in every procedure in every module without using a central exception handler!

Figure 3-1   A central exception handler makes it easy to display comprehensive error messages.

Notice the use of *Me.Name* in the call to the exception handler, which makes the line of code a bit more portable. You can copy the *Catch* statement as well as this statement to the Clipboard and paste it into other procedures. This enables you to write the exception handlers in your various procedures more quickly and allows you to change the way exceptions are handled or displayed by changing code in one location rather than in hundreds or thousands of locations.

The Exception object tracks the procedure in which an exception occurs (*e.TargetSite.Name*), but it doesn't keep track of the object (module) involved. This is why the reference to *Me.Name* is in the code shown previously.

For modules other than forms, *Name* doesn't work, so you have to use the literal class name. However, in this situation it's best to create a module-level constant and use the constant so that you don't have to modify the exception handlers' code if a module's name is changed. If you use a generic constant name (such as *mc_Module*), you can copy the *Catch* and *Call HandleException* statements from one module and paste them into another module without having to make any modifications.

Although the central exception handler shown earlier displays the error message to the user in a consistent fashion, you must determine the code that each exception handler will have in addition to calling the *HandleException* method. For instance, what additional code (if any) should go in the *Catch* block? What code should go in the *Finally* block? You should make your exception handlers as generic as possible, but you also should make sure that each one is appropriate for the procedure in which it resides.

Logging Exceptions to a Text File

It's often useful to have a log of any exceptions that occur. For instance, during the testing phase of your project, you need to know as much as you can about any errors that happen. You usually can't rely on reports from users. When it's critical that you know about every exception in your program, you should use a central exception handler to create an exception log.

Creating an exception log is simple. First create a central exception handler as discussed earlier. Then, within the central exception handler, devise a mechanism to log the exceptions to a text file. The following code illustrates one way to log exceptions to a text file. This code is shown as it would appear as part of the central exception handler shown previously. It assumes that there is a global variable in the project called *g_strExceptionLogFileName* that contains the path and name of the exception log file.

```
' Open a new stream writer to the log file.
Dim objStream As New System.IO.StreamWriter(g_strExceptionLogFileName, _
                                            True)

Dim strLogText As String

' Create the log text.
strLogText = DateTime.Now & ControlChars.CrLf & _
             "Exception: " & e.Message & ControlChars.CrLf & _
             "Module: " & strModule & ControlChars.CrLf & _
             "Method: " & e.TargetSite.Name & ControlChars.CrLf & _
             "Stack: " & e.StackTrace & ControlChars.CrLf

' Write the exception message.
objStream.WriteLine(strLogText)

' Flush the text to the log file.
objStream.Flush()

' Close the log file.
objStream.Close()
```

If the file does not exist, the StreamWriter creates it. If the file exists, text is appended to it. Once the file is opened, a log entry is written. Here is a sample of a text file created using the previous code:

```
4/8/2002 11:43:00 PM
Exception: Arithmetic operation resulted in an overflow.
Module: Form1
Method: Button1_Click
Stack:    at Hungarian.Form1.Button1_Click(Object sender, EventArgs
e) in C:\Documents and Settings\James Foxall\My Documents\Visual
```

(continued)

```
Studio Projects\Form1.vb:line 97

4/8/2002 11:46:47 PM
Exception: Arithmetic operation resulted in an overflow.
Module: Form1
Method: Button1_Click
Stack:     at Hungarian.Form1.Button1_Click(Object sender, EventArgs
e) in C:\Documents and Settings\James Foxall\My Documents\Visual
Studio Projects\Form1.vb:line 97

4/8/2002 11:47:31 PM
Exception: Funky crazy custom error
Module: Form1
Method: Button1_Click
Stack:     at Hungarian.Form1.Button1_Click(Object sender, EventArgs
e) in C:\Documents and Settings\James Foxall\My Documents\Visual
Studio Projects\Form1.vb:line 96
```

You can start to see a trend in this exception log. Whoever wrote the Form1 module needs to spend a little more time with the code. The information shown here is the minimum amount you'd want to include in a text file; you might want to include much more. For instance, you might want to include the user name of the person running the program when the exception occurs, or you might want to include the machine name in the log entry. The possibilities are endless. Whatever you choose to put into the text file, make sure it's pertinent information that will help you find and correct the problem.

For clarity, the following is the complete exception handler shown previously, with the inclusion of the exception log code:

```
Friend Sub HandleException(ByVal strModule As String, ByVal e As Exception)
  ' Purpose   :   Provide a central error-handling mechanism.
  ' Accepts   :   strModule - the module in which the error was
  '                   encountered (form, class, standard, and so on.)
  '                   e - the exception that occurred.
  Dim strMessage As String
  Dim strCaption As String

  Try
      ' Build the error message.
      strMessage = "Exception: " & e.Message & vbCrLf & vbCrLf & _
                  "Module: " & strModule & vbCrLf & _
                  "Method: " & e.TargetSite.Name & vbCrLf & vbCrLf & _
                  "Please notify My Software's tech support " & _
                  "at 555-1213 about this issue." & vbCrLf & _
                  "Please provide the support technician with " & _
                  "information shown in " & vbCrLf & "this dialog " & _
                  "box as well as an explanation of what you " & _
```

```
                            "were" & vbCrLf & "doing when this " & _
                            "error occurred."

            ' Build the title bar text for the message box. The text includes
            ' the version number of the program.
            With System.Reflection.Assembly.GetExecutingAssembly.GetName.Version
                strCaption = "Unexpected Exception! Version: " & _
                              .Major & "." & _
                              .Minor & "." & _
                              Format(.Revision, "0000")
            End With

            ' Open a new stream writer to the log file.
            Dim objStream As New System.IO.StreamWriter(g_strExceptionLogFileName, _
                                                        True)

            Dim strLogText As String

            ' Create the log text.
            strLogText = DateTime.Now & ControlChars.CrLf & _
                         "Exception: " & e.Message & ControlChars.CrLf & _
                         "Module: " & strModule & ControlChars.CrLf & _
                         "Method: " & e.TargetSite.Name & ControlChars.CrLf & _
                         "Stack: " & e.StackTrace & ControlChars.CrLf

            ' Write the exception message.
            objStream.WriteLine(strLogText)
            ' Flush the text to the log file.
            objStream.Flush()
            ' Close the log file.
            objStream.Close()

            ' Show the error to the user.
            MessageBox.Show(strMessage, strCaption, MessageBoxButtons.OK, _
                            MessageBoxIcon.Exclamation)

        Finally

        End Try

    End Sub
```

Once your application is logging error messages, you must decide what you want to do with those logs. If you're on-site with the program, you can manually retrieve copies of the exception logs. Or you can have users e-mail you their logs if they encounter problems. You might even write a program that automatically e-mails the logs to you on a preset schedule, or you might want to write an e-mail interface directly into the central exception handler. Log files can be very useful for locating specific bugs as well as general program errors, and they trivially easy to create; you should seriously consider adding this feature to your programs. You might even elect to include the logging code but turn off the feature by default. You could then enable or disable log file generation via your program's interface or a registry setting.

Goals of Exception Handling

The goals of utilizing exception handling are

- Preventing your program from crashing

- Gracefully correcting mistakes whenever possible

- Notifying the user when exceptions occur so that the problems can be addressed

---

Directives

3.1 Use *Try...Catch...Finally* to handle unexpected as well as anticipated exceptions.

Most exception handlers are designed to trap exceptions that aren't anticipated at design time. Use a *Try...Catch...Finally* structure to catch all unanticipated exceptions.

Incorrect:

```
Private Sub btnSelectPicture_Click(ByVal sender As System.Object, _
                                   ByVal e As System.EventArgs) Handles _
                                   btnSelectPicture.Click
    ' Purpose   :  Open the selected picture and display it in the
    '              picture box.

    ' Show the open file dialog box.
    If ofdSelectPicture.ShowDialog = DialogResult.OK Then
        ' Load the picture into the picture box.
        picShowPicture.Image = Image.FromFile(ofdSelectPicture.FileName)
        ' Show the name of the file in the form's caption.
        Me.Text = "Picture Viewer(" & ofdSelectPicture.FileName & ")"
    End If

End Sub
```

Correct:
```
Private Sub btnSelectPicture_Click(ByVal sender As System.Object, _
                          ByVal e As System.EventArgs) Handles _
                          btnSelectPicture.Click
    ' Purpose   : Open the selected picture and display it in the
    '             picture box.

    Try
        ' Show the open file dialog box.
        If ofdSelectPicture.ShowDialog = DialogResult.OK Then
            ' Load the picture into the picture box.
            picShowPicture.Image = Image.FromFile(ofdSelectPicture.FileName)
            ' Show the name of the file in the form's caption.
            Me.Text = "Picture Viewer(" & ofdSelectPicture.FileName & ")"
        End If

    Catch ex As Exception
        MessageBox.Show("Error: " & e.Message, "Error!", _
                        MessageBoxButtons.OK, MessageBoxIcon.Exclamation)
    End Try
End Sub
```

3.2 Use a consistent format when dealing with unanticipated exceptions.

When you use *Try...Catch...Finally*, it's important to use a consistent format for handling unanticipated exceptions. *It's best to use a central exception handler,* but if you don't use one, create an exception handler like this typical *Catch* block:

```
Catch ex As Exception
    MessageBox.Show("Exception: " & ex.Message & ControlChars.CrLf & _
                    ControlChars.CrLf & _
                    "Module: " & modulename & ControlChars.CrLf & _
                    "Method: " & ex.TargetSite.Name)
```

The only part of the *MessageBox.Show* statement that should be modified for each procedure is the module.

You can add code to the *Catch* block at your discretion, such as invoking a rollback on a database transaction. Of course, the necessary code will vary from procedure to procedure, and some code might best be placed in the *Finally* block, depending on the situation at hand.

Creating a central exception handler eliminates the necessity to micromanage the exception handler in every procedure. However, if you don't use a central exception handler, you must handle and display exceptions in a consistent manner.

Incorrect:

```
Catch ex As Exception
    MessageBox.Show("An unexpected exception has occurred." & _
                    ControlChars.CrLf & ex.Message)

Catch ex As Exception
    MessageBox.Show("An error has occurred!", "Error!", _
                    MessageBoxButtons.OK, MessageBoxIcon.Exclamation)
```

Correct:

```
Catch ex As Exception
    MessageBox.Show("Exception: " & ex.Message & _
                    ControlChars.CrLf & ControlChars.CrLf & _
                    "Module: " & Me.Name & ControlChars.CrLf & _
                    "Method: " & ex.TargetSite.Name)


Catch ex As Exception
    MessageBox.Show("Exception: " & ex.Message & _
                    ControlChars.CrLf & ControlChars.CrLf & _
                    "Module: " & mc_ModuleName & ControlChars.CrLf & _
                    "Method: " & ex.TargetSite.Name)
```

3.3 Never blame the user.

When you display an error message to a user, never blame the user or make the user feel he or she did something wrong. If the exception that has been caught was not anticipated, the fault lies with the programmer. If the exception was a result of "bad" user input, find a way to politely inform the user of the situation rather than make the user feel as bad as the data. Make sure the user can tell the difference between a programming error and a legitimate exception (an anticipated error).

Incorrect:

```
Dim intTotal As Integer
Dim intPeriods As Integer

Try
    ' Get the total and number of periods from the user.
    intTotal = CInt(txtTotal.Text)
    intPeriods = CInt(txtPeriods.Text)

    ' Display the payment.
    MessageBox.Show("Each payment is: " & _
                    CSng(intTotal / intPeriods), _
                    "Payment Info", MessageBoxButtons.OK, _
                    MessageBoxIcon.Information)
```

```vbnet
Catch ex As InvalidCastException
    ' The user didn't enter a numeric value!
    MessageBox.Show("The total can't be computed because you " & _
                    "failed to enter a numeric value.", _
                    "User Error", MessageBoxButtons.OK, _
                    MessageBoxIcon.Warning)

Catch ex As Exception
    MessageBox.Show("Exception: " & ex.Message & ControlChars.CrLf & _
                    ControlChars.CrLf & _
                    "Module: " & "test" & ControlChars.CrLf & _
                    "Method: " & ex.TargetSite.Name)
End Try
```

Correct:

```vbnet
Dim intTotal As Integer
Dim intPeriods As Integer

Try
    ' Get the total and number of periods from the user.
    intTotal = CInt(txtTotal.Text)
    intPeriods = CInt(txtPeriods.Text)

    ' Display the payment.
    MessageBox.Show("Each payment is: " & _
                    CSng(intTotal / intPeriods), _
                    "Payment Info", MessageBoxButtons.OK, _
                    MessageBoxIcon.Information)

Catch ex As InvalidCastException
    ' The user didn't enter a numeric value.
    MessageBox.Show("Please enter a numeric value in each " & _
                    "required field.", "MyApplication", _
                    MessageBoxButtons.OK, _
                    MessageBoxIcon.Information)

Catch ex As Exception
    MessageBox.Show("Exception: " & ex.Message & ControlChars.CrLf & _
                    ControlChars.CrLf & _
                    "Module: " & "test" & ControlChars.CrLf & _
                    "Method: " & ex.TargetSite.Name)
End Try
```

> **Tip**   Whenever possible, offer the user practical advice for dealing with an exception.

Reading 4

Arrays, Lists, and Collections

The .NET Framework doesn't merely include classes for managing system objects, such as files, directories, processes, and threads. It also exposes objects, such as complex data structures (queues, stacks, and hash tables), that help developers solve recurring problems.

Many real-world applications use arrays and collections, and the .NET Framework support for arrays and collection-like objects is really outstanding. It can take a while for you to get familiar with the many possibilities that the .NET runtime offers, but this effort pays off nicely at coding time.

The Array Class

The Array class has no public constructor because its New procedure has a Protected scope. In practice, this is no problem because you create an array using the standard Visual Basic syntax, and, you can even use initializers:

```
' An array initialized with the powers of 2
Dim intArr() As Integer = {1, 2, 4, 8, 16, 32, 64, 128, 256, 512}
' Noninitialized two-dimensional array
Dim lngArr(10, 20) As Long
' An empty array
Dim dblArr() As Double
```

From *Programming Microsoft Visual Basic .NET* by Francesco Balena. pp. 385-418. (Redmond: Microsoft Press. 2002.) Copyright © 2002 by Francesco Balena.

A variation of this syntax lets you create an array and initialize it on the fly, which is sometimes useful for passing an argument or assigning a property that takes an array without having to create a temporary array. Consider the code at the top of the next page.

```
' Create a temporary array.
Dim tmp() As Integer = {2, 5, 9, 13}
' The obj.ValueArray property takes an array of Integer.
obj.ValueArray = tmp
' Clear the temporary variable.
tmp = Nothing
```

The ability to create and initialize an array in a single statement makes the code more concise, even though the syntax you need isn't exactly intuitive:

```
obj.ValueArray = New Long() {2, 5, 9, 13}
```

As in Visual Basic 6, you get an error if you access an empty array, which is an array that has no elements. Because the array is an object, you can test it using a plain Is operator and use ReDim on the array if necessary:

```
If dblArr Is Nothing Then
    ReDim dblArr(100)                 ' Note: no As clause in ReDims
End If
```

You can query an array for its rank (that is, the number of dimensions) by using its Rank property, and you can query the total number of its elements by means of its Length property:

```
' ...(Continuing preceding example)...
Console.WriteLine(lngArr.Rank)     ' => 2
' lngArr has 11*21 elements.
Console.WriteLine(lngArr.Length)    ' => 231
```

The GetLength method returns the number of elements along a given dimension, whereas GetLowerBound and GetUpperBound return the lowest and highest index along the specified dimension. Unlike values returned by the LBound and UBound functions, the dimension number is 0-based, not 1-based:

```
' ...(Continuing previous example)...
Console.WriteLine(lngArr.GetLength(0))     ' => 11
Console.WriteLine(lngArr.GetLowerBound(1))  ' => 0
Console.WriteLine(lngArr.GetUpperBound(1))  ' => 20
```

You can visit all the elements of an array using a single For Each loop and a strongly-typed variable; this is an improvement on Visual Basic 6, which forces you to use a Variant (and therefore late binding) when working with numeric or string arrays. This technique also works with multidimensional arrays, so you can process all the elements in a two-dimensional array with just one loop:

```
Dim strArr(,) As String = {{"00", "01", "02"}, {"10", "11", "12"}}
Dim s As String
For Each s In strArr
    Console.Write(s & ",")        ' => 00,01,02,10,11,12
Next
```

For Each loops on multidimensional arrays work in previous language versions as well, with an important difference: Visual Basic 6 visits array elements in a column-wise order (all the elements in the first column, then all the elements in the second column, and so on), whereas Visual Basic .NET follows the more natural row-wise order.

Creating Nonzero-Based Arrays

The GetLowerBound method might look unnecessary because all Visual Basic arrays have indexes beginning with 0. However, it turns out that you can create arrays with arbitrary starting indexes by means of the shared Array.CreateInstance method, even though the required syntax isn't exactly straightforward:

```
Sub TestArraysWithNonZeroLBound()
    ' Create a bidimensional array that is equivalent
    ' to the following Visual Basic 6 declaration:
    '     Dim(1 To 5, -10 To 10) As Integer

    ' Prepare an auxiliary array with the length along each direction.
    Dim lengths() As Integer = {5, 21}
    ' An auxiliary array with the starting index along each direction
    Dim lbounds() As Integer = {1, -10}
    ' Create a generic Array object from the shared CreateInstance method.
    Dim arrObj As Array = _
        Array.CreateInstance(GetType(Integer), lengths, lbounds)
    ' Assign it to an array with the right rank.
    Dim arr(,) As Integer = CType(arrObj, Integer(,))

    ' Prove that it worked.
    Console.WriteLine(arr.GetLowerBound(0))    ' => 1
    Console.WriteLine(arr.GetUpperBound(0))    ' => 5
    Console.WriteLine(arr.GetLowerBound(1))    ' => -10
    Console.WriteLine(arr.GetUpperBound(1))    ' => 10
    ' Assign an element, and read it back.
    arr(1, -1) = 1234
    Console.WriteLine(arr(1, -1))              ' => 1234
End Sub
```

Now that I have shown you how to create arrays with nonzero lower bounds, I ask you not to use them for anything other than impressing your friends at the local VB user group. The main problem with this technique is that it works well only with multidimensional arrays: when you use it with one-dimensional arrays it forces you to read and write array elements by calling the GetValue and SetValue methods, a rather clumsy practice. (This difference is caused by the fact that one-dimensional arrays, also known as vectors in .NET, are implemented differently from other arrays.) In addition, arrays with a lower index other than 0 aren't Common Language Specification (CLS) compliant, so you might have problems sharing them with other .NET languages.

Finally, a nonzero lower index changes the way some methods of the Array class work. For example, the IndexOf method (see later in the "Searching Values" section) is expected to return −1 if an element isn't found, which apparently makes it unusable with arrays whose lowest index is a negative number. The truth is, IndexOf returns the lowest index minus 1 when an element isn't found and therefore does work correctly even with these arrays, but this detail makes working with them even more confusing.

Copying Arrays

The Array class supports the ICloneable interface, so you can create a shallow copy of an array using the Clone instance method.

```
' This works if Option Strict is Off.
Dim anotherArray(,) As Integer = arr.Clone

' This is the required syntax if Option Strict is On.
' (You can also use CType instead of DirectCast.)
Dim anotherArray(,) As Integer = DirectCast(arr.Clone, Integer())
```

You can copy a one-dimensional array to another, and you decide the starting index in the destination array:

```
' Create and initialize an array (10 elements).
Dim sourceArr() As Integer = {1, 2, 3, 5, 7, 11, 13, 17, 19, 23}
' Create the destination array (must be same size or larger).
Dim destArr(20) As Integer
' Copy the source array into the second half of the destination array.
sourceArr.CopyTo(destArr, 10)
```

Pay attention to an important detail: the index in the target array is actually the offset from the array starting index. If the target array is 0-based (as are all the arrays created with the Dim statement), you can safely pass the index of the first element that will be overwritten in the target array. However, if you used Array.CreateInstance to create an array whose lowest index is a number other than 0, you must modify the second argument of the CopyTo method accordingly. For example, if the array is 1-based, pass the value 9 so that destArr(10) is the first overwritten element.

Sorting Elements

The Array class offers several shared methods for processing arrays quickly and easily. One is the Array.Sort method. You can sort arrays of objects using an arbitrary group of keys by means of the IComparable and IComparer interfaces. The Sort method is even more flexible than anything you've seen so far. For example, you can sort just a portion of an array:

```
' Sort only elements [10,100] of the targetArray.
' Second argument is starting index; last argument is length of the subarray.
Array.Sort(targetArray, 10, 91)
```

You can also sort an array of values using another array that holds the sorting keys, which lets you sort arrays of structures or objects. To see how this overloaded version of the Sort method works, let's start defining a structure:

```
Structure Employee
    Public FirstName As String
    Public LastName As String
    Public HireDate As Date

    Sub New(ByVal firstName As String, ByVal lastName As String, _
        ByVal hireDate As Date)
        Me.FirstName = firstName
        Me.LastName = lastName
        Me.HireDate = hireDate
    End Sub

    ' A function to display an element's properties easily
    Function Description() As String
        Return FirstName & " " & LastName & _
            " (hired on " & HireDate.ToShortDateString & ")"
    End Function
End Structure
```

The following code creates a main array of Employee structures, then creates an auxiliary key array that holds the hiring date of each employee, and finally sorts the main array using the auxiliary array:

```
' Create a test array.
Dim employees() As Employee = { _
```

(continued)

```
        New Employee("Joe", "Doe", #3/1/2001#), _
        New Employee("Robert", "Smith", #8/12/2000#), _
        New Employee("Ann", "Douglas", #11/1/1999#)}

' Create a parallel array of hiring dates.
Dim hireDates(UBound(employees)) As Date
Dim j As Integer
For j = 0 To employees.Length - 1
    hireDates(j) = employees(j).HireDate
Next
' Sort the array of Employees using HireDates to provide the keys.
Array.Sort(hireDates, employees)
' Prove that the array is sorted on the HireDate field.
For j = 0 To employees.Length - 1
    Console.WriteLine(employees(j).Description)
Next
```

Interestingly, the key array is sorted as well, so you don't need to initialize it again when you add another element to the main array:

```
' Add a fourth employee.
ReDim Preserve employees(3)
employees(3) = New Employee("Chris", "Doe", #5/9/2000#)
' Extend the key array as well - no need to reinitialize it.
ReDim Preserve hireDates(3)
hireDates(3) = employees(3).HireDate
' Re-sort the new, larger array.
Array.Sort(hireDates, employees)
```

An overloaded version of the Sort method lets you sort a portion of an array of values for which you provide an array of keys. This is especially useful when you start with a large array that you fill only partially:

```
' Create a test array with a lot of room.
Dim employees(1000) As Employee
' Initialize only its first four elements.
 ⋮
' Sort only the portion actually used.
Array.Sort(hireDates, employees, 0, 4)
```

All the versions of the Array.Sort method that you've seen so far can take an additional IComparer object, which dictates how the array elements or keys are to be compared with one another.

The Array.Reverse method reverses the order of elements in an array or in a portion of an array, so you can apply it immediately after a Sort method to get descending sorting:

```
' Sort an array of Integers in reverse order.
Array.Sort(intArray)
Array.Reverse(intArray)
```

You pass the initial index and number of elements to reverse only a portion of an array:

```
' Reverse only the first 10 elements in intArray.
Array.Reverse(intArray, 0, 10)
```

You have a special case when you reverse only two elements, which is the same as swapping two consecutive elements, a frequent operation when you're working with arrays:

```
' Swap elements at indexes 5 and 6.
Array.Reverse(intArray, 5, 2)
```

Clearing, Copying, and Moving Elements

You can clear a portion of an array with the Clear method, without a For loop:

```
' Clear elements [10,100] of an array.
Array.Clear(arr, 10, 91)
```

The Array.Copy method lets you copy elements from a one-dimensional array to another. There are two overloaded versions for this method. The first version copies a given number of elements from the source array to the destination array:

```
Dim intArr() As Integer = {1, 2, 3, 4, 5, 6, 7, 8, 9, 10}
Dim intArr2(20) As Integer
' Copy the entire source array into the first half of the target array.
Array.Copy(intArr, intArr2, 10)
Dim i As Integer
For i = 0 To 20
    Console.Write(CStr(intArr2(i)) & " ")
        ' => 1 2 3 4 5 6 7 8 9 10 0 0 0 0 0 0 0 0 0 0 0
Next
```

The second version lets you decide the starting index in the source array, the starting index in the destination array (that is, the index of the first element that will be overwritten), and the number of elements to copy:

```
' Copy elements at indexes 5-9 to the end of destArr.
Array.Copy(intArr, 5, intArr2, 15, 5)
' This is the first element that has been copied.
Console.WriteLine(intArr2(15))                ' => 6
```

You get an exception of type ArgumentOutOfRangeException if you provide wrong values for the indexes or the destination array isn't large enough, and you get an exception of type RankException if either array has two or more dimensions.

The Copy method works correctly even when source and destination arrays have a different type, in which case it attempts to cast each individual source element to the corresponding element in the destination array. The actual behavior depends on many factors, though, such as whether the source or the destination is a value type or a reference type. For example, you can always copy from any array to an Object array, from an Integer array to a Long array, and from a Single array to a Double array because they are widening conversions and can't fail. Copy throws an exception of type TypeMismatchException when you attempt a narrowing conversion between arrays of value types, even though individual elements in the source array might be successfully converted to the destination type:

```
' This Copy operation succeeds even if array types are different.
Dim intArr3() As Integer = {1, 2, 3, 4, 5, 6, 7, 8, 9, 10}
Dim lngArr3(20) As Long
Array.Copy(intArr3, lngArr3, 10)

' This Copy operation fails with TypeMismatchException.
'    (But you can carry it out with an explicit For loop.)
Dim lngArr4() As Long = {1, 2, 3, 4, 5, 6, 7, 8, 9, 10}
Dim intArr4(20) As Integer
Array.Copy(lngArr4, intArr4, 10)
```

Conversely, if you copy from and to an array of reference type, the Array.Copy method attempts the copy operation for each element; if an Invalid-CastException object is thrown for an element, the method copies neither that element nor any of the values after the one that raised the error. For more details about the Array.Copy method, see the .NET Framework SDK documentation.

The SDK documentation doesn't mention one of the most important features of the Array.Copy method: the ability to copy a portion of an array over itself. In this case, the Copy method performs a "smart copy," in the sense that elements are copied correctly, in ascending order when you're copying to a lower index and in reverse order when you're copying to a higher index. So you can use the Copy method to delete one or more elements and fill the hole that would result by shifting all subsequent elements one or more positions toward lower indexes:

```
Dim lngArr5() As Long = {1, 2, 3, 4, 5, 6, 7, 8, 9, 10}
' Delete element at index 4.
Array.Copy(lngArr5, 5, lngArr5, 4, 5)
' Complete the delete operation by clearing the last element.
Array.Clear(lngArr5, lngArr5.GetUpperBound(0), 1)
' Now the array contains: {1, 2, 3, 4, 6, 7, 8, 9, 10, 0}
```

You can use this code as the basis for a reusable routine that works with any type of array:

```
Sub ArrayDeleteElement(ByVal arr As Array, ByVal index As Integer)
    ' Shift elements from arr(index+1) to arr(index).
    Array.Copy(arr, index + 1, arr, index, UBound(arr) - Index)
    ' Clear the last element.
    arr.Clear(arr, arr.GetUpperBound(0), 1)
End Sub
```

Inserting an element is also easy, and again you can create a generic routine that works with arrays of any type:

```
Sub ArrayInsertElement(ByVal arr As Array, ByVal index As Integer, _
    Optional ByVal newValue As Object = Nothing)
    ' Shift elements from arr(index) to arr(index+1) to make room.
    Array.Copy(arr, index, arr, index + 1, arr.Length - index - 1)
    ' Assign the element using the SetValue method.
    arr.SetValue(newValue, index)
End Sub
```

The Array class exposes the SetValue and GetValue methods to assign and read elements; you don't normally use these methods in regular programming, but they turn out to be useful in generic routines (such as the two preceding routines) that work with any type of array. SetValue and GetValue are also useful for working with elements of non-CLS-compliant arrays with a nonzero lowest index. (See "Creating Nonzero-Based Arrays" earlier in this reading.)

You can also use Copy with multidimensional arrays, in which case the array is treated as if it were a one-dimensional array with all the rows laid down in memory one after the other.

Searching Values

The IndexOf method searches an array for a value and returns the index of the first element that matches or −1 if the search fails:

```
Dim strArray() As String = {"Robert", "Joe", "Ann", "Chris", "Joe"}
Console.WriteLine(Array.IndexOf(strArray, "Ann"))    ' => 2
' Note that string searches are case sensitive.
Console.WriteLine(Array.IndexOf(strArray, "ANN"))    ' => -1
```

More precisely, IndexOf returns the lowest index value minus 1 when the search fails; this difference is important only when the array isn't 0-based. You can also specify a starting index and an optional ending index; if an ending index is omitted, the search continues until the end of the array.

You can use this overloaded form to find all the values in the array with a given value:

```
' Search for all the occurrences of the "Joe" string.
Dim index As Integer = -1
Do
    ' Search next occurrence.
    index = Array.IndexOf(strArray, "Joe", index + 1)
    ' Exit the loop if not found.
    If index = -1 Then Exit Do
    Console.WriteLine("Found at index {0}", index)
Loop
```

The preceding loop displays the following messages in the console window:

```
Found at index 1
Found at index 4
```

The LastIndexOf method is similar to IndexOf except that it returns the index of the last occurrence of the value. Because the search is backward, you must pass a start index higher than the end index:

```
' A revised version of the search loop, which searches
' from higher indexes toward the beginning of the array.
index = strArr.Length
Do
    index = Array.LastIndexOf(strArr, "Joe", index - 1)
    If index = -1 Then Exit Do
    Console.WriteLine("Found at index {0}", index)
Loop
```

The IndexOf and LastIndexOf methods perform a linear search, so their performance degrades linearly with larger arrays. You deliver much faster code if the array is sorted and you use the BinarySearch method:

```
' Binary search on a sorted array
Dim strArr2() As String = {"Ann", "Chris", "Joe", "Robert", "Sam"}
Console.WriteLine(Array.BinarySearch(strArr2, "Chris"))      ' => 1
```

If the binary search fails, the method returns a negative value that's the bit-wise complement of the index of the first element that's larger than the value being searched. This feature lets you determine where the value should be inserted in the sorted array:

```
index = Array.BinarySearch(strArr2, "David")
If index >= 0 Then
    Console.WriteLine("Found at index {0}", index)
Else
    ' Negate the result to get the index for the insertion point.
    index = Not index
    Console.WriteLine("Not Found. Insert at index {0}", index)
```

```
           ' => Not found. Insert at index 2
End If
```

You can pass a start index and the length of the portion of the array to the point at which you want to perform the search, which is useful when you're working with an array that's only partially filled:

```
Console.Write(Array.BinarySearch(strArr2, 0, 3, "Chris"))   ' => 1
```

Finally, both syntax forms for the BinarySearch method support an IComparer object at the end of the argument list, which lets you determine how array elements are to be compared. In practice, you can use the same IComparer object that you passed to the Sort method to have the array sorted.

Arrays of Arrays

Visual Basic .NET also supports arrays of arrays, that is, arrays whose elements are arrays. This is a familiar concept to most C++ programmers, but it might be new to many Visual Basic programmers. In my book *Programming Microsoft Visual Basic 6*, I showed how you can create such structures in previous versions of the language by using the ability to store arrays in Variants. The good news is that Visual Basic .NET supports arrays of arrays natively, so you don't have to resort to any hack.

Arrays of arrays—also known as *jagged arrays*—are especially useful when you have a two-dimensional matrix whose rows don't have the same length. You can render this structure by using a standard two-dimensional array, but you'd have to size it to accommodate the row with the highest number of elements, which would result in a waste of space. The arrays of arrays concept isn't limited to two dimensions only, and you might need three-dimensional or four-dimensional jagged arrays. Here is an example of a "triangular" matrix of strings:

```
"a00"
"a10"   "a11"
"a20"   "a21"   "a22"
"a30"   "a31"   "a32"   "a33"
```

Even though Visual Basic .NET supports arrays of arrays natively, I can't consider their syntax to be intuitive. The next code snippet shows how you can initialize the preceding structure and then process it by expanding its rows:

```
Sub TestJaggedArray()
    ' Initialize an array of arrays.
    Dim arr()() As String = {New String() {"a00"}, _
        New String() {"a10", "a11"}, _
        New String() {"a20", "a21", "a22"}, _
        New String() {"a30", "a31", "a32", "a33"}}
```

(continued)

```
                   ' Show how you can reference an element.
                   Console.WriteLine(arr(3)(1))                      ' => a31

                   ' Assign an entire row.
                   arr(0) = New String() {"a00", "a01", "a02"}

                   ' Read an element just added.
                   Console.WriteLine(arr(0)(2))                      ' => a02

                   ' Expand one of the rows.
                   ReDim Preserve arr(1)(3)
                   ' Assign the new elements. (Currently they are Nothing.)
                   arr(1)(2) = "a12"
                   arr(1)(3) = "a13"
                   ' Read back one of them.
                   Console.WriteLine(arr(1)(2))                      ' => a12
               End Sub
```

The System.Collections Namespace

The System.Collections namespace exposes many classes that can work as generic data containers, such as collections and dictionaries. You can learn the features of all these objects individually, but a smarter approach is to learn about the underlying interfaces that these classes might implement.

The ICollection, IList, and IDictionary Interfaces

All the collection classes in the .NET Framework implement the ICollection interface, which inherits from IEnumerable and defines an object that supports enumeration through a For Each loop. The ICollection interface exposes a read-only Count property and a CopyTo method, which copies the elements from the collection object to an array.

The ICollection interface defines the minimum features that a collection-like object should have. The .NET Framework exposes two more interfaces whose methods add power and flexibility to the object: IList and IDictionary.

Many classes in the framework implement the IList interface. This interface inherits from ICollection, and therefore from IEnumerable, and represents a collection of objects that can be individually indexed. All the implementations of the IList interface fall into three categories:

■ **Read-only** The collection's elements can't be modified or deleted, nor can new elements be inserted.

- **Fixed-size**   Existing items can be modified, but elements can't be added or removed.

- **Variable-size**   Items can be modified, added, and removed.

Table 4-1 summarizes the main properties and methods of the IList interface. You should already be familiar with most of them because they're implemented in many other collection-like objects that you've worked with in the past, most notably Collection and Dictionary objects in Visual Basic 6.

Table 4-1   Members of the IList Interface

Syntax	Description
Count	Returns the number of elements in the collection (inherited from ICollection).
CopyTo(array, index)	Copies elements from the collection to an array, starting at the specified index in the array (inherited from ICollection).
Item(index)	Gets or sets the element at the specified 0-based index. This is the default member.
Clear	Removes all items from the collection.
Add(object)	Appends an element after the last element in the collection and returns the index where it was inserted.
Insert(index, object)	Inserts an element at a given index.
Remove(object)	Removes an object from the collection.
RemoveAt(index)	Removes an element at the specified index.
Contains(object)	Returns True if an object is in the collection.
IndexOf(object)	Returns the index of the object in the collection, or –1 if not found.
IsFixedSize	Returns True if no item can be added to the collection.
IsReadOnly	Returns True if items can't be written to.

The IDictionary interface defines a collection-like object that contains one or more (key, value) pairs for which the key can be any object (not just a string in Visual Basic 6 collections). The IDictionary interface inherits from ICollection and extends it using the methods defined in Table 4-2. As for the IList interface, implementations of the IDictionary interface can be read-only, fixed-size, or variable-size.

Table 4-2   **Members of the IDictionary Interface**

Syntax	Description
Count	Returns the number of elements in the dictionary (inherited from ICollection).
CopyTo(array, index)	Copies elements from the dictionary to an array, starting at the specified index in the array (inherited from ICollection).
Item(key)	Gets or sets the element associated with the specified key. This is the default member.
Clear	Removes all items from the dictionary.
Add(key, value)	Inserts a (key, value) pair into the dictionary; key must not be Nothing.
Remove(key)	Removes the dictionary element associated with a given key.
Contains(key)	Returns True if an element with the specified key is in the dictionary.
Keys	Returns an ICollection object that contains all the keys in the dictionary.
Values	Returns an ICollection object that contains all the values in the dictionary.
IsFixedSize	Returns True if no item can be added to the dictionary.
IsReadOnly	Returns True if items can't be written to.

A class that implements the ICollection, IList, or IDictionary interface isn't required to expose all the interface's properties and methods as Public members. For example, the Array class implements IList, but the Add, Insert, and Remove members don't appear in the Array class interface because the array has a fixed size. (You get an exception if you try to access these methods by casting an array to an IList variable.)

A trait that all the classes in System.Collections except the BitArray class have in common is that they can store Object values. (As its name implies, the BitArray class stores Boolean values.) This means that you can store any type of value inside them and even mix data types inside the same structure. In this sense, they're similar to the Collection object in Visual Basic 6, which used Variants internally and could therefore store numbers, strings, dates, and objects.

The BitArray Class

The BitArray object can hold a large number of Boolean values in a compact format, using a single bit for each element. This class implements IEnumerable (and thus supports For Each), ICollection (and thus supports indexing of individual elements), and ICloneable (and thus supports the Clone method). You can create a BitArray object in many ways:

```
' Provide the number of elements (all initialized to False).
Dim ba As New BitArray(1024)
' Provide the number of elements, and initialize them to a value.
Dim ba2 As New BitArray(1024, True)

' Initialize the BitArray from an array of Boolean, Byte, or Integer.
Dim boolArr(1023) As Boolean
' ...(Initialize the boolArr array)...
Dim ba3 As New BitArray(boolArr)

' Initialize the BitArray from another BitArray object.
Dim ba4 As New BitArray(ba)
```

You can retrieve the number of elements in a BitArray by using either the Count property or the Length property. The Get method reads and the Set method modifies the element at the specified index:

```
' Set element at index 9, and read it back.
ba.Set(9, True)
Console.WriteLine(ba.Get(9))      ' => True
```

The CopyTo method can move all elements back to an array of Booleans, or it can perform a bitwise copy of the BitArray to a 0-based Byte or Integer array:

```
' Bitwise copy to an array of Integers
Dim intArr(31) As Integer       ' 32 elements * 32 bits each = 1024 bits
' Second argument is the index in which the copy begins in target array.
ba.CopyTo(intArr, 0)
' Check that bit 9 of first element in intArr is set.
Console.WriteLine(intArr(0))     ' => 512
```

The Not method complements all the bits in the BitArray object:

```
ba.Not()                          ' No arguments
```

The And, Or, and Xor methods let you perform the corresponding operation on pairs of Boolean values stored in two BitArray objects:

```
' Perform an AND operation of all the bits in the first BitArray
' with the complement of all the bits in the second BitArray.
ba.And(ba2.Not)
```

Finally, you can set or reset all the bits in a BitArray class using the SetAll method:

```
' Set all the bits to True.
ba.SetAll(True)
```

The BitArray class doesn't expose any methods that let you quickly determine how many True (or False) elements are in the array. You can take advantage of the IEnumerator support of this class and use a For Each loop:

```
Dim b As Boolean
Dim TrueCount As Integer
For Each b In ba
    If b Then TrueCount += 1
Next
Console.Write("Found {0} True values.", TrueCount)
```

The Stack Class

In Visual Basic 6, you can simulate a last-in-first-out (LIFO) structure by using an array and an Integer variable that works as the pointer to the current element. Under Visual Basic .NET, you can build a stack structure by simply instantiating a System.Collections.Stack object:

```
' Define a stack with initial capacity of 50 elements.
Dim st As New Stack(50)
```

The three basic methods of a Stack object are Push, Pop, and Peek; the Count property returns the number of elements currently in the stack:

```
' Create a stack that can contain 100 elements.
Dim st As New Stack(100)
' Push three values onto the stack.
st.Push(10)
st.Push(20)
st.Push(30)
' Pop the value on top of the stack, and display its value.
Console.WriteLine(st.Pop)        ' => 30
' Read the value on top of the stack without popping it.
Console.WriteLine(st.Peek)       ' => 20
' Now pop it.
Console.WriteLine(st.Pop)        ' => 20
' Determine how many elements are now in the stack.
Console.WriteLine(st.Count)      ' => 1
' Pop the only value still on the stack.
Console.WriteLine(st.Pop)        ' => 10
' Check that the stack is now empty.
Console.WriteLine(st.Count)      ' => 0
```

The only other method that can prove useful is Contains, which returns True if a given value is currently in the stack:

```
' Is the value 10 somewhere in the stack?
If st.Contains(10) Then Console.Write("Found")
```

The Queue Class

A first-in-first-out (FIFO) structure, also known as a *queue* or *circular buffer*, is often used to solve recurring programming problems. You need a queue structure when a portion of an application inserts elements at one end of a buffer and another piece of code extracts the first available element at the other end. This situation occurs whenever you have a series of elements that you must process sequentially but you can't process immediately.

In Visual Basic 6, you typically implement queues by using an array for holding elements; a pointer to the element added, or *enqueued*, more recently; and another pointer to the element about to be extracted, or *dequeued*, from the queue. When you're creating a circular buffer, you must anticipate several potential error conditions, such as the attempt to extract an element from an empty queue, and decide what to do when the array is full. (Should you refuse the insertion, or should you extend the buffer?)

You don't need to write any code to render a queue in Visual Basic .NET because you can leverage the System.Collections.Queue object. Queue objects have an initial capacity, but the internal buffer is automatically extended if the need arises. You create a Queue object by specifying its initial capacity and an optional growth factor:

```
' A queue with initial capacity of 200 elements; a growth factor equal to 1.5
' (When new room is needed, the capacity will become 300, then 450, 675, etc.)
Dim qu As New Queue(200, 1.5)
' A queue with 100 elements and a default growth factor of 2
Dim qu As New Queue(100)
' A queue with 32 initial elements and a default growth factor of 2
Dim qu As New Queue()
```

The key methods of a Queue object are Enqueue, Peek, and Dequeue. Check the output of the following code snippet, and compare it with the behavior of the Stack object:

```
Dim qu As New Queue(100)
' Insert three values in the queue.
qu.Enqueue(10)
qu.Enqueue(20)
qu.Enqueue(30)
' Extract the first value, and display it.
Console.WriteLine(qu.Dequeue)    ' => 10
' Read the next value, but don't extract it.
Console.WriteLine(qu.Peek)       ' => 20
' Extract it.
Console.WriteLine(qu.Dequeue)    ' => 20
' Check how many items are still in the queue.
Console.WriteLine(qu.Count)      ' => 1
' Extract the last element, and check that the queue is now empty.
```

(continued)

```
Console.WriteLine(qu.Dequeue)     ' => 30
Console.WriteLine(qu.Count)       ' => 0
```

The Queue object also supports the Contains method, which checks whether an element is in the queue, and the Clear method, which clears the queue's contents.

The ArrayList Class

You can think of the ArrayList class as a hybrid of the Array and Collection objects, in that it lets you work with a set of values as if it were an array and a collection at the same time. For example, you can address elements by their indexes, sort and reverse them, and search a value sequentially or by means of a binary search as you do with an array; you can append elements, insert them in a given position, or remove them as you do with a collection.

The ArrayList object has an initial capacity—in practice, the number of slots in the internal structure that holds the actual values—but you don't need to worry about that because an ArrayList is automatically expanded as needed, as all collections are. However, you can optimize your code by choosing an initial capability that offers a good compromise between used memory and the overhead that occurs whenever the ArrayList object has to expand:

```
' Create an ArrayList with default initial capacity of 16 elements.
Dim al As New ArrayList
' Create an ArrayList with initial capacity of 1000 elements.
Dim al2 As New ArrayList(1000)
```

You can modifiy the capacity at any moment to enlarge the internal array or shrink it, by assigning a value to the Capacity property. However, you can't make it smaller than the current number of elements actually stored in the array (which corresponds to the value returned by the Count property):

```
' Have the ArrayList take just the memory that it strictly needs.
al.Capacity = al.Count
' Another way to achieve the same result
al.TrimToSize
```

When the current capacity is exceeded, the ArrayList object doubles its capacity automatically. You can't control an ArrayList's growth factor as you can a Queue object's, so it's critical that you set the Capacity property to a suitable value in order to avoid time-consuming memory allocations.

Another way to create an ArrayList object is by means of its shared Repeat method, which lets you determine an initial value for the specified number of elements:

```
' Create an ArrayList with 100 elements equal to a null string.
Dim al As ArrayList = ArrayList.Repeat("", 100)
```

The ArrayList class fully implements the IList interface, so you're already familiar with its basic methods. You add elements to an ArrayList object by using the Add method (which appends the new element after the last item) or the Insert method (which inserts at the specified index). You remove a specific object by using the Remove method, remove the element at a given index by using the RemoveAt method, or remove all elements by using the Clear method:

```
' Be sure that you start with an empty ArrayList.
al.Clear
' Append the elements "Joe" and "Ann" at the end of the ArrayList.
al.Add("Joe")
al.Add("Ann")
' Insert "Robert" item at the beginning of the list. (Index is 0-based.)
al.Insert(0, "Robert")
' Remove "Joe" from the list.
al.Remove("Joe")
' Remove the first element of the list ("Robert" in this case).
al.RemoveAt(0)
```

The Remove method removes only the first occurrence of a given object, so you need a loop to remove all the elements with a given value. You can't simply iterate through the loop until you get an error, however, because the Remove method doesn't throw an exception if the element isn't found. Therefore, you must use one of these two approaches:

```
' Using the IndexOf method is concise but not very efficient.
' (You can use also the Contains method.)
Do While al.IndexOf("element to remove") >= 0
    al.Remove("element to remove")
Loop

' A more efficient technique: loop until the Count property becomes constant.
Dim saveCount As Integer
Do
    saveCount = al.Count
    al.Remove("element to remove")
Loop While al.Count < saveCount
```

You can read and write any ArrayList element using the Item property. This property is the default property, so you can omit it and deal with this object as if it were a standard 0-based array. The main difference between a real array and an ArrayList object is that an element in an ArrayList object is created only when you invoke the Add method, so you can't reference an element whose index is equal to or higher than the ArrayList's Count property:

```
al(0) = "first element"
```

As with collections, the preferred way to iterate over all elements is through the For Each loop:

```
Dim o As Object
For Each o In al
    Console.WriteLine(o)
Next
```

The ArrayList class exposes methods that allow you to manipulate ranges of elements in one operation. The AddRange method appends to the current ArrayList object all the elements contained in another object that implements the ICollection interface. Many .NET classes other than those described in this chapter implement ICollection, such as the collection of all the items in a List-Box control and the collection of nodes in a TreeView control. The following routine takes two ArrayList objects and returns a third ArrayList that contains all the items from both arguments:

```
Function ArrayListJoin(ByVal al1 As ArrayList, ByVal al2 As ArrayList) _
    As ArrayList
    ' Note how we avoid time-consuming reallocations.
    ArrayListJoin = New ArrayList(al1.Count + al2.count)
    ' Append the items in the two ArrayList arguments.
    ArrayListJoin.AddRange(al1)
    ArrayListJoin.AddRange(al2)
End Function
```

The InsertRange method works in a similar way but lets you insert multiple elements at any index in the current ArrayList object:

```
' Insert all the items of al2 at the beginning of the current ArrayList.
al.InsertRange(0, al2)
```

RemoveRange deletes multiple elements in the current ArrayList object:

```
' Delete the last four elements (assumes there are at least four elements).
al.RemoveRange(al.Count - 4, 4)
```

You can quickly extract all the items in the ArrayList object by using the ToArray method or the CopyTo method. Both of them support one-dimensional target arrays of any compatible type, but the latter also allows you to extract a subset of ArrayList:

```
' Extract elements to an Object array (never raises an error).
Dim objArr() As Object = al.ToArray()
' Extract elements to a String array (might throw an exception
' of type InvalidCastException).
' (Requires CType or DirectCast if Option Strict is On.)
Dim strArr() As String = CType(al.ToArray(GetType(String)), String())
```

(continued)

```
' Same as above but uses the CopyTo method.
' (Note that the target array must be large enough.)
Dim strArr2(al.Count) As String
al.CopyTo(strArr2)
' Copy only items [1,2], starting at element 4 in the target array.
Dim strArr3() As String = {"0", "1", "2", "3", "4", "5", "6", "7", "8", "9"}
' Syntax is: sourceIndex, target, destIndex, count.
al.CopyTo(0, strArr3, 4, 2)
```

The ArrayList class supports other useful methods, such as Sort, SortRange, BinarySearch, IndexOf, LastIndexOf, and Reverse. I've already described most of these methods in depth in the section devoted to arrays, so I won't repeat their description here.

The last feature of the ArrayList class that's worth mentioning is its Adapter shared method. This method takes an IList-derived object as its only argument and creates an ArrayList wrapper around that object. In other words, instead of creating a copy of the argument, the Adapter method creates an ArrayList object that "contains" the original collection: all the changes you make on the outer ArrayList object are duplicated in the inner collection. The reason you might want to use the Adapter method is that the ArrayList class implements several methods—Reverse, Sort, BinarySearch, ToArray, IndexOf, and LastIndexOf, just to name a few—that are missing in the inner IList object. The following code sample demonstrates how you can use this technique to reverse (or sort, and so on) all the items in a ListBox control:

```
' Create a wrapper around the Listbox.Items IList collection.
Dim lbAdapter As ArrayList = ArrayList.Adapter(ListBox1.Items)
' Reverse their order.
lbAdapter.Reverse()
```

If you don't plan to reuse the ArrayList wrapper further, you can make this code even more concise:

```
ArrayList.Adapter(ListBox1.Items).Reverse()
```

The Hashtable Class

The Hashtable class implements the IDictionary interface, and it behaves much like the Scripting.Dictionary object you might have used from Visual Basic 6 days. (The Dictionary object can be found in the Microsoft Scripting Runtime library; see Chapter 4 in my *Programming Microsoft Visual Basic 6*.) All objects based on IDictionary manage two internal series of data, values and keys, and you can use a key to retrieve the corresponding value. The actual implementation of the methods in this interface depends on the specific object; for example, the Hashtable class uses an internal hash table, a well-known data structure that has been studied for decades by computer scientists and has been thoroughly described in countless books on algorithms.

When a (key, value) pair is added to a Hashtable object, the position of an element in the internal array is based on the numeric hash code of the key. When you later search for that key, the key's hash code is used again to locate the associated value as quickly as possible, without sequentially visiting all the elements in the hash table. Collection objects in Visual Basic 6 use a similar mechanism except that the key's hash code is derived from the characters in the key and the key must necessarily be a string. Conversely, the .NET Hashtable class lets you use *any* object as a key as long as its hash code can't change during the application's lifetime. Behind the scenes, the Hashtable object uses the key object's GetHashCode, a method that all objects inherit from System.Object, so you can even affect the way in which hash codes are used by overriding the GetHashCode method of the objects you're going to store in the Hashtable.

Depending on how the hash code is evaluated, it frequently happens that multiple keys map to the same slot (or *bucket*) in the hash table: in this case, you have a *collision*. The Hashtable object uses double hashing to minimize collisions, but it can't avoid collisions completely. To get optimal performance you must select an adequate initial capacity for the hash table: a larger table doesn't speed up searches remarkably, but it makes insertions faster.

You can also get better performance by selecting a correct *load factor* when you create a Hashtable object. This number determines the maximum ratio between values and buckets before the hash table is automatically expanded: the smaller this value is, the more memory is allocated to the internal table and the fewer collisions occur when you're inserting or searching for a value. The default load factor is 1.0, which in most cases delivers a good-enough performance, but you can set a smaller load factor when you create the Hashtable if you're willing to trade memory for better performance. You can initialize a Hashtable object in many ways:

```
' Default load factor and initial capacity
Dim ht As New Hashtable
' Default load factor and specified initial capacity
Dim ht2 As New Hashtable(1000)
' Specified initial capability and custom load factor
Dim ht3 As New Hashtable(1000, 0.8)
```

You can also initialize the Hashtable by loading it with the elements contained in any other object that implements the IDictionary interface (such as another Hashtable or a SortedList object). This technique is especially useful when you want to change the load factor of an existing hash table:

```
' Decrease the load factor of the current Hashtable.
ht = New HashTable(ht, 0.5)
```

Other, more sophisticated, variants of the constructor let you pass an IComparer object to compare keys in a customized fashion or an IHashCodeProvider object to supply a custom algorithm for calculating hash codes of keys.

The Hashtable object is very similar to the Scripting.Dictionary object in that you can add a key and value pair, read or modify the value associated with a given key through the Item property, and remove an item with the Remove method:

```
' Syntax for Add method is Add(key, value).
ht.Add("Joe", 12000)
ht.Add("Ann", 13000)
' Referencing a new key creates an element.
ht.Item("Robert") = 15000
' Item is the default member, so you can omit its name.
ht("Chris") = 11000
Console.Write(ht("Joe"))      ' => 12000
' The Item property lets you overwrite an existing element.
' (You need CInt or CType if Option Strict is On.)
ht("Ann") = CInt(ht("Ann")) + 1000
' Note that keys are compared in case-insensitive mode,
' so the following statement creates a *new* element.
ht("ann") = 15000
' Reading a nonexistent element doesn't create it.
Console.WriteLine(ht("Lee"))      ' Doesn't display anything.

' Remove an element given its key.
ht.Remove("Chris")
' How many elements are now in the hashtable?
Console.WriteLine(ht.Count)      ' => 4

' Adding an element that already exists throws an exception.
ht.Add("Joe", 11500)             ' Throws ArgumentException.
```

As I explained earlier, you can use virtually anything as a key, including a numeric value. When you're using numbers as keys, a Hashtable looks deceptively similar to an array:

```
ht(1) = 123
ht(2) = 345
```

But never forget that the expression between parentheses is just a key and not an index; thus, the ht(2) element isn't necessarily stored "after" the ht(1) element. As a matter of fact, the elements in a Hashtable object aren't stored in a particular order, and you should never write code that assumes that they are.

This is the main difference between the Hashtable object and the SortedList object (which is described next).

The Hashtable object implements the IEnumerable interface, so you can iterate over all its elements with a For Each loop. Each element of a Hashtable is a DictionaryEntry object, which exposes a Key and a Value property:

```
Dim de As DictionaryEntry
For Each de In ht
    Console.WriteLine("ht('{0}') = {1}", de.Key, de.Value)
Next
```

The Hashtable's Keys and Values properties return an ICollection-based object that contains all the keys and all the values, respectively, so you can assign them to any object that implements the ICollection interface. Or you can use these properties directly in a For Each loop:

```
' Display all the keys in the Hashtable.
Dim o As Object
For Each o In ht.Keys          ' Or use ht.Values for all the values.
    Console.WriteLine(o)
Next
```

One last note: by default, keys are compared in a case-sensitive way, so *Joe, JOE,* and *joe* are considered distinct keys. You can create case-insensitive instances of the Hashtable class through one of its many constructors, or you can use the CreateCaseInsensitiveHashtable shared method of the System.Collections.Specialized.CollectionsUtil, as follows:

```
Dim ht2 As Hashtable = _
    Specialized.CollectionsUtil.CreateCaseInsensitiveHashtable()
```

The SortedList Class

The SortedList object is arguably the most versatile collection-like object in the .NET Framework. It implements the IDictionary interface, like the Hashtable object, and also keeps its elements sorted. Alas, you pay for all this power in terms of performance, so you should use the SortedList object only when your programming logic requires an object with all this flexibility.

The SortedList object manages two internal arrays, one for the values and one for the companion keys. These arrays have an initial capacity, but they automatically grow when the need arises. Entries are kept sorted by their key, and you can even provide an IComparer object to affect how complex values (an object, for example) are compared and sorted. The SortedList class provides several constructor methods:

```
' A SortedList with default capacity (16 entries)
Dim sl As New SortedList()
```

```
' A SortedList with specified initial capacity
Dim s12 As New SortedList(1000)

' A SortedList can be initialized with all the elements in an IDictionary.
Dim ht As New Hashtable()
ht.Add("Robert", 100)
ht.Add("Ann", 200)
ht.Add("Joe", 300)
Dim s13 As New SortedList(ht)
```

As soon as you add new elements to the SortedList, they're immediately sorted by their key:

```
' Iterate over all the DictionaryEntry items in a SortedList.
Dim de As DictionaryEntry
For Each de In s13
    Console.WriteLine("s13('{0}') = {1}", de.Key, de.Value)
Next
```

Here's the result that appears in the console window:

```
s13('Ann') = 200
s13('Joe') = 300
s13('Robert') = 100
```

Keys are sorted according to the order implied by their IComparable interface, so numbers and strings are always sorted in ascending order. If you want a different order, you must create an object that implements the IComparer interface. For example, you can use the following class to invert the natural string ordering:

```
Class ReverseStringComparer
    Implements IComparer

    Function CompareValues(ByVal x As Object, ByVal y As Object) As Integer _
        Implements IComparer.Compare
        ' Just change the sign of the StrComp function's result.
        Return -StrComp(x.ToString, y.ToString)
    End Function
End Class
```

You can pass an instance of this object to one of the two overloaded constructors that take an IComparer object:

```
' A SortedList that sorts elements through a custom IComparer
Dim s14 As New SortedList(New ReverseStringComparer)

' Here's a SortedList that loads all the elements in a Hashtable and
' sorts them with a custom IComparer object.
Dim s15 As New SortedList(ht, New ReverseStringComparer)
```

Here are the elements of the resulting SortedList object:

```
sl5('Robert') = 100
sl5('Joe') = 300
sl5('Ann') = 200
```

Table 4-3 summarizes the most important properties and methods of the SortedList class. You have already met most of them, and the ones you never met before are almost self-explanatory, so I won't describe them in detail.

The SortedList class compares keys in case-sensitive mode, with lowercase characters coming before their uppercase versions (for example with *Ann* coming before *ANN*, which in turn comes before *Bob*). If you want to compare keys without taking case into account, you can create a case-insensitive SortedList object using the auxiliary CollectionsUtil object in the System.Collections.Specialized namespace:

```
Dim sl6 As SortedList = _
    Specialized.CollectionsUtil.CreateCaseInsensitiveSortedList()
```

In this case, trying to add two elements whose keys differ only in case throws an ArgumentException object.

> **Note** As I said before, the SortedList class is the most powerful collection-like object, but it's also the most demanding in terms of resources and CPU time. To see what kind of overhead you can expect when using a SortedList object, I created a routine that adds 100,000 elements to an ArrayList object, a Hashtable object, and a SortedList object. The results were pretty interesting: The ArrayList object was about 4 times faster than the Hashtable object, which in turn was from 8 to 100 times faster than the SortedList object. Even though you can't take these ratios as reliable in all circumstances, you clearly should never use a more powerful data structure if you don't really need its features.

Table 4-3   Properties and Methods of the SortedList Class

Syntax	Description
Capacity	Sets or returns the capacity of the SortedList object.
Count	Returns the number of elements currently in the SortedList object.
Item(key)	Sets or returns a value given its key (default member).

Table 4-3   Properties and Methods of the SortedList Class *(continued)*

Syntax	Description
Keys	Returns all the keys in the SortedList object as an ICollection object.
Values	Returns all the values in SortedList as an ICollection object.
Add(key, value)	Adds a (key, value) pair to SortedList.
Clear	Removes all the elements from SortedList.
Clone	Creates a shallow copy of the SortedList object.
Contains(key)	Returns True if a given key exists.
ContainsKey(key)	Returns True if a given key exists (same as Contains).
ContainsValue(value)	Returns True if a given value exists.
CopyTo(array, index)	Copies all the DictionaryEntries elements to a one-dimensional array, starting at a specified index in the target array.
GetByIndex(index)	Retrieves a value by its index. (Similar to the Item property but works with the index instead of the key.)
GetKey(index)	Retrieves the key associated with the element at the given index.
GetKeyList	Returns all the keys as an IList object; all the changes in SortedList are reflected in this IList object. (Similar to the Keys property but returns an IList object instead of an ICollection object, and the result continues to be linked to the list of keys.)
GetValueList	Returns all the values as an IList object; all the changes in the SortedList are reflected in this IList object. (Similar to Values property but returns an IList object instead of an ICollection object, and the result continues to be linked to the list of values.)
IndexOfKey(key)	Returns the 0-based index of an element with a given key, or −1 if the key isn't in the SortedList object.
IndexOfValue(value)	Returns the 0-based index of the first occurrence of the specified value, or −1 if the value isn't in the SortedList object.
Remove(key)	Removes the element associated with a given key.
RemoveAt(index)	Removes the element at the given index.
SetByIndex(index, value)	Assigns a new value to the element at the specified index. (Similar to the Item property but works with the index instead of the key.)
TrimToSize	Sets the capacity to the current number of elements in the SortedList object.

The StringCollection and StringDictionary Classes

The StringCollection class (contained in the System.Collections.Specialized namespace) is a low-overhead class that manages a small collection of strings in a very efficient way. It exposes most of the properties and methods of the

ArrayList class: Item, Count, Clear, Add, AddRange, Insert, Remove, RemoveAt, IndexOf, Contains, and CopyTo. The Capacity property is missing, however, and the constructor takes no arguments:

```
' Create a StringCollection (no support for initial capability).
Dim sc As New System.Collections.Specialized.StringCollection

' Fill it with month names in current language, in one operation.
' (We leverage the DateFormatInfo object's MonthNames method, which
'  returns an array of strings, which in turn implements the IList interface.)
sc.AddRange(System.Globalization.DateTimeFormatInfo.CurrentInfo.MonthNames())

' Display the elements in the StringCollection.
Dim s As String
For Each s In sc
    Console.WriteLine(s)
Next
```

In general, you should prefer StringCollection objects to more resource-intensive objects, such as the ArrayList object, when you're working with small sets of elements (say, 100 elements or fewer). If a StringCollection object resolves the majority (but not all) of your programming tasks, consider using a temporary ArrayList object for implementing missing functionality. For example, say that a StringCollection satisfies your needs except that you need to sort its elements once in a while during the application's lifetime. Because the StringCollection object implements the IList interface, you can pass it to the shared ArrayList.Adapter method to create a temporary ArrayList that does what you need:

```
' A temporary ArrayList that wraps around the StringCollection object
Dim al As ArrayList = ArrayList.Adapter(sc)
' Sort the inner StringCollection in reverse order through the wrapper.
al.Sort
al.Reverse
' Destroy the wrapper object, which isn't necessary any longer.
al = Nothing
```

The temporary ArrayList object works as a wrapper for the inner String-Collection object, so all the operations you perform on the ArrayList are actually carried out in the StringCollection object instead.

The StringDictionary class, a lightweight version of the Hashtable object, takes only string keys and values. It exposes only the IEnumerable interface (to support For Each loops) and the following properties and methods: Item, Count, Add, Remove, Clear, ContainsKey, ContainsValue, Keys, and Values. The StringDictionary object compares keys in case-insensitive mode and throws an exception if you add two elements whose keys differ only in case:

```
Dim sd As New System.Collections.Specialized.StringDictionary
sd.Add("Ann", "Marketing")
sd.Add("Joe", "Sales")
sd.Add("Robert", "Administration")

Dim de As DictionaryEntry
For Each de In sd
    Console.WriteLine("{0} = {1}", de.Key, de.Value)
Next
```

The System.Collections.Specialized namespace offers two more light-weight classes: ListDictionary and NameValueCollection. The ListDictionary class is a lightweight implementation of the IDictionary interface. It offers a sub-set of the properties and methods of the Hashtable object but should be used only for very small sets of elements because its performance degrades with more than 10 elements. This object can take both object keys and object values.

The NameValueCollection class is a lightweight sorted collection of strings that can be retrieved by their key or index. Its peculiarity is the capability to store multiple string values under the same key.

Custom Collection and Dictionary Classes

You can create your own collection classes by implementing the IEnumerable interface for adding support for the For Each statement. In most cases, however, creating a collection class is as simple as inheriting from one of the special abstract classes that the .NET Framework kindly provides. These classes provide much of the functionality you need in a collection-like object, and you simply have to add the missing pieces. In this section, I'll describe three such objects: the CollectionBase class, for implementing full-featured collection classes; the ReadOnlyCollectionBase class, which is more convenient for collection classes with fixed membership (that is, collections you can't add items to or remove items from); and the DictionaryBase class, for implementing dictionary-like objects.

The ReadOnlyCollectionBase Abstract Class

Let's start with a simple collection with fixed membership that contains all the powers of 2, up to a given maximum exponent whose value is passed in the collection's constructor. This class inherits from the ReadOnlyCollectionBase abstract class, and its code for this class couldn't be simpler:

```
Class PowersOfTwoCollection
    Inherits System.Collections.ReadOnlyCollectionBase
```

(continued)

```
Sub New(ByVal MaxExponent As Integer)
    MyBase.New()

    ' Fill the inner ArrayList object.
    Dim index As Integer
    For Index = 0 To MaxExponent
        ' InnerList is a protected member of the base class.
        InnerList.Add(2 ^ Index)
    Next
End Sub


' Add support for the Item element (read-only).
Default ReadOnly Property Item(ByVal Exponent As Integer) As Long
    Get
        Return CLng(InnerList.Item(Exponent))
    End Get
End Property
End Class
```

InnerList is a protected property through which the derived class can access the internal ArrayList object that actually contains the values. You reference this internal ArrayList both when you're loading values in the constructor method and when you're returning them in the Item property.

In this specific example, the Item property is marked ReadOnly because a client isn't supposed to change the powers of 2 once the collection has been initialized. But don't confuse this ReadOnly attribute with the fact that the collection inherits from ReadOnlyCollectionBase: when applied to a collection, read-only means that the collection has a fixed size, not that individual elements aren't writable. Note that the Item property returns a Long data type, rather than the Object data type, as all default collections do: in fact, one of the main reasons for implementing a custom collection class is to make it strongly typed. The following code snippet uses the collection just created:

```
' Display powers of 2 up to 2^20.
Dim powers As New PowersOfTwoCollection(20)
' The Count property is provided by the base class.
Console.WriteLine(powers.Count)     ' => 21


' For Each support is also provided by the base class.
Dim n As Long
For Each n In powers
    Console.WriteLine(n)
Next


' Assign the value of 2^15 to a variable.
' (No casting is required because the collection is strongly typed.)
Dim lngValue As Long = powers(15)
```

The CollectionBase Abstract Class

You can create a regular read/write, strongly typed collection by inheriting a class from CollectionBase: you just need to implement an Add method that takes an argument of the expected type, and an Item property that sets or returns an element. The following code defines a simple Square class and a SquareCollection collection class:

```
Class Square
    Public Side As Single

    ' A simple constructor
    Sub New(ByVal side As Single)
        Me.Side = side
    End Sub
End Class

' A collection object that can store only Square objects
Class SquareCollection
    Inherits System.Collections.CollectionBase

    ' The Item property sets or returns a Square object.
    Default Property Item(ByVal index As Integer) As Square
        Get
            Return CType(InnerList.Item(index), Square)
        End Get
        Set(ByVal Value As Square)
            InnerList.Item(index) = Value
        End Set
    End Property

    ' You can add only Square objects to this collection.
    Sub Add(ByVal value As Square)
        InnerList.Add(value)
    End Sub
End Class
```

The SquareCollection class doesn't need to override the RemoveAt method because this method doesn't take or return a typed object, and therefore the base class can implement it:

```
Dim squares As New SquareCollection()
squares.Add(New Square(10))
squares.Add(New Square(20))
squares.Add(New Square(30))

' The RemoveAt method is provided by the base class.
Squares.RemoveAt(0)
```

You aren't limited to the members that a generic collection exposes. For example, you might add a Create method that works as a constructor for a Square object that's then added to the collection. (Methods like this are also called *factory methods*.)

```
' ...(Add this method to the SquareCollection class.)...
Function Create(ByVal Side As Single) As Square
    Dim sq As New Square(Side)
    Add(sq)
    Return sq
End Function
```

With this factory method, adding new elements to the collections is even simpler:

```
squares.Create(40)
squares.Create(50)
```

The CollectionBase abstract class exposes several protected methods that let the derived class take control when an operation is performed on the collection. For example, say that the SquareCollection class exposes the TotalArea read-only property, which contains the sum of the area of all the squares in the collection. You must modify the Add method to implement this new property:

```
' Keep track of the total area of squares.
Dim m_TotalArea As Single

Sub Add(ByVal value As Square)
    InnerList.Add(value)
    ' Keep the total area updated.
    m_TotalArea += (value.Side * value.Side)
End Sub

ReadOnly Property TotalArea() As Single
    Get
        Return m_TotalArea
    End Get
End Property
```

The next problem to solve is that the m_TotalArea variable must be updated when an element is removed from the collection. You achieve this behavior by overriding the OnRemoveComplete protected method, which runs after an item has been removed from the collection:

```
Protected Overrides Sub OnRemoveComplete(ByVal index As Integer, _
    ByVal value As Object)
    ' Get a reference to the square being removed.
    Dim sq As Square = CType(value, Square)
```

```
' Keep the total area updated.
    m_TotalArea -= (sq.Side * sq.Side)
End Sub
```

These are the protected methods you can override in classes that derive from CollectionBase: OnInsert, OnInsertComplete, OnClear, OnClearComplete, OnRemove, OnRemoveComplete, OnSet, OnSetComplete, and OnValidate.

The DictionaryBase Abstract Class

Now that you know the mechanism, you should have no problem grasping how you can use the DictionaryBase class to implement a strongly typed, custom dictionary-like object. Again, all you have to do is provide your custom Add and Item procedures, and reference the protected Dictionary object that you inherit from DictionaryBase. The following example creates a SquareDictionary object that can manage Square objects and associate them with a string key:

```
Class SquareDictionary
    Inherits System.Collections.DictionaryBase

    Sub Add(ByVal key As String, ByVal value As Square)
        Dictionary.Add(key, value)
    End Sub

    Function Create(ByVal key As String, ByVal side As Single) As Square
        Create = New Square(side)
        ' Use the function name as a local variable.
        Dictionary.Add(key, Create)
    End Function

    Default Property Item(ByVal key As String) As Square
        Get
            Return CType(Dictionary.Item(key), Square)
        End Get
        Set(ByVal Value As Square)
            Dictionary.Item(key) = Value
        End Set
    End Property
End Class
```

Here's a sample of client code:

```
Dim sq As New SquareDictionary()
sq.Create("First", 10)
sq.Create("Second", 20)
sq.Create("Third", 30)

Console.WriteLine(sq("Second").Side)      ' => 20
```

The custom SquareDictionary class should be completed with properties such as Values and Keys, and a few other methods that aren't implemented in the DictionaryBase class. As with the CollectionBase class, you can intervene when an operation is performed on the inner dictionary object through several protected methods, such as OnClear, OnClearComplete, OnGet, OnInsert, OnInsert-Complete, OnRemove, OnRemoveComplete, OnSet, and OnSetComplete.

At this point, you have added many new classes to your data structure arsenal and you should have become more familiar with how things work in the .NET world, such as how you use inheritance to derive new and more powerful data classes. It's now time to start working with other classes in the .NET Framework, such as files and directories.

Reading 5

Windows Forms Applications

In spite of the potential that Visual Basic has now in areas such as component and Internet programming, I expect that many developers will continue to use the language to create standard Win32 applications. The .NET Framework offers a lot in this area and lets you create applications with a rich user interface without the annoyances and limitations of previous language versions. To qualify as a Visual Basic 6 user-interface wiz, you had to learn a lot of tricks and advanced techniques, such as tons of Windows API calls and subclassing. Now you need only to use correctly the classes and methods defined in the System.Windows.Forms namespace.

Form Basics

A Visual Basic .NET form is nothing but a class that inherits from the System.Windows.Forms.Form class; it isn't special in comparison with other .NET classes. For example, there's no global variable named after the form class (as happens in Visual Basic 6), so you can't display an instance of a form named Form1 by simply executing Form1.Show. Instead, you have to correctly create an instance of the proper form class, as in this code:

```
Dim frm As New Form1
frm.Show
```

From *Programming Microsoft Visual Basic .NET* by Francesco Balena. pp. 675-691. (Redmond: Microsoft Press. 2002.) Copyright © 2002 by Francesco Balena.

The Form Designer

Visual Studio .NET comes with a designer similar to the one provided with earlier versions of Visual Basic. Behind the scenes, however, things work very differently. The Visual Studio .NET designer is a sophisticated code generator: when you set a control's property in the Properties window, you're just creating one or more Visual Basic statements that assign a value to that property after the form has been created.

Code Generation

For example, the code that follows is generated for a form named Form1 that contains a Label, a TextBox, and a Button control. (See Figure 5-1.) The designer encloses the generated code in a collapsed #Region so that you can't modify it accidentally:

```
Public Class Form1
    Inherits System.Windows.Forms.Form

#Region " Windows Form Designer generated code "

    Public Sub New()
        MyBase.New()

        'This call is required by the Windows Form Designer.
        InitializeComponent()

        'Add any initialization after the InitializeComponent() call.

    End Sub

    'Form overrides dispose to clean up the component list.
    Protected Overloads Overrides Sub Dispose(ByVal disposing As Boolean)
        If disposing Then
            If Not (components Is Nothing) Then
                components.Dispose()
            End If
        End If
        MyBase.Dispose(disposing)
    End Sub
    Friend WithEvents btnOK As System.Windows.Forms.Button
    Friend WithEvents txtValue As System.Windows.Forms.TextBox
    Friend WithEvents lblMessage As System.Windows.Forms.Label

    'Required by the Windows Form Designer
    Private components As System.ComponentModel.Container
```

```
'NOTE: The following procedure is required by the Windows Form Designer.
'It can be modified using the Windows Form Designer.
'Do not modify it using the code editor.
<System.Diagnostics.DebuggerStepThrough()> _
Private Sub InitializeComponent()
    Me.btnOK = New System.Windows.Forms.Button()
    Me.txtValue = New System.Windows.Forms.TextBox()
    Me.lblMessage = New System.Windows.Forms.Label()
    Me.SuspendLayout()
    '
    'lblMessage
    '
    Me.lblMessage.Location = New System.Drawing.Point(16, 16)
    Me.lblMessage.Name = "lblMessage"
    Me.lblMessage.Size = New System.Drawing.Size(352, 40)
    Me.lblMessage.TabIndex = 0
    Me.lblMessage.Text = "Type your value here"
    '
    'txtValue
    '
    Me.txtValue.Location = New System.Drawing.Point(16, 64)
    Me.txtValue.Name = "txtValue"
    Me.txtValue.Size = New System.Drawing.Size(352, 20)
    Me.txtValue.TabIndex = 1
    Me.txtValue.Text = ""
    '
    'btnOK
    '
    Me.btnOK.Location = New System.Drawing.Point(400, 16)
    Me.btnOK.Name = "btnOK"
    Me.btnOK.Size = New System.Drawing.Size(88, 32)
    Me.btnOK.TabIndex = 2
    Me.btnOK.Text = "OK"
    '
    'Form1
    '
    Me.AcceptButton = Me.btnOK
    Me.AutoScaleBaseSize = New System.Drawing.Size(5, 13)
    Me.ClientSize = New System.Drawing.Size(496, 141)
    Me.Controls.AddRange(New System.Windows.Forms.Control() _
        {Me.lblMessage, Me.txtValue, Me.btnOK})
    Me.Name = "Form1"
    Me.Text = "First Windows Forms example"
    Me.ResumeLayout(False)
End Sub
#End Region


End Class
```

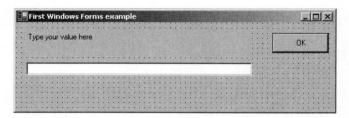

Figure 5-1.   A simple form in the Visual Studio form designer.

The listing shows a few interesting features of the Form class:

- The Sub New procedure is where you can put initialization code; it broadly corresponds to the Form_Initialize event in Visual Basic 6.

- The Sub Dispose procedure is where you put cleanup code; it corresponds to the Visual Basic 6 Form_Terminate event.

- A control on the form is just an object of the proper control class, which the form instantiates in the InitializeComponent procedure and assigns to a WithEvents variable named after the control itself. By default, control variables are Friend members of the form class, but you can change this by assigning a different scope to the control's Modifiers property in the Properties window.

- Property values are set through regular assignments in code; Visual Basic .NET source code modules don't contain hidden sections that you can't load in Visual Studio's editor.

- After assigning property values, the code produced by the designer inserts individual control objects into the form's Controls collection, using a single AddRange method for best performance.

I'll talk about other interesting new properties—for example, the Size and Location properties—later in this chapter.

New Designer Features

The Visual Studio .NET form designer is virtually identical to the designer in Visual Basic 6, with a few interesting new features. For example, controls that are invisible at run time are displayed on the component tray, near the bottom border of the designer. This area isn't normally visible until you drop an invisible control, such as a Timer control, on the designer.

You can save some time by arranging the TabIndex property in a visual manner, using the Tab Order command on the View menu. This command displays little numbered labels over each control, and you can create the correct

TabIndex sequence by simply clicking on each control in the order you want it to appear in relation to the others. As you see in Figure 5-2, controls that are themselves a container have a TabIndex subsequence. You terminate the Tab Order command by pressing the Esc key.

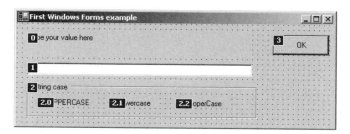

Figure 5-2.   Arrange the TabIndex property using the Tab Order command.

Another timesaving feature is the ability to resize multiple controls by using the mouse. Just select multiple controls—by clicking on each one while pressing the Ctrl or the Shift key, or by pressing the Ctrl+A key combination to select all the controls on the form—and then use the mouse to resize one of them: all the selected controls will be sized accordingly. (You can't do this in Visual Basic 6.)

Finally, note that you can lock each individual control (so as not to accidentally move or resize it with the mouse) by setting its Locked property to True in the Properties window. Visual Basic 6 allows you to lock only all controls or none. (You can still lock controls Visual Basic 6–style in Visual Basic .NET by using the Lock Controls command on the Format menu.)

The Windows Forms Class Hierarchy

The classes in the System.Windows.Forms namespace make up a fairly complex hierarchy, at the root of which is the System.Windows.Forms.Control class. (See Figure 5-3.) The Control class inherits from the System.Component-Model.Component class, which represents an object that can be placed on a container.

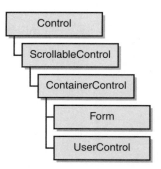

Figure 5-3. A partial view of the Windows Forms class hierarchy.

You might be surprised to see that the Form object is a descendant of the Control object; you might have expected a relationship in the opposite direction. Keep in mind that this is an inheritance diagram, not a containment diagram. The Control, ScrollableControl, and ContainerControl classes are generic objects that expose properties that are inherited by more specific controls. These classes aren't abstract classes, and you can actually create an instance of each class, even though there's no point in doing so. (You must do this from code, however, because these classes don't appear in the Toolbox.)

Even if you don't work with these classes in code directly, it's interesting to see the functionality of each class because it's inherited by other classes further down the hierarchy.

The Control class defines a generic Windows Forms control, which is an object that can be hosted in Visual Studio's Toolbox and placed on the form designer's surface. It has methods such as BringToFront and SendToBack (for controlling Z-ordering), properties such as Location and Size (for defining position and dimension), and many others. Many actual controls that don't require advanced functionality—for example, the Label and PictureBox controls—inherit directly from the System.Windows.Forms.Control class. (Note that the Visual Basic .NET PictureBox control can't work as a container for other controls.) But even a few sophisticated controls inherit directly from Control, including the DataGrid control.

The ScrollableControl class inherits all the members of the Control class, to which it adds the ability to scroll its own contents. It exposes properties such as AutoScrollPosition and methods such as ScrollControlIntoView. The Panel control—which replaces the Visual Basic 6 Frame control—inherits directly from the ScrollableControl class.

The ContainerControl class represents an object that can contain other controls. It exposes properties such as ActiveControl and BindingContext, and the Validate method. The Form class inherits directly from the ContainerControl class.

Windows Forms Controls

The System.Windows.Forms.dll library includes 46 controls, most of which are similar to their Visual Basic counterparts and most of which have retained the same names. (See Figure 5-4.)

Figure 5-4.   All the Windows Forms controls as they appear in the Visual Studio Toolbox.

The Label, Button, TextBox, CheckBox, RadioButton, PictureBox, ListBox, ComboBox, HScrollBar, VScrollBar, and Timer controls are virtually identical to the intrinsic controls in Visual Basic 6, but they often have additional features and different method syntax. CheckedListBox controls replace ListBox controls with the Style property set to 1-CheckBox. The old Frame control is gone and has been replaced by two new controls, GroupBox and Panel. Both these controls work as containers for other controls, but the Panel control is also scrollable. In a difference from previous Visual Basic versions, you now have two explicit menu controls, MainMenu and ContextMenu.

The majority of Windows Common Controls are available in the default Toolbox, so you don't have to reference another library. This group includes the following controls: ImageList, ListView, TreeView, ProgressBar, TrackBar (SlideBar), RichTextBox, TabControl (TabStrip), ToolBar, StatusBar, DateTimePicker, and MonthCalendar (MonthView). (The names in parentheses are the old Visual Basic 6 versions.)

The new NumericUpDown control replaces the combination of a TextBox control and an UpDown control. The new DomainUpDown is like a single-row list box. The DataGrid control has more or less the same functionality as the old control of the same name. The old CommonDialog control has been replaced by six more-specific controls: OpenFileDialog, SaveFileDialog, FontDialog, ColorDialog, PrintDialog, and PageSetupDialog.

There are also a few brand-new controls. The LinkLabel control is an enhanced label control that can be used to implement Web-like hyperlinks to other portions of the application or to URLs on the Internet. The Splitter control lets you create resizeable regions on your form. The NotifyIcon control enables your program to create those little icons in the Windows taskbar and to react to mouse actions on them.

The PrintPreviewDialog control works together with the PrintPreviewControl object to provide a WYSIWYG preview of printed documents. You can simplify actual printing operations by using the PrintControl object, and you can create complex reports using the CrystalReportViewer control.

Finally, there are three controls known as *extender provider controls* because they augment the functionality of other controls on the form. The ToolTip control displays a tooltip message when the mouse hovers over any other control. The HelpProvider control provides help functionality (and therefore replaces the help functionality previously in the CommonDialog control). The ErrorProvider control can display a red icon beside controls that don't pass input validation.

A few Visual Basic 6 controls aren't available any longer: DriveList, DirListBox, FileListBox, OLE container, UpDown, Animation, the two flat scroll bars, MSFlexGrid, and a bunch of others. Windows Forms don't support windowless controls, which explains why the Line and Shape controls aren't supported any longer. The Image control is also gone, but its lightweight capabilities have been embedded in the new PictureBox control. All the Data, RDO Data, and ADO Data controls have been dumped (even though Windows Forms still support data binding).

Common Properties

Because all controls inherit most of their functionality from System.Windows. Forms.Control, they expose a similar set of properties. I gathered in Table 5-1 the properties that the majority of controls have in common. The third column lists the corresponding Visual Basic 6 properties, if there are any, to help you in understanding what each property does and to speed up porting of applications from previous language versions.

Table 5-1   Properties Common to Most Controls

Category	Name	VB6 Property	Description
Size and position	Location	Left and Top	The location of the object, expressed as a Point object that exposes the X and Y properties.
	Size	Width and Height	The dimension of the object. The Size object exposes the Width and Height properties.
	Left, Top, Width, Height	Left, Top, Width, Height	Individual coordinates and dimensions of the control.
	Right	Left+Width	The X coordinate of the right border.
	Bottom	Top+Height	The Y coordinate of the bottom border.
	Bounds		The rectangle that defines position and size of the control in its container's coordinate system.
	ClientRectangle		The client rectangle of the control.
	ClientSize		A Size object that defines the dimension of the client rectangle.
	Anchor		From which edges of the container this control maintains a fixed distance (bit-coded).
	Dock		Which borders of this control are docked to its container (bit-coded).
	Parent	Container	The parent for this control.
Text	Text	Caption or Text	The text string displayed in the control.
	Font	Font	The font used to display text in the control. Font properties are Name, Size, Bold, Italic, Strikeout, Underline, and Unit. (Unit can be Point, Pixel, Inch, Millimeter, Document, or World.)
	RightToLeft	RightToLeft	True if the control should draw text right-to-left for right-to-left (RTL) languages.

(continued)

Table 5-1   Properties Common to Most Controls   *(continued)*

Category	Name	VB6 Property	Description
	IMEMode		The Input Method Editor status of the object when selected. (Used for alphabets such as Japanese, Chinese, and Korean.)
Color and graphic	ForeColor	ForeColor	The foreground color.
	BackColor	BackColor	The background color.
Focus	TabIndex	TabIndex	The index in tab order for this control.
	TabStop	TabStop	True if the user can use the Tab key to give focus to the control.
	Visible	Visible	True if the control is visible or hidden.
	Enabled	Enabled	True if the control is enabled.
	Cursor		The Cursor object that represents the mouse state, position, and size.
	ShowFocusCues		True if the user interface is in a state to show focus rectangles (read-only).
	ShowKeyboard Cues		True if the user interface is in a state to show keyboard accelerators (read-only).
	CausesValidation	CausesValidation	True if the control causes a validation event.
Keyboard and mouse	ModifierKeys		The current state of Shift, Ctrl, and Alt keys (bit-coded).
	MouseButtons		The current state of mouse buttons (bit-coded).
	MousePosition		The current mouse position in screen coordinates (returns a Point object).
Accessibility	AccessibleName		The name reported to accessibility clients.
	Accessible Description		The description reported to accessibility clients.
	AccessibleRole		The role reported to accessibility clients (Default, Alert, Text, Graphic, Sound, and so on).

Table 5-1   Properties Common to Most Controls *(continued)*

Category	Name	VB6 Property	Description
	AccessibleDefault-ActionDescription		The description of the default action of the control.
	IsAccessible		True if this control should be accessible to accessibility applications.
Creation	Created		True if the control has been created.
	Disposing		True if the control is being disposed of (destroyed).
	Disposed		True if the control has been disposed of (destroyed).
Miscellaneous	Name	Name	The name of the control.
	AllowDrop	OLEDropMode	True if the control receives drag-and-drop notifications.
	ContextMenu		The pop-up menu to display when the user right-clicks on the control.
	ProductName		The name of this specific component.
	ProductVersion		The version of this specific component.
	CompanyName		The company name of this specific component.
Design only	Modifiers		The visibility level of the control (Public, Protected, Friend, or Private).
	Locked		True if the control can't be resized or moved on its container.
Run time only	Focused	ActiveControl (of parent form)	True if the control has the input focus.
	Handle	hWnd	The handle of the Windows control.
	CanFocus		True if the control can receive the focus.
	CanSelect		True if the control can be selected.
	Capture		True if the control has captured the mouse and receives all mouse events (read/write).

Common Methods

Table 5-2 lists the most important methods in common among controls. Once again, I indicated the corresponding Visual Basic 6 method if possible.

Table 5-2 **Methods Common to Most Controls**

Category	Name	VB6 Method	Description
Size and position	BringToFront	ZOrder	Brings the control to the front of the Z-order.
	SendToBack	ZOrder 1	Sends the control to the back of the Z-order.
	FindForm	Parent	Returns the form this control is on.
	GetContainer	Container	Returns the container for the control.
	GetContainerControl	Container	Returns the closest ContainerControl in the control's chain of parent controls and forms.
	PointToClient(point)		Converts a point from screen coordinates to client coordinates.
	PointToScreen(point)		Converts a point from client coordinates to screen coordinates.
	RectangleToClient(rect)		Converts a rectangle from screen coordinates to client coordinates.
	RectangleToScreen(rect)		Converts a rectangle from client coordinates to screen coordinates.
	SetBounds(left,top,width, height)	Move	Sets the bounding rectangle (same as assigning the Bounds property).
	SetSize(width,height)	Move	Sets the size of the control (same as assigning the Size property).
	SetClientSizeCore (width,height)		Sets the client size of the control.

Table 5-2   Methods Common to Most Controls *(continued)*

Category	Name	VB6 Method	Description
Child controls	Scale(horiz [,vert])		Resizes the control and its children according to the specified ratio values. (If only one value is provided, it's used as both vertical and horizontal ratio.)
	SetNewControls(ctrlarray)		Sets the array of child controls contained in this control.
	GetChildAtPoint(point)		Returns the child control at the specified client coordinates.
	Contains(ctrl)		Checks whether this control contains another control.
	ActivateControl(ctrl)		Activates a child control.
Appearance	Invalidate	Refresh	Invalidates the control and forces a repaint.
	Refresh	Refresh	Forces the control to invalidate and immediately repaint itself and its children.
	Update	Refresh	Forces the control to repaint any currently invalid areas.
	Show		Shows the control; same as setting Visible property to True.
	Hide		Hides the control; same as setting Visible property to False.
	ResetForeColor		Resets the ForeColor property to reflect the parent's foreground color.
	ResetBackColor		Resets the BackColor property to reflect the parent's background color.

(continued)

Table 5-2 **Methods Common to Most Controls** *(continued)*

Category	Name	VB6 Method	Description
	ResetCursor		Resets Cursor property to its default value.
	ResetText		Resets the Text property to its default value.
Focus	Focus	SetFocus	Attempts to give input focus to this control.
	ContainsFocus		Returns True if the control or one of its child controls has the focus.
	GetNextControl		Returns the next control in tab order.
	Select		Selects this control.
	SelectNextControl		Gives input focus to next control in tab order.
Miscellaneous	CallWndProc(msg,wParam, lParam)		Dispatches a message to the control's window procedure directly.
	CreateControl		Forces the creation of the control, including its child controls.
	CreateGraphics		Returns the Graphics object that can be used to draw on the control's surface.
	Dispose		Destroys the control.
	DoDragDrop (allowedEffects)	OLEDrag	Begins a drag operation; the argument determines which drag operation can occur.

Common Events

Table 5-3 lists all the events common to the majority of controls, together with the corresponding Visual Basic 6 event if there is one. Keep in mind that all events receive exactly two arguments—sender and *xxxx*EventArgs—where the former is a reference to the control raising the event and the latter is an object that might contain additional information about the event. The descriptions of individual events explain which values are passed in this second argument, if any. Notice that you can create an event template in Visual Studio by selecting the (Base Class Events) element in the leftmost combo box on the right.

Table 5-3   Events Common to Most Controls

Category	Name	VB6 Event	Description
Focus	GotFocus	GotFocus	The control receives the focus.
	LostFocus	LostFocus	The control loses the focus; this event occurs after the Validated event.
	Enter		The control is entered; this event occurs before the GotFocus event.
	Leave		The control is left; this event occurs before the Validating event.
	Validating	Validate	The control is being validated.
	Validated		The control has completed validation.
	ChangeUICues		Focus cue, keyboard cue, or both cues have changed (useful only when creating custom controls).
Keyboard and Mouse	Click	Click	The control is clicked.
	DoubleClick	DblClick	The control is double-clicked.
	MouseDown	MouseDown	A mouse button has been pressed; it receives Button, Clicks, Delta, X, and Y values.
	MouseUp	MouseUp	A mouse button has been released; it receives the same values as MouseDown.
	MouseMove	MouseMove	The mouse is moved over the control; it receives the same values as MouseDown.
	MouseWheel		The mouse wheel has been rotated while the control has the focus; it receives the same values as MouseDown.
	MouseEnter		The mouse enters the control.
	MouseLeave		The mouse leaves the control.
	MouseHover		The mouse hovers over the control.

(continued)

Table 5-3 **Events Common to Most Controls** *(continued)*

Category	Name	VB6 Event	Description
	KeyDown	KeyDown	A key is pressed while the control has the focus; it receives Alt, Control, Shift, Modifiers, KeyCode, KeyData, and Handled values.
	KeyUp	KeyUp	A key is released while the control has the focus; it receives the same values as KeyDown.
	KeyPress	KeyPress	A printable key is pressed while the control has the focus; it receives KeyChar and Handled values.
	HelpRequested		The user requests help for the control.
Drag and drop	DragDrop	OLEDragDrop	A drag-and-drop operation is complete; it receives AllowedEffect, Data, Effect, KeyState, X, and Y values.
	DragEnter	OLEDragOver, with state = vbEnter	An object is dragged into the control's border; it receives the same values as DragDrop.
	DragLeave	OLEDragOver, with state = vbLeave	An object is dragged out of the control's border; it receives the same values as DragDrop.
	DragOver	OLEDragOver, with state = vbOver	An object is being dragged over the control's border; it receives the same values as DragDrop.
	GiveFeedback	OLEGive Feedback	Occurs during a drag operation; it gives the source control a chance to change the cursor's appearance.
	QueryContinue-Drag		Occurs during a drag operation; it gives the source control a chance to cancel the operation.
Appearance	Paint	Paint	The control is being repainted; it receives ClipRectangle and Graphics values.

Table 5-3   Events Common to Most Controls *(continued)*

Category	Name	VB6 Event	Description
	Invalidated		The control has been invalidated; it receives an Invalid-Rect value.
	Move		The control has been moved.
	Resize	Resize	The control is resized.
	Layout		Occurs when a control has to lay out its child controls.
Container controls	ControlAdded		A new control is added; it receives a Controlvalue
	ControlRemoved		A control is removed; it receives a Control argument.
Miscellaneous	HandleCreated		A handle is created for the control.
	HandleDestroyed		The control's handle is destroyed.
	PropertyChanged		A control's property has been changed; it receives a PropertyName value.

✳✳✳

Using Menus

Menus allow users to access critical, top-level commands and functions in a familiar, easy to understand interface. A well designed menu that exposes your application's functionality in a logical, consistent manner will make your application easy to learn and use. If you offer a poorly designed menu, users will avoid it whenever possible and work with it reluctantly only when necessary.

When designing menus, you should take into account the logical flow of the application. Menu items should be grouped according to related functionality. Using access keys to enable keyboard shortcuts to menu items will also make the use of your application easier.

Creating Menus at Design Time

With the *MainMenu* component, you can rapidly and intuitively create menus for your forms at design time. The *MainMenu* component contains and manages a collection of *MenuItem* controls, which form the visual element of a menu at run time.

Using the MainMenu Component

The *MainMenu* control allows you to do the following at design time:

- Create new menus and menu bars.

- Add new menu items to existing menus.

- Modify the properties of menus and menu items via the Properties window.

- Create event handlers to handle the Click event and other events for menu items.

To create a new menu, add a *MainMenu* component to your form. The component appears in the component tray, and a box with the text **Type Here** appears in the menu bar of the form. The menu appears on your form as it would at run time. To create a menu item, type in the box where indicated. As you type, additional boxes are created beneath and to the right of the first menu item.

Adapted from *Developing Windows-Based Applications with Microsoft Visual Basic .NET and Microsoft Visual C# .NET.* pp. 75-83. (Redmond: Microsoft Press. 2002.) Copyright © 2002 by Microsoft Corporation.

Submenus are created the same way. If you want to create a submenu, simply type an entry to the right of the menu item that you want to expand. Figure 5-5 shows how to use the *MainMenu* component.

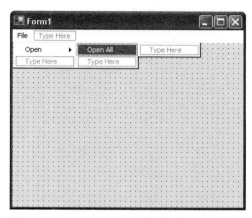

Figure 5-5. Creating menus with the MainMenu component

When an item is added to a menu, the designer creates an instance of a *MenuItem* object. Each *MenuItem* object has its own properties and members that can be set in the Properties window. The *Text* property represents the text that will be displayed at run time and is automatically set to the text that you type. The *Name* property indicates how you will refer to this object in code and is automatically given a default value that can be changed if desired.

To create main menus at design time, follow these steps:

1.   In the Toolbox, add a *MainMenu* component to the form either by double-clicking the *MainMenu* tool or by dragging it onto the form. A *MainMenu* component appears in the component tray.

2.   In the designer, type the text for the first menu item in the box presented on the form's menu bar. As additional boxes appear, add additional menu items until the structure of your menu is complete.

3.   In the Properties window, set any of the properties that you want to change for your menu items.

4.   In the Properties window of the form, make sure that the *Menu* property of the form is set to the menu you want to display. If you have multiple menus on a form, only the designated menu will be displayed.

Separating Menu Items

You can separate menu items with a separator, a horizontal line between items on a menu. You can use separator bars to divide menu items into logical groups on menus that contain multiple items, as shown in Figure 5-6. To add a separator to your menus, enter a hyphen as the text of a menu item at the point where you want the separator to be.

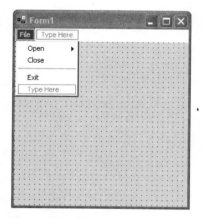

Figure 5-6. Separator bars on menus

Menu Access and Shortcut Keys

You can enable keyboard access to your menus through the use of Access and Shortcut keys.

Access Keys

Access keys allow the user to open a menu by pressing the Alt key and typing a designated letter. When the menu is open, you can select a menu command by pressing the Alt key and the correct access key. For example, in most programs the Alt+F key opens the File menu. When it is open, you can choose Alt+N to create a new item. Access keys are displayed on the form as an underlined letter on the menu items.

You can use the same access key for different menu items as long as the menu items are contained in different menu groups. For example, you might want to use Alt+C to access the Close command on the File menu group and the Copy command on the Edit menu group. You should avoid using the same access key for multiple items on a menu group, such as using Alt+C for both the Cut and the Copy commands of an Edit menu group. If you do use the same access key combination for two items on a menu group, you will be able to use the access key to toggle your selection between the items, but you will not be able to select the item without pressing the Enter key.

To assign an access key to a menu item go to the designer and click the menu item that you want to assign an access key. Type an ampersand (&) in front of the desired letter for the access key.

Shortcut Keys

Shortcut keys enable instant access to menu commands and can be useful for providing a keyboard shortcut for frequently used menu commands. Shortcut key assignments can either be single keys—such as Delete, F1, or Insert—or key combinations, such as Ctrl+A, Ctrl+F1, or Ctrl+Shift+X. When a shortcut key is designated for a menu item, it is shown to the right of the menu item. The shortcut key combination will not be displayed if the *ShowShortcut* property of the menu item is set to false.

To assign a shortcut key, select the menu item for which you want to enable a shortcut key and select the *Shortcut* property n the Properties window. Choose the appropriate shortcut key combination from the drop-down menu.

Menu Item Events

You can create event handlers for menu items in the same manner in which you create event handlers for other controls. The most frequently used event is the *Click* event. The *Click* event handler should contain the code to be executed when the menu item is clicked. This code will also execute when a shortcut key combination is used.

The *Select* event is raised when a menu item is highlighted, either with the mouse or through the use of access keys. You might create an event handler that provides detailed help regarding the use of a menu command when selected.

The *Popup* event is raised just before a menu item's list is displayed. You can use this event to enable and disable menu items at run time before the menu is displayed.

Context Menus

Context menus are menus that appear when an item is right-clicked. You create context menus with the *ContextMenu* component, which is edited in exactly the same way as the *MainMenu* component. The *ContextMenu* appears at the top of the form, and you can add menu items by typing them on the control.

Context menus are similar to main menus in many respects. Both contain and manage a collection of menu item controls. You can enable shortcut keys for menu items in a context menu, but not access keys. To associate a context menu with a particular form or control, set the *ContextMenu* property of that form or control to the appropriate menu.

To create a context menu, follow these steps:

1. In the Toolbox, add a *ContextMenu* component to the form, either by double-clicking the *ContextMenu* tool or by dragging it onto the form. A *ContextMenu* component appears in the component tray.

2. In the designer, type the text for the first menu item in the box presented on the form's menu bar. As additional boxes appear, add additional menu items until the structure of your menu is complete.

3. In the Properties window, set any of the properties that you want to change for your menu items.

4. Select the form or control you want to associate the context menu with. In the Properties window for the control, set the *ContextMenu* property to your context menu. The context menu will be displayed at run time when the control is right-clicked. You can associate a single context menu with several controls, but only one context menu per control.

Modifying Menus at Run Time

You can dynamically manipulate your menus to respond to run-time conditions. For example, if your application is unable to complete a certain command, you can disable the menu item that calls that command. You can display a check mark next to a menu item or a radio button to provide information to the user; make menu items invisible at times that it might not be appropriate to choose them. You can also add menu items at run time, and menus can be cloned or merged with one another at run time.

Enabling and Disabling Menu Commands

Every menu item has an *Enabled* property. When this property is set to false, the menu is disabled and does not respond to user actions. Access and shortcut key actions are also disabled for this menu item, and it appears dimmed on the user interface. The following code disables a menu item at run time.

Visual Basic .NET

```
MenuItem1.Enabled = False
```

Visual C#

```
menuItem1.Enabled = false;
```

Displaying Check Marks on Menu Items

You can use the *Checked* property to display a check mark next to a menu item, such as displaying a check mark to indicate that a particular option has been selected. Use the following code to select and clear a menu item.

Visual Basic .NET

```
' Checks the menu item
MenuItem1.Checked = True
' Unchecks the menu item
MenuItem1.Checked = False
```

Visual C#

```
// Checks the menu item
MenuItem1.Checked = true;
// Unchecks the menu item
MenuItem1.Checked = false;
```

Displaying Radio Buttons on Menu Items

A radio style button can be displayed instead of a check mark. To display radio buttons, set the *RadioCheck* property for the menu item to true. The menu item will then display a radio button instead of a check mark when the *Checked* property is set to true. When the *Checked* property is false, neither a check mark nor a radio button will appear.

Radio buttons are frequently used to display exclusive options, such as the choice of background colors. If you want to display radio buttons next to mutually exclusive options, you must write code that clears other options when one option is selected.

Making Menu Items Invisible

You can make your menu items invisible by setting the Visible property to false. Use this property to modify your menus at run time in response to changing conditions. The following code demonstrates how to make a menu item invisible.

Visual Basic .NET

```
MenuItem1.Visible = False
```

Visual C#

```
menuItem1.Visible = false;
```

Note that making a menu item invisible at run time removes it from the menu bar. Any submenus contained by that menu item will also be inaccessible.

Cloning Menus

You can make a copy of existing menu items at run time. For example, you might want to clone an Edit menu item (and its associated submenus) from a main menu to serve as a context menu for a control. You can create a new menu item by using the *CloneMenu* method. It creates a copy of the specified menu item and all of its members, including contained menu items, properties, and event handlers. Thus, all events that are handled by the original menu item will be handled in the same way by the cloned menu item. The newly created context menu can then be assigned to a control. Use the following code to clone a menu item as a new context menu at run time.

Visual Basic .NET

```
' The following example assumes the existence of a menu item called
' fileMenuItem and a control called myButton
' Declares and instantiates a new context menu
Dim myContextMenu as New ContextMenu()
' Clones fileMenuItem and fills myContextMenu with the cloned item
myContextMenu.MenuItems.Add(fileMenuItem.CloneMenu())
' Assigns the new context menu to myButton
myButton.ContextMenu = myContextMenu
```

Visual C#

```
// The following example assumes the existence of a menu item called
// fileMenuItem and a control called myButton
// Declares and instantiates a new context menu
ContextMenu myContextMenu = new ContextMenu();
// Clones fileMenuItem and fills myContextMenu with the cloned item
myContextMenu.MenuItems.Add(fileMenuItem.CloneMenu());
// Assigns the new context menu to myButton
myButton.ContextMenu = myContextMenu;
```

Merging Menus at Run Time

At times, you might want to display multiple menus as a single menu at run time. The *MergeMenu* method allows you to combine menus and display them as one. You can merge multiple main or context menus with each other, merge menus with menu items, or merge multiple menu items. To merge menus at run time, call the *MergeMenu* method of the menu or menu item that will be displayed. Supply the menu or menu item to be incorporated as the argument.

Visual Basic .NET

```
MainMenu1.MergeMenu(ContextMenu1)
```

Visual C#

```
mainMenu1.MergeMenu(contextMenu1);
```

Adding Menu Items at Run Time

You can dynamically add new items to an existing menu at run time. For example, you might add menu items that display the pathnames of the most recently opened files. New menu items will not have any event handlers associated with them, but you can specify a method to handle the *Click* event as an argument to the constructor of the new menu item. This method must be a *Sub (void)* method and have the same signature as other event handlers. The following code is an example of an appropriate method.

Visual Basic .NET

```
Public Sub ClickHandler (ByVal sender As Object, ByVal e As _
    System.EventArgs)
    ' Implementation details omitted
End Sub
```

Visual C#

```
public void ClickHandler (object sender, System.EventArgs e)
{
    // Implementation details omitted
}
```

To add menu items at run time, begin by declaring and instantiating a new menu item. You can specify a method to handle the *Click* event at this time if you choose. Next add the new method to the menuitems collection of the menu you want to modify.

Visual Basic .NET

```
' This example assumes the existence of a method called myClick
' which has the correct event handler signature
Dim myItem as MenuItem
myItem = New MenuItem("Item 1", New EventHandler(AddressOf myClick))

MainMenu1.MenuItems.Add(myItem)
```

Visual C#

```
// This example assumes the existence of a method called myClick
// which has the correct event handler signature
MenuItem myItem;
myItem = new MenuItem("Item 1", new EventHandler(myClick));

MainMenu1.MenuItems.Add(myItem);
```

Part II

Object-Oriented Programming

Reading 6

Object-Oriented Programming in Visual Basic .NET

You really can't do anything in Visual Basic .NET without coming face to face with objects. When you create a standard form in a new project, you have access to the code for the form's class. While this code was present in classic Visual Basic, it was hidden from a programmer's view. Now it is presented to you in the integrated development environment (IDE). A solid understanding of object-oriented programming is a prerequisite for getting the most from Visual Basic .NET. If you are new to object-oriented programming (sometimes abbreviated OOP) or up till now have tried to avoid using it directly, this chapter will make you a believer, and you'll see that it's pretty straightforward, which wasn't the case at first for me.

An Object Lesson

When I started to learn object-oriented programming about 10 years ago, I found its concepts somewhat difficult. I read every book I could get my hands on and thought about all that I'd read, but it still didn't make sense. I performed due diligence and put in the time, but for some reason OOP didn't click. "What's this business about creating a class and calling methods? After all, didn't I do the same thing with C math libraries for years?"

Then one day I had a revelation! All at once I realized how simple the concepts of object-oriented programming really are, and I became a believer. I spent time reflecting on why I took so long to understand a concept that turned out to be so simple and realized that the reason was twofold. First, the authors of the books I read seemed to obfuscate OOP by using terms such as overloading, encapsulation, inheritance, and polymorphism all over the place before they were clearly defined (at least for me). While I might have muddled my way through this terminological maze, the knockout punch was the examples the authors provided, which were contrived and never about anything that could be used by a programmer to solve real problems. Although I tried to match alien concepts with contrived and overly difficult examples (again, at least to me), OOP didn't sink in. I had pictures of cookie cutters, stars, and rectangles dancing in my head. These images were the hands-down favorites of every author discussing object-oriented programming. To me, they hadn't made any sense.

To save you the time I spent scratching my head and thinking about objects until my brain hurt, I'll use prefabricated objects such as a Windows form and a few control objects to illustrate object-oriented concepts. By working with something that you already use in your programming, the jump to thinking about objects is much, much easier. Over time, I've found this approach to be the clearest way to illustrate the principles of OOP.

I'll cover objects and classes, properties, methods, inheritance, overloading, polymorphism, and sharing, all within the context of what you know.

Starting Out with Objects

Let's start out by describing our terms. Many beginners have a difficult time sorting out the difference between a class and an object. I hear them using the terms interchangeably. Remember that a class contains the instructions for how to construct an object in the computer's memory. Here's an analogy.

A Class Is Really Only a Blueprint

Think of a class as a blueprint for building a house. A blueprint isn't a house; it's a sheaf of papers with drawings and dimensions that tell a contractor how to build a house. When the contractor follows the blueprints and builds the house, you have an object. An object is a physical manifestation of a class, just like a house is a physical manifestation of a blueprint.

A blueprint might indicate the location for each window and the type of window to use. A class can include the types of controls and their positions on a form, as well as various data types to use. A house is built with the appropriate windows in the right location. A form object is created with the controls displayed as the form class directed. Of course, contractors use the same blueprints to build several houses, as shown in Figure 6-1. Likewise, you can create several objects from the same class. Because the objects follow the same class blueprint, each of the objects will look and function in the same way.

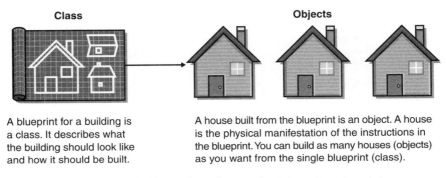

A blueprint for a building is a class. It describes what the building should look like and how it should be built.

A house built from the blueprint is an object. A house is the physical manifestation of the instructions in the blueprint. You can build as many houses (objects) as you want from the single blueprint (class).

Figure 6-1   A blueprint is like a class; houses built from the blueprints are like objects.

Let's Talk Objects

The best way to introduce a few of the key object-oriented concepts is with an example. Start up Visual Studio .NET and follow these steps:

1.   Create a new Windows Application project. You'll have a blank form.

2.   Drag a button control from the tool palette to the form. If you've worked with Visual Basic 6, this is old hat to you. Keep the default names of the form and the button control.

> **Note**   There are three ways to add a control to a form. You can double-click the control, you can click once on the control and then once on the form, or you can click the control and then drag it to the form.

3.   Double-click the button control. Double-clicking the control automatically adds the *Click* event handler to the form's class.

4.   Click the Form1.vb tab and modify the *Text* property of both the button and the form objects. For the form, change the *Text* property to "Mirror Image". For the button, change the value to "&Clone Me!" You can tell the form and the button are both objects because you can set their properties and see that both have inherited the know-how to do things such as resize themselves.

> **Note**   The ampersand (&) used in the button's *Text* property automatically provides an *accelerator* key combination for power users. Visual Basic .NET adds an underscore to the character that immediately follows the ampersand when the text is displayed on the control. A user can press Alt plus the accelerator key to simulate clicking the button.

5. Size the form and button so that they look something like what's shown in Figure 6-2.

Figure 6-2   Your form should look like this.

Our Form as an Object

All objects are created as identical copies of their class; they are mirror images. Your form is a perfect example of an object. Once you instantiate an object from your class, however, the object is separate from any other object you instantiate from the class. After your form is created in your project, you can resize it in the Designer, for example. The form itself is responsible for handling the implementation of how it is resized and redrawn. It is born knowing how to do that and everything else a form does, such as displaying its own default menu and dismissing itself when you click its Close button.

A key point you should understand about objects is that they are a combination of data and code. The fundamental advantage of OOP is that the data and the operations that manipulate the data are both contained in the object. An object can be treated as a self-contained unit.

Objects are the building blocks of an object-oriented program, and an object-oriented program is essentially a collection of objects. In the simple program we just created, we have a button object on a form object. When the form appears, it has a color, size, and position on the screen. These characteristics are among what are called its *properties*. Properties define the state of an object.

The form also knows how to minimize and maximize itself and how to resize itself when you drag its edges with a mouse. In other words, the form has a set of built-in behaviors, and these behaviors are implemented by what are called *methods*. Methods tell an object how to do things.

Seeing Properties and Methods in the IDE

The IntelliSense feature in the IDE puts everything the form is or can do at your fingertips. For example, when you enter "Form1" in the code editor, Visual Basic .NET knows that this refers to an object because you've defined *Form1* as such—an object that inherits from the *Windows.Forms.Form* class. The IDE displays each legitimate property or method when you enter a dot (.) after *Form1*. The dot, or *scope resolution modifier*, separates the object from its methods or properties. The general form is *Object.Method* or *Object.Property*. Properties are marked by an icon of a hand holding a card, while methods are indicated by purple flying bricks.

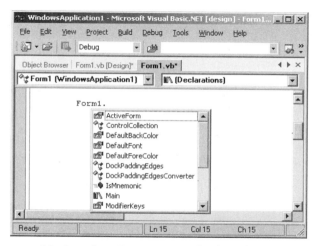

Notice that *Form1* was declared with an uppercase "F," but you could have entered *form1* with a lowercase "f." Unlike C, C++, or C#, Visual Basic is not case sensitive, but the IDE will automatically correct your typing and make the spelling consistent.

You could create five forms, each of a different size and with different captions, so that each has its own *Size* and *Text* properties set to a different value. Each object contains its own properties. Each is a self-contained black box of functionality that contains data (its size and color) and code for how it does things (resizing or redrawing itself, for example).

If you've programmed before in classic Visual Basic, these concepts might be familiar. For example, any time you placed a list box control on a form and changed its name or size, you were modifying its properties. Whenever you added an item to the list box with *AddItem*, you were calling one of the list box's methods.

So, just to summarize, the key elements of an object are

- **Properties.**   A characteristic of a form (or other object), such as its size, color, and position or the font used for displaying text. Properties contain values that are unique to each object. Most visual controls, such as our form, expose properties to define their appearance.

- **Methods.**   Something an object knows how to do. A form object, for example, can resize itself, display a menu, or hide itself.

Reading, Writing, Invoking

You communicate with an object programmatically by reading and writing its properties and invoking its methods. If you wanted to read the current *Height* property of a form and display it in a message box, you would write the following line in the *Load* event of the form:

```
Private Sub Form1_Load(ByVal sender As System.Object,
    ByVal e As System.EventArgs) Handles MyBase.Load
    MessageBox.Show("Form1's height is " & _
        Me.Height, Me.Text)
End Sub
```

> **Note**   The keyword might look strange to those of you new to OOP. *Me* is the equivalent of the *this* pointer in C++. *Me* is used to reference the current object, which happens to be a form. The *Me* keyword is one of the first elements you will have to become familiar with in Visual Basic .NET.

The first call in this code fragment is to the *Show* method of the *MessageBox* class, new to Visual Basic .NET. The *Show* method knows how to display a message box. The first parameter is what will be displayed as the message. Because we want to display the height of the form, we read its *Height* property as the second parameter of the *Show* method. The code *Me.Height* reads the form's *Height* property. The final parameter of the *Show* method is the title to show in the message box's caption. The code *Me.Text* reads the form's *Text* property. Now when you run the program, the dialog box shown in Figure 6-3 appears.

Figure 6-3   This message box displays the form's height.

If you wanted to change the form's *Height* property—write to it instead of read it—you simply assign a new value to the property. To change the form's height from 115 pixels to 203 pixels when the user clicks the button, you would write this code:

```
Protected Sub Button1_Click(ByVal sender As Object, _
    ByVal e As System.EventArgs)

    Me.Height = 203
    MessageBox.Show("Form1's height is " & _
        Me.Height, Me.Text)
End Sub
```

When the user clicks the button, the first line of code assigns the value 203 to the form's *Height* property, invoking the form's *Size* method. The form immediately adjusts to the new size. The message box displays the height, confirming that the form resized itself, as shown in Figure 6-4. All you did was assign a new property value; the form object already knew how to resize itself through its *Size* method.

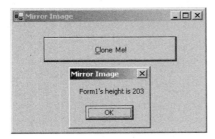

Figure 6-4   The resized form.

The form object automatically knows whether you are reading or writing a value by the position of the object reference relative to the equal sign (=). To assign a value to a property, you use code like the following:

```
Me.Height = 203
```

With the object reference on the left side of the equal sign, the object knows you are assigning a value to the property.

To read the value of a property, you use code like the following:

```
MyVariable = Me.Height
```

Here the object reference is on the right side of the equal sign, which means you're reading the property's value. As I stressed before, you don't know how the property is stored inside the object. It might be stored in Portuguese, pig Latin, or any language at all. All you know is that you can read an integer from the property or write an integer to set the property. How the object performs these operations is its business. An object can seem very much like the Wizard of Oz when he says, "Pay no attention to the man behind the curtain."

This kind of implementation is one of the productive aspects of working with objects. To use an object you simply read or write its properties and call the methods that it exposes. The object is responsible for doing the real work. An object might be prepackaged like a form, or it might be one you write yourself.

Inheritance

As you can see, a form is a pretty smart object. It has all sorts of properties and methods that you can use immediately because they are part of the *base class* (also known as the *parent class*) that the form object inherits from. As I've said, inheritance is one of the fundamental tenets of object-oriented programming. Through inheritance, you can derive classes from other classes that have already been written. In our example, the base class is *System.Windows.Forms.Form*.

```
Public Class Form1
    Inherits System.Windows.Forms.Form
```

When a class inherits from a base class, it inherits the properties and methods of that class. Properties and methods are often referred to as the *members* of a class. You can then use or add to these members in your own class in whatever way you need.

The Buffed Up Message Box

The message box we're using in this example is a tried and true friend of the Visual Basic programmer, but a few changes have been made to the message box that classic Visual Basic programmers should note. In Visual Basic 6, the *MsgBox* function supported optional arguments to specify a Help topic that would be displayed when the user pressed F1. Because the underlying mechanism for displaying Help topics has changed significantly in Visual Basic .NET, the *HelpFile* and *Context* arguments have been eliminated.

The older *MsgBox* syntax is still available in Visual Basic .NET. The *Microsoft.VisualBasic.Interaction* class exposes a *MsgBox* method that approximates the functionality of the Visual Basic 6 *MsgBox* function. However, I suggest you move to the new *MessageBox* class. It's entirely possible that in later versions of Visual Basic .NET, legacy Visual Basic syntax will be eliminated. By using the *Show* method of the *MessageBox* class, *System.Windows.Forms.MessageBox* provides fairly extensive support for informing and instructing the user.

Sometimes a user must dismiss a message box before continuing. Forms and dialog boxes can be displayed as either *modal* or *modeless* (the default). A modal form or dialog box must be closed (hidden or unloaded) before you can continue working with the application. Most forms, however, are displayed as modeless forms, which means that you can switch from one form to another by simply clicking the form you want to be active. Dialog boxes or message boxes that display important messages should always be modal. The user should always be required to close the dialog box or respond to its message before proceeding.

At times you might want to show a form modally, such as a form you've customized for entering a password or logging in. You want the user to address this form before moving on. Simply call the form's *ShowDialog* method to accomplish this.

```
mydialog = New Dialog1()
mydialog.ShowDialog()
```

Understanding Namespaces

A large part of the power of Visual Basic .NET comes from the base classes supplied by the Microsoft .NET Framework. Microsoft has provided a vast array of ready-built classes for your use. The .NET Framework includes a variety of base classes that encapsulate data structures, perform I/O, give you access to information about a loaded class, and provide ways for you to perform rich GUI generation and data access and develop server controls. These built-in types are designed to be the foundation on which all .NET applications, components, and controls are built.

These base classes are simple to use, and you can easily derive from them to include their functionality in your own specialized classes. To bring some order to this power, the .NET base classes are grouped into what are called *namespaces*. As I mentioned earlier, our form is an instance of the *System.Windows.Forms.Form* class. In other words, the form lives in the .NET Framework namespace dedicated to Windows client user interface programming.

Think of a namespace as a container for related classes in the same way that a folder on your hard drive contains related files. In a .NET program you'll make use of many of the base classes, and any significant Visual Basic .NET program that you develop will have many more of your own namespaces. Having a firm understanding of the concept of namespaces is required before you do just about anything in Visual Basic .NET.

Because we need a way to identify and find the built-in items required for a program, the .NET Framework types are named using a dot-syntax naming scheme that connotes a naming hierarchy. You can see this syntax in the familiar class *System.Windows.Forms.Form*.

```
Public Class Form1
    Inherits System.Windows.Forms.Form
```

This syntax tells us that the *Form* class is related to other classes that use the *System.Windows.Forms* namespace. These classes, representing objects such as graphical controls, are all part of the namespace. The part of the name up to the last dot (*System.Windows.Forms*) is referred to as the *namespace* name, and the last part (*Form*) as the *class* name. These naming patterns group related classes into namespaces and are used to build and document class libraries. This naming syntax has no effect on a class's visibility, how you access its members, how your classes inherit from the class, or how the linker binds your code.

As you've seen, the root namespace for the types in the .NET Framework is the *System* namespace. This namespace includes classes that represent the base data types used by all applications. These include *Object* (the root of the inheritance hierarchy), *Byte, Char, Array, Int32, String,* and so on.

Along with the base data types, the *System* namespace itself includes almost 100 classes. These classes range from those for handling exceptions (errors) and events to those dealing with core run-time concepts such as application domains and the automatic memory manager. Since it's impossible to cover everything about .NET in a single book, my goal is for you to work with these built-in classes enough that you'll be able to find what you need on your own.

In addition to the base data types touched on above, the *System* namespace contains 24 second-level namespaces. Table 6-1 lists the categories of functionality that are built in and the namespaces in each category.

Table 6-1   Second-Level Namespaces in the *System* Namespace

Category	Namespace
Data	*System.Data*
	System.Xml
	System.Xml.Serialization
Component model	*System.CodeDom*
	System.ComponentModel
Configuration	*System.Configuration*
Framework services	*System.Diagnostics*
	System.DirectoryServices
	System.Management
	System.ServiceProcess
	System.Messaging
	System.Timers
Globalization	*System.Globalization*
	System.Resources
Network programming	*System.NET*
Programming basics	*System.Collections*
	System.IO
	System.Text
	System.Text.RegularExpressions
	System.Threading

(continued)

Table 6-1 **Second-Level Namespaces in the *System* Namespace** *(continued)*

Category	Namespace
Reflection	*System.Reflection*
Rich, client-side GUI	*System.Drawing*
	System.Windows.Forms
Run-time infrastructure services	*System.Runtime.CompilerServices*
	System.Runtime.InteropServices
	System.Runtime.Remoting
	System.Runtime.Serialization
Security services	*System.Security*
Web services	*System.Web*
	System.Web.Services

Revisiting the Solution Explorer

Open the Solution Explorer by selecting View | Solution Explorer in the IDE. Click the References entry to expand it, and you'll see the items shown in the following illustration. The list contains the default references for a project. Even though namespaces live in assemblies (i.e., files), the Solution Explorer displays the namespaces, and it's more helpful to us to know the namespace than it is to know the particular assembly.

Revisiting the Solution Explorer *(continued)*

Of course, if you use any of the base classes that are defined in libraries, you need to ensure that the Visual Basic .NET compiler knows where to look for them—you need to understand how the compiler finds the namespaces you import. In more sophisticated projects later in the book, you'll import namespaces that are not among the defaults. You'll have to add references to these namespaces so that the compiler can probe the assemblies and find them. To add a reference, right-click References in the Solution Explorer and select Add Reference to open the Add Reference dialog box, shown here.

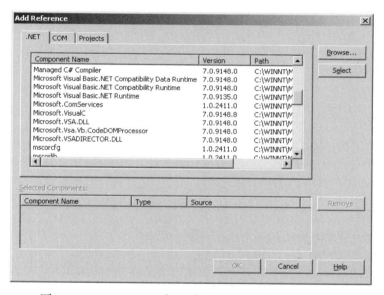

The namespaces are listed in the Component Name column. You can also see the version and the path that provides the fully qualified reference to the assembly file where the namespace items are housed. Don't select anything now. This glimpse is just to round out our exploration of the IDE for a project.

※※※

Polymorphism

The term *polymorphism* comes from the Greek language and literally means "many forms." In the context of object-oriented programming, it means "do the right thing." For example, many classes can provide the same property or method, and a caller doesn't have to know what class an object belongs to before calling the property or method. A programmer might call *Form1.Size* or *Text1.Size* and know that the object will do what's right to resize itself.

Most object-oriented programming systems provide polymorphism through inheritance. For example, you might have two forms that inherit from the *Windows.Forms.Form* class. Each form could override the class's *Close* method. When the *Close* method is invoked for *Form1*, it might ensure that all database connections are closed. The *Close* method of *Form2* might display a message box. The user simply closes each form, and then each form does the right thing. Not too terribly difficult, eh?

While you can implement polymorphism through inheritance, you can also use it through a programming interface that you can write. With polymorphism you can create hierarchies of classes and then treat the objects in the hierarchy as either similar or different depending on your needs. As we delve more deeply into classes later in the book, I'll examine this concept in more detail. The endgame, however, is the same. A program calls the same method on a different object and the right thing happens. Polymorphism is another large word for a straightforward concept.

The Three Pillars of Object-Oriented Programming: As Easy as PIE

Object-oriented programming is as easy as *PIE*. That's Polymorphism, Inheritance, and Encapsulation. We just covered the three cornerstones of all object-oriented programming.

- **Polymorphism.** Overriding methods of the same name for different objects to perform different actions.

- **Inheritance.** Deriving an object from a base class to inherit its properties and methods.

- **Encapsulation.** Hiding data within a class so that it can be manipulated only by subroutines or functions within the class itself.

Reading 7
Inheritance

To the majority of developers, the most important new feature of Visual Basic is implementation inheritance. In a nutshell, inheritance is the ability to derive a new class (the *derived* or *inherited* class) from a simpler class (the *base* class). The derived class inherits all the fields, properties, and methods of the base class and can modify the behavior of any of those properties and methods by *overriding* them. And you can also add new fields, properties, and methods to the inherited class.

Inheritance is especially effective for rendering an *is-a* relationship between two classes. For example, you can create a Bird class from the Animal class because a bird is an animal and therefore inherits the characteristics and behaviors of the generic animal, such as the ability to move, sleep, feed itself, and so on. You can then extend the new Bird class with new properties and methods, such as the Fly and LayEgg methods. Once the Bird class is in place, you can use it as the base class for a new Falcon class, and so on. A more business-oriented example of inheritance is an Employee class that derives from the Person class, an example that we will use often in the following sections.

A few programming languages, such as Microsoft Visual C++, support multiple-class inheritance, by which a class can derive from more than one base class. All .NET languages, however, support at most single-class inheritance.

Inheritance in Previous Visual Basic Versions

Inheritance is an effective way to reuse code in a class. Visual Basic 6 and previous versions offered no native support for inheritance, but you could simulate it, to an extent at least, by writing a good amount of code. It's interesting to revisit this technique because in some cases you'll find it useful in Visual Basic .NET as well.

From *Programming Microsoft Visual Basic .NET* by Francesco Balena. pp. 237-277. (Redmond: Microsoft Press. 2002.) Copyright © 2002 by Francesco Balena.

Inheritance by Delegation

Say you have a Person class that exposes properties such as FirstName, Last-Name, Address, and BirthDate, and you want to create a new Employee class that exposes these properties and a few additional ones, such as BaseSalary and HourlySalary. Under Visual Basic 6, you have only two choices: you can copy the Person source code into the Employee class—an approach some developers ironically call *cut-and-paste inheritance*—or you can use a coding technique called *inheritance by delegation*. In the latter case, the derived class delegates all the inherited properties and methods to an instance of the base class, which is conveniently instantiated in the Class_Initialize event (or through an auto-instancing variable, as in the following code snippet).

```
' A Visual Basic 6 version of the Employee class
'
' The inner object of the base class
Private Person As New Person

' A FirstName property that delegates to the inner object
Property Get FirstName() As String
    FirstName = Person.FirstName
End Property
Property Let FirstName(ByVal newValue As String)
    Person.FirstName = newValue
End Property
' Add here other delegated properties and methods.
⋮
```

Inheritance and Late-Bound Polymorphic Code

Another benefit of inheritance—including simulated inheritance achieved through delegation—is that you can create polymorphic code that can operate on both the base class and the derived class. In Visual Basic 6, such polymorphic code must use a variable of type Variant or Object, and therefore, you can refer to the actual object's methods and properties only through late binding. Thus, the downside is that you have polymorphism at the expense of performance and robustness:

```
' This procedure works with both Person and Employee objects.
Sub DisplayName(obj As object)
    ' This code uses late binding.
    Print obj.FirstName & " " obj.LastName
End Sub
```

The delegation technique works well and is flexible enough to handle all cases, but it has two severe shortcomings: it requires that you manually write a lot of code, and it requires that you modify the derived class whenever you add or delete a member in the base class. Moreover, all the delegation code tends to slow down your applications, so you can't use it in time-critical cases.

Early-Bound Polymorphic Code

Visual Basic 6 developers can implement yet another variant of inheritance, the so-called *interface inheritance*, a fancy name for a very common way to use the Implements keyword. In this case, you "inherit" only the methods' signature from the base class, not their implementation. Again, it's up to you to write all the code that performs the actual operation:

```
' A Visual Basic 6 class that inherits Person's interface
Implements Person
' Private members
Private m_FirstName As String
Private m_LastName As String
⋮

Private Property Get Person_FirstName() As String
    Person_FirstName = m_FirstName
End Property
Private Property Let Person_FirstName(ByVal RHS As String)
    m_FirstName = RHS
End Property
' Add here other properties and methods.
⋮
```

This coding technique lets you write more efficient polymorphic code that uses early binding:

```
' You can pass either a Person or an Employee object
' to this procedure.
Sub DisplayName(p As Person)
    ' This code uses early binding.
    Print p.FirstName & " " p.LastName
End Sub
```

Finally, you can mix the two techniques—inheritance by delegation and the interface implementation—and have the methods in the Person interface delegate their action to an inner Person object. This latter approach offers the best in terms of code reuse but requires that you write a large amount of code. Or you can switch to Visual Basic .NET.

Inheritance in Visual Basic .NET

To see how inheritance works in Visual Basic .NET, let's start by defining a simple Person base class:

```
Class Person
    ' Fields visible from outside the class
    Public FirstName As String
    Public LastName As String
End Class
```

You don't have to write any delegation code to implement inheritance in Visual Basic .NET because all you need is an Inherits clause immediately after the Class statement:

```
' The Employee class inherits from Person
Class Employee
    Inherits Person
    ⋮
End Class
```

Or you can use the following syntax to convince your C# colleagues that Visual Basic. NET is a first-class language:

```
' A more C++-like syntax
Class Employee: Inherits Person
    ⋮
End Class
```

The great thing about inheritance in Visual Basic .NET is that you can inherit from *any* object, including objects for which you don't have the source code, because all the plumbing code is provided by the .NET Framework. The only exception to this rule occurs when the author of the class you want to derive from has marked the class *sealed*, which means that no other class can inherit from it. (You'll find more information later in this reading about sealed classes.)

The derived class inherits all the Public and Friend fields, properties, and methods of the base class. Note that inheriting a field could be a problem because a derived class becomes dependent on that field, and the author of the base class can't change the implementation of that field—for example, to make it a calculated value—without breaking the derived class. For this reason, it's usually preferable that classes meant to work as base classes should include only Private fields. You should always use a property instead of a field to make a piece of data visible outside the class because you can always change the internal implementation of a property without any impact on derived classes. (To save space and code, some of the examples in this section use fields instead of properties: in other words, do as I say, not as I do.)

Extending the Derived Class

You can extend the derived class with new fields, properties, and methods simply by adding these new members anywhere in the class block:

```
Class Employee
    Inherits Person

    ' Two new public fields
    Public BaseSalary As Single
    Public HoursWorked As Integer
    ' A new private field
    Private m_HourlySalary As Single

    ' A new property
    Property HourlySalary() As Single
        Get
            Return m_HourlySalary
        End Get
        Set(ByVal Value As Single)
            m_HourlySalary = Value
        End Set
    End Property

    ' A new method
    Function Salary() As Single
        Return BaseSalary + m_HourlySalary * HoursWorked
    End Function
End Class
```

Using the Derived Class

You can use the new class without even knowing that it derives from another class. However, being aware of the inheritance relationship between two classes helps you write more flexible code. For example, inheritance rules state that you can always assign a derived object to a base class variable. In this case, the rule guarantees that you can always assign an Employee object to a Person variable:

```
Sub TestInheritance()
    Dim e As New Employee
    e.FirstName = "Joe"
    e.LastName = "Doe"
    ' This assignment always works.
    Dim p As Person = e
    ' This proves that p points to the Employee object.
    Console.WriteLine(p.CompleteName)    '=> Joe Doe
End Sub
```

The compiler knows that Person is the base class for Employee, and it therefore knows that all the properties and methods that you can invoke through the p variable are exposed by the Employee object as well. As a result, these calls can never fail. This sort of assignment is always successful also when the derived class inherits from the base class indirectly. *Indirect inheritance* means that there are intermediate classes along the inheritance path, such as when you have a PartTimeEmployee class that derives from Employee, which in turn derives from Person.

A consequence of this rule is that you can assign any object reference to an Object variable because all .NET classes derive from System.Object either directly or indirectly:

```
' This assignment *always* works, regardless of
' the type of sourceObj.
Dim o As Object = sourceObj
```

Assignments in the opposite direction don't always succeed, though. Consider this code:

```
' This code assumes that Option Strict is Off.

Dim p As Person
If Math.Rnd < .5 Then
    ' Sometimes P points to an Employee object.
    p = New Employee()
Else
    ' Sometimes P points to a Person object.
    p = New Person()
End If
' This assignment fails with an InvalidCastException
' error if Math.Rnd was >= .5.
Dim e As Employee = p
```

The compiler can't determine whether the reference assigned to the e variable points to an Employee or a Person object, and the assignment fails in the latter case. For this reason, this assignment is rejected if Option Strict is on. (You should set Option Strict On for all the files in the project or from inside the Build page of the project Property Pages dialog box.) An assignment that is accepted by the compiler regardless of the Option Strict setting requires that you perform an explicit cast to the destination type, using the CType or the DirectCast operator:

```
' This statement works also when Option Strict is On.
Dim e As Employee = DirectCast(p, Employee)
```

Inheriting Events

A derived class inherits also the events defined in the base class. Let's make a concrete example and assume that the base class exposes a GotMail event:

```
Class Person
    ⋮
    Event GotMail(ByVal msgText As String)

    Sub NotifyNewMail(ByVal msgText As String)
        ' Let all listeners know that we got mail.
        RaiseEvent GotMail(msgText)
    End Sub

End Class
```

If Employee inherits from Person, you can use an Employee object in the following way:

```
Dim WithEvents anEmployee As Employee

Sub TestInheritance2()
    ' Create the event sink.
    anEmployee = New Employee()
    anEmployee.FirstName = "Joe"
    anEmployee.LastName = "Doe"

    ' Notify this employee that he got new mail.
    ' (This indirectly raises the event.)
    anEmployee.NotifyNewMail("Message from VB2TheMax")
End Sub

' The event procedure
Sub Employee_NewMail(ByVal msgText As String) Handles anEmployee.GotMail
    Console.WriteLine("NEW MAIL: " & msgText)
End Sub
```

Inheriting Shared Members

A derived class inherits all the shared methods of the base class. For example, let's enhance the Person class with a shared method that returns True when two persons are brothers (where brotherhood is defined as having at least one parent in common). To implement this shared function, we have to add two fields to the Person base class:

```
Class Person
    ⋮
    ' Public fields
    Public Father As Person
    Public Mother As Person
```

(continued)

```
        Shared Function AreBrothers(ByVal p1 As Person, ByVal p2 As Person) _
            As Boolean
                Return (p1.Father Is p2.Father) Or (p1.Mother Is p2.Mother)
        End Function
End Class
```

Because the Employee class inherits from Person, you can check whether two employees are brothers using this code:

```
Sub TestInheritance3()
    Dim e1 As New Employee()
    e1.FirstName = "Joe"
    e1.LastName = "Doe"

    Dim e2 As New Employee()
    e2.FirstName = "Robert"
    e2.LastName = "Doe"

    Dim e3 As New Employee()
    e3.FirstName = "Ann"
    e3.LastName = "Doe"

    ' Joe is Robert and Ann's father.
    e2.Father = e1
    e3.Father = e1
    ' Call the inherited shared method in the Employee class.
    Console.WriteLine(Employee.AreBrothers(e2, e3))    ' => True
End Sub
```

Polymorphic Behavior

As I mentioned previously, inheriting from a base class implicitly adds a degree of polymorphism to your code. Under Visual Basic 6, you achieve efficient early-bound polymorphism by having the derived class expose the base class as a secondary interface. (See "Early-Bound Polymorphic Code" earlier in this section.) Visual Basic .NET doesn't require any interface gimmick to get the same behavior:

```
Dim p As Person
If Math.Rnd < .5 Then
    ' Sometimes P points to an Employee object.
    p = New Employee()
Else
    ' Sometimes P points to a Person object.
    p = New Person()
End If
' In either case, this polymorphic code uses early binding.
Console.WriteLine(p.FirstName & " " & p.LastName)
```

Notice that a base class variable can't access methods defined only in the derived class. For example, the following code doesn't compile:

```
' *** This code doesn't compile because you're trying to access
'     a method defined in the Employee class through a Person variable.
p.BaseSalary = 10000
```

As an exception to this rule, you can access—more precisely, you can try to access—any member in any class via an Object variable and late binding as long as Option Strict is Off:

```
' *** This code requires that Option Strict be Off.
⋮
Dim o As Object = New Employee()
' The following statement uses late binding.
o.BaseSalary = 10000
```

Overriding Members in the Base Class

The derived class can modify the behavior of one or more properties and methods in the base class. Visual Basic .NET requires that you slightly modify your code in both the base class and the derived class to implement this new behavior. For example, say that you have a CompleteName method in the Person class. You must prefix it with the Overridable keyword to tell the compiler that this method can be overridden:

```
' ...(In the Person (base) class)...
Overridable Function CompleteName() As String
    Return FirstName & " " & LastName
End Function
```

You must use the Overrides keyword to redefine the behavior of this method in the derived class:

```
' ...(In the Employee (derived) class)...
Overrides Function CompleteName() As String
    Return LastName & ", " & FirstName
End Function
```

Another common term for such a method is *virtual* method. Your code won't compile if you omit either the Overridable keyword in the base class or the Overrides keyword in the derived class. This behavior is a nuisance when you're creating large classes meant to work as base classes because you must remember to use the Overridable keyword for each and every member.

Visual Studio offers a simple and effective way to create the template code for an overridden method: click the down arrow for the Class Name drop-down list, scroll until you find the name of the derived class, and click the (Overrides) element immediately below it. (See Figure 7-1.) Then click the down arrow for the Method Name drop-down list, and click the method you want to override. You can use this technique also to generate the template for event handlers and for procedures that implement methods of a secondary interface.

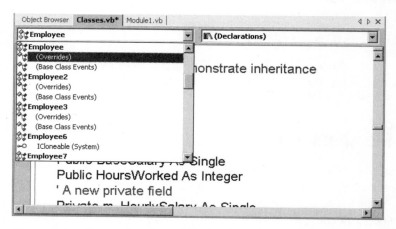

Figure 7-1.   Generating the template code for an overridden method in Visual Studio.

Visual Basic .NET also supports the NotOverridable keyword, which explicitly states that a method can't be overridden; however, this is the default behavior, and in fact you can use this keyword only in conjunction with the Overrides keyword, as I explain in the following section.

When you override a property in the base class, you can redefine its internal implementation, but you can't alter the read or write attribute. For example, if the base class exposes a ReadOnly property, you can't make it writable by overriding it in the derived class. Similarly, you can't define a read-write property that overrides a WriteOnly property in the base class. Along the same lines, if you're overriding a default member in the base class, the method in the derived class must be the default member in the derived class and requires the Default keyword.

Note that you can't override fields, constants, or shared members defined in the base class.

Override Variations

By default, a method marked with the Overrides keyword is itself overridable, so you never need both the Overrides and Overridable keywords in the same procedure definition, even though using both is legal. You need the NotOverridable keyword to explicitly tell the compiler that an overridden method isn't overridable in derived classes:

```
' This procedure overrides a procedure in the base class, but this
    ' procedure can't be overridden in any class that inherits from the current
    ' class.
NotOverridable Overrides Sub MyProc()
    ⋮
End Sub
```

You need neither the Overrides keyword in the derived class nor the Overridable keyword in the base class if you're adding a member with the same name but a different signature. For example, if the Employee class contains a CompleteName method with one argument, it doesn't override the parameterless method with the same name in the Person class, and therefore no special keyword is necessary in either class. Oddly enough, however, the method in the derived class does require the Overloads keyword:

```
' ...(In the Person (base) class)...
' Note: no Overridable keyword
Function CompleteName() As String
    Return FirstName & " " & LastName
End Function

' ...(In the Employee (derived) class)...
' Note: no Overrides keyword, but Overloads is required.
Overloads Function CompleteName(ByVal title As String) As String
    Return title & " " & LastName & ", " & FirstName
End Function
```

The general rule is therefore as follows: you don't need the Overloads keyword when a class defines multiple members with identical names, but you need the Overloads keyword in the derived class when the derived class exposes multiple members with the same name, regardless of whether they're inherited from the base classes or added in the derived class. However, you must use Overrides in the derived class (and Overridable in the base class) only if the derived class is redefining an overloaded method that already exists in the base class with the same argument signature.

> **Note** The compiler can generate more efficient code when calling nonoverridable methods instead of overridable methods (also known as virtual methods), so you might want to avoid using the Overridable keyword if you can. For example, the JIT compiler can inline regular methods but not virtual methods. (*Inlining* is an optimization technique through which the compiler moves code from the called method into the caller's procedure.) In addition, allocating an object that contains virtual methods takes slightly longer than the allocation of an object that has no virtual methods.
>
> However, benchmarks prove that invoking a nonoverridable method is less than 15 percent faster than invoking an empty method marked with the Overridable keyword, and in practice the difference is hardly noticeable with actual nonempty methods in real-world applications. In absolute terms, the difference in timing is so small that you can disregard it unless you're performing millions of method calls.
>
> While we're talking performance, remember that calling a virtual method on a value type forces the compiler to consider it a reference type, which causes the object to be boxed in the heap and therefore degrades the overall execution speed. For example, this happens when you call the ToString method on a value type such as a Structure, as you can easily see by looking at the IL code produced by such a call.

The MyBase Keyword

The MyBase keyword is useful when you want to reference a field, property, or method of the base object. If a member hasn't been overridden in the derived class, the expressions *Me.membername* and *MyBase.membername* refer to the same member and execute the same code. However, when *membername* has been redefined in the inherited class, you need the MyBase keyword to access the member as defined in the base class. Consider the following method:

```
' ...(In the Person (base) class)...
Overridable Function CompleteName() As String
    Return FirstName & " " & LastName
End Function
```

Now, let's assume that the Employee class overrides this method to prefix the complete name with the employee's title. Here's a not-so-smart implementation of this method:

```
' ...(In the Employee (derived) class)...
Public Title As String

Overrides Function CompleteName() As String
    If Title <> "" Then CompleteName = Title & " "
    CompleteName &= FirstName & " " & LastName
End Function
```

The preceding solution isn't optimal because it doesn't reuse any code in the base class. In this particular case, the code in the base class is just a string concatenation operation, but in a real class it might be dozens or hundreds of statements. Worse, if you later change or improve the implementation of the CompleteName function in the base class, you must dutifully apply these changes to all the classes that inherit from Person. The MyBase keyword lets you implement a better solution:

```
Overrides Function CompleteName() As String
    If Title <> "" Then CompleteName = Title & " "
    CompleteName &= MyBase.CompleteName
End Function
```

If you worked with simulated inheritance under Visual Basic 6, you see that the coding pattern is the same as the one you used with inheritance by delegation, for which MyBase corresponds to the private instance of the base class managed by the inherited class.

.NET programming guidelines dictate that an inherited class that overrides the IDisposable.Dispose method of its base class should manually invoke its base class's Dispose method:

```
Overrides Sub Dispose()
    ' Put your cleanup code here.
    ⋮
    ' Call the base class's Dispose method.
    MyBase.Dispose
End Sub
```

Constructors in Derived Classes

Even though you declare constructor procedures with the Sub keyword, they aren't ordinary methods and aren't inherited from the base class in the way all other methods are. It's up to you to provide the derived class with one or more constructors if you want the derived class to be creatable using the same syntax as the base class.

If the base class has no constructor method or has a Sub New procedure that takes no arguments, you don't strictly need to define an explicit constructor for the derived class. As a matter of fact, all the preceding examples show that you can create an instance of the Employee class without defining a constructor for it:

```
Dim e As Employee = New Employee()
```

Things are different when the base class doesn't include a parameterless constructor method either implicitly or explicitly. In this case, the derived class has to contain a constructor method, and the very first executable line of this method must be a call to the base class's constructor. Say that the Person2 class has the following constructor method:

```
Class Person2
    Sub New(ByVal firstName As String, ByVal lastName As String)
        Me.FirstName = firstName
        Me.LastName = lastName
    End Sub
    ' ...(other properties and methods as in Person class) ...
    ⋮
End Class
```

The derived Employee2 class must therefore contain the following code:

```
Class Employee2
    Inherits Person2

    Sub New(ByVal firstName As String, ByVal lastName As String)
        ' The first executable statement *must* be a call
        ' to the constructor in the base class.
        MyBase.New(firstName, lastName)
        ' You can continue with the initialization step here.
        ⋮
    End Sub
    ' ...(other properties and methods) ...
    ⋮
End Class
```

The constructor in the derived class can have a different argument signature from the constructor in the base class, but also in this case the first executable statement must be a call to the base class's constructor:

```
Public Title As String                  ' A new field

Sub New(ByVal firstName As String, ByVal lastName As String, _
    ByVal title As String)
    MyBase.New(firstName, lastName)
    Me.Title = title
End Sub
```

Sometimes you're forced to create auxiliary functions whose only purpose is to comply with the requirement that the first executable statement be a call to the base class's constructor.

Finalizers in Derived Classes

A well-written class that uses unmanaged resources (files, database connections, Windows objects, and so on) should implement both a Finalize method and the IDisposable.IDispose method. If you're inheriting from a class that uses unmanaged resources, you should check whether your inherited class uses any additional unmanaged resources. If not, you don't have to write any extra code because the derived class will inherit the base class's implementation of both the Finalize and the Dispose methods. However, if the inherited class does use additional unmanaged resources, you should override the implementation of these methods, correctly release the unmanaged resources that the inherited class uses, and then call the base class's corresponding method. For example, the Finalize method should always call the base class's Finalize procedure:

```
Protected Overrides Sub Finalize()
    ' Release unmanaged resources created by the inherited class.
    ⋮
    ' Ask the base class to release its own unmanaged resources.
    MyBase.Finalize()
End Sub
```

You can use a generic technique for correctly implementing these methods in a class, based on an overloaded Dispose method that contains the code for both the IDisposable.Dispose and the Finalize methods. As it happens, this overloaded Dispose method has a Protected scope, so in practice you can correctly implement the Dispose-Finalize pattern in derived classes by simply overriding one method:

```
Class BetterDataFile2
    Inherits DataFile2

    ' Insert here regular methods, some of which may allocate additional
    ' unmanaged resources.
    ⋮

    ' The only method we need to override to implement the Dispose-Finalize
    ' pattern for this class.
    Protected Overloads Overrides Sub Dispose(ByVal disposing As Boolean)
        ' Exit now if the object has been already disposed.
        ' (The disposed variable is declared as Protected in the base class.)
```

(continued)

```
            If disposed Then Exit Sub

            If disposing Then
                ' The object is being disposed, not finalized.
                ' It is safe to access other objects (other than the base
                ' object) only from inside this block.
                ⋮
            End If

            ' Perform clean up chores that have to be executed in either case.
            ⋮

            ' Call the base class's Dispose method.
            MyBase.Dispose(disposing)
        End Sub
    End Class
```

The MyClass Keyword

You can easily miss a subtle but important detail of inheritance: when a client calls a nonoverridden method of an inherited class, the code runs in the base class (as you would expect) but in the context of the derived class.

The simplest way to explain this concept is through an example, once again based on the Person-Employee pair. Let's define a Person3 base class exposing a TitledName method that returns the complete name of the person, prefixed with his or her title if one has been specified:

```
Enum Gender
    NotSpecified
    Male
    Female
End Enum

Class Person3
    ' (In a real-world class, these would be properties.)
    Public FirstName As String
    Public LastName As String
    Public Gender As Gender = Gender.NotSpecified
    ' ...(other members omitted for brevity) ...
    ⋮

    Dim m_Title As String
    Overridable Property Title() As String
        Get
            Return m_Title
        End Get
```

```
        Set(ByVal Value As String)
            m_Title = Value
        End Set
    End Property

    ' Prefix the name with a title if one has been specified.
    Function TitledName() As String
        If Title <> "" Then
            Return Title & " " & FirstName & " " & LastName
        Else
            Return FirstName & " " & LastName
        End If
    End Function
End Class
```

The derived Employee3 class doesn't override the TitledName method, but it does override the Title property, so it's never an empty string:

```
Class Employee3
    Inherits Person3

    ' Always provide a title if one hasn't been assigned.
    Overrides Property Title() As String
        Get
            If MyBase.Title <> "" Then
                Return MyBase.Title
            ElseIf Gender = Gender.Male Then
                Return "Mr."
            ElseIf Gender = Gender.Female Then
                Return "Mrs."
            End If
        End Get
        Set(ByVal Value As String)
            MyBase.Title = Value
        End Set
    End Property
End Class
```

Because the derived class doesn't override the TitledName property, the version in the base class is used. However, that code runs in the context of the derived class, and therefore, it uses the overridden version of the Title property, the one defined in Employee3 instead of the one defined in Person3:

```
Dim e As New Employee3("Joe", "Doe")
e.Gender = Gender.Male
' The TitledName method defined in Person3 uses the overridden
' version of Title property defined in Employee3.
Console.WriteLine(e.TitledName)    ' => Mr. Joe Doe
```

A better way to anticipate the effect of inheritance is to pretend that all the nonoverridden routines in the base class have been pasted inside the derived class. So if they reference another property or method, they call the version of that member that's defined in the derived class—not the original one defined in the base class.

However, sometimes you want a piece of code in the base class to use the nonoverridden version of the properties and methods it references. Let's use another example to clarify this concept. Let's say that a person can vote only if he or she is 18 years old, so the Person3 class contains this code:

```
' This code assumes that the following Imports statement has been used.
Imports Microsoft.VisualBasic

Class Person3
    ⋮
    Public BirthDate As Date

    ' Age is defined as the number of whole years passed from BirthDate.
    Overridable ReadOnly Property Age() As Integer
        Get
            Age = CInt(DateDiff(DateInterval.Year, BirthDate, Now()))
            If Month(Now) < Month(Birthdate) Or _
                (Month(Now) = Month(BirthDate) And _
                Day(Now) < Day(BirthDate)) Then
                ' Correct if this year's birthday hasn't occurred yet.
                Age = Age - 1
            End If
        End Get
    End Property

    ReadOnly Property CanVote() As Boolean
        Get
            Return (Age >= 18)
        End Get
    End Property
End Class
```

The Employee3 class uses a looser definition of the age concept and overrides the Age property with a simpler version that returns the difference between the current year and the year when the employee was born:

```
Class Employee3
    ⋮

    ' Age is defined as difference between the current year
    ' and the year the employee was born.
    Overrides ReadOnly Property Age() As Integer
```

```
        Get
            Age = CInt(DateDiff(DateInterval.Year, BirthDate, Now()))
        End Get
    End Property
End Class
```

Do you see the problem? The CanVote property incorrectly uses the Age property defined in the Employee3 class rather than the original version in the Person3 class. To see what kind of bogus result this logical error can cause, run this code:

```
Sub TestMyClassKeyword()
    ' Create a person and an employee.
    Dim p As New Person3("Joe", "Doe")
    Dim e As New Employee3("Robert", "Smith")
    ' They are born on the same day.
    p.BirthDate = #12/31/1984#
    e.BirthDate = #12/31/1984#
    ' (Assuming that you run this code in the year 2002...)
    ' The person can't vote yet (correct).
    Console.WriteLine(p.CanVote)           ' => False
    ' The employee appears to be allowed to vote (incorrect).
    Console.WriteLine(e.CanVote)           ' => True
End Sub
```

Once you understand where the problem is, its solution is simple: you must use the MyClass keyword to be sure that a method in a base class always uses the properties and methods in that base class (as opposed to their overridden version in the inherited class). Here's how to fix the problem in our example:

```
    ' ...(In the Person3 class)...
    ReadOnly Property CanVote() As Boolean
        Get
            ' Ensure that it always uses the nonoverridden
            ' version of the Age property.
            Return (MyClass.Age >= 18)
        End Get
    End Property
```

Member Shadowing

.NET lets you inherit from a class in a compiled DLL for which you neither have nor control the source code. This raises an interesting question: what happens if you extend the base class with a method or a property and then the author of the base class releases a new version that exposes a member with the same name?

Visual Basic copes with this situation in such a way that the application that uses the derived class isn't broken by changes in the base class. If the derived class has a member with the same name as a member in the base class, you get a compilation warning, but you are still able to compile the two classes. In this case, the member in the derived class is said to be *shadowing* the member with the same name in the base class. Visual Basic offers three different syntax forms of shadowing:

■ A member in the derived class shadows all the members in the base class with the same name, regardless of their parameter signatures; as I've explained, you get a compilation warning that doesn't prevent successful compilation (unless you select the Treat Compiler Warnings As Errors check box on the Build page of the project Property Pages dialog box).

■ A member in the derived class marked with the Shadows keyword hides all the members in the base class with the same name, regardless of their signatures; the effect is exactly the same as in the preceding case. In addition, you don't get any compilation warning, so you should use the Shadows keyword to make it clear that you are intentionally shadowing one or more members in the base class.

■ A member in the derived class marked with the Overloads keyword shadows only the member in the base class that has the same name and argument signature. (Note that you can apply the Shadows and Overloads keywords to the same member.)

Shadowing can be quite confusing, so it's best to look at a concrete example:

```
Class AAA
    Sub DoSomething()
        Console.WriteLine("AAA.DoSomething")
    End Sub
    Sub DoSomething(ByVal msg As String)
        Console.WriteLine("AAA.DoSomething({0})", msg)
    End Sub

    Sub DoSomething2()
        Console.WriteLine("AAA.DoSomething2")
    End Sub
    Sub DoSomething2(ByVal msg As String)
        Console.WriteLine("AAA.DoSomething2({0})", msg)
    End Sub
End Class
```

```
Class BBB
    Inherits AAA

    Overloads Sub DoSomething()
        Console.WriteLine("BBB.DoSomething")
    End Sub
    Shadows Sub DoSomething2()
        Console.WriteLine("BBB.DoSomething2")
    End Sub
End Class
```

The following routine calls the methods in the two classes:

```
Sub TestMemberShadowing()
    Dim b As New BBB()
    b.DoSomething()          ' => BBB.DoSomething
    b.DoSomething("abc")     ' => AAA.DoSomething(abc)
    b.DoSomething2()         ' => BBB.DoSomething2
End Sub
```

As you see, the DoSomething procedure in class BBB shadows the procedure DoSomething with zero arguments in class AAA, but the procedure that takes one argument isn't shadowed and can be accessed as usual. This behavior contrasts with the DoSomething2 procedure in class BBB, which is declared with the Shadows keyword and therefore hides both procedures with the same name in class AAA; for this reason, the following statement raises a compilation error:

```
' *** This statement doesn't compile.
b.DoSomething2("abc")
```

If you drop the Shadows keyword in class BBB, the overall effect is the same, the only difference being that the call to DoSomething2 causes a compilation warning.

You've just seen that you can shadow a property or a method even if the procedure isn't marked with Overridable (or is marked with NotOverridable Overrides) in the base class. This raises an interesting question: what is the point of omitting the Overridable keyword, then?

In practice, member shadowing makes it impossible for a developer to prevent a method from being overridden, at least from a logical point of view. In fact, let's say that by omitting the Overridable keyword, the author of the Person3 class makes the Address property not overridable:

```
Class Person3
    ⋮
    Dim m_Address As String
```

(continued)

```
Property Address() As String
    Get
        Return m_Address
    End Get
    Set(ByVal Value As String)
        m_Address = Value
    End Set
End Property
End Class
```

The author of the Employee3 class can still override the Address property—for example, to reject null string assignments—by using the Shadows keyword (to suppress compilation warnings) and manually delegating to the base class using the MyBase.Address expression:

```
Class Employee3
    Inherits Person3

        ⋮

    Shadows Property Address() As String
        Get
            Return MyBase.Address
        End Get
        Set(ByVal Value As String)
            If Value = "" Then Throw New ArgumentException()
            MyBase.Address = Value
        End Set
    End Property
End Class
```

Here's the client code that uses the Address property:

```
Sub TestShadows()
    ' Create a Person3 object.
    Dim p As New Person3("Joe", "Doe")
    ' You can assign a null string to its Address property
    ' without raising any error.
    p.Address = ""

    ' Create an Employee3 object.
    Dim e As New Employee3("Ann", "Doe")
    ' Show that Employee overrides the (nonoverridable) Address property.
    ' NOTE: Next statement throws an exception because the code in
    '       Employee3 trapped the invalid assignment.
    e.Address = ""
End Sub
```

As you see, you can't prevent a class member from being overridden. However, you see a different behavior when you access the member through a base class variable, depending on whether you override the member in the standard way or you shadow it implicitly or explicitly using the Shadows keyword. When a member has been overridden with Overrides, you always access the member in the derived class, even if you're referencing it through a base class variable. When a member has been shadowed (with or without the Shadows keyword), no inheritance relationship exists between the two members and therefore you access the member in the base class. An example can make this concept clearer:

```
Sub TestShadows2()
    Dim e As New Employee3("Joe", "Doe")
    ' This statement correctly raises an ArgumentException
    ' because of the code in the Employee class.
    e.Address = ""

    ' Access the same object through a base class variable.
    Dim p As Person3 = e
    ' This raises no run-time error because the Address property procedure
    ' in the base class is actually executed.
    p.Address = ""
End Sub
```

If the Address property had been redefined using the Overrides keyword, the last statement would invoke the Address property procedure in the derived class, not in the base class.

Because the redefined method in the derived class has nothing to do with the original method in the base class, the two members can have different scope qualifiers, which isn't allowed if the method in the derived class overrides the method in the base class. For example, you can have a Public method in the derived class that shadows (and possibly delegates to) a Protected method in the base class. However, keep in mind that a Private member in the derived class does not shadow a member in the base class: in other words, the Shadows keyword has no effect on Private members.

One last detail on shadowing: you can't shadow a method that is defined as MustOverridable in the base class. In this case, the compiler expects a method marked with the Overrides keyword and flags the derived class as incomplete.

Redefining Shared Members

You can use neither the Overridable nor the Overrides keyword with shared members because shared members can't be overridden. Either they're inherited as they are or they must be shadowed and redefined from scratch in the derived class.

You *cannot* use the *MyBase* variable to invoke shared methods defined in the base class if you're redefining them in the derived class because *MyBase* is forbidden in shared methods. For example, say that you have a Person class with the following shared method:

```
' ...(In the Person (base) class)...
Shared Function AreBrothers(ByVal p1 As Person, ByVal p2 As Person) As Boolean
    Return (p1.Father Is p2.Father) Or (p1.Mother Is p2.Mother)
End Function
```

In addition, you have an Employee class that inherits from Person and that redefines the AreBrothers shared method so that two Employee objects can be considered brothers if they have one parent in common and the same family name. The following code builds on the AreBrothers shared method in the Person class so that if you later change the definition in the Person class, the Employee class automatically uses the new definition:

```
' In the Employee (derived) class
Shared Shadows Function AreBrothers(ByVal e1 As Employee, _
    ByVal e2 As Employee) As Boolean
    Return Person.AreBrothers(e1, e2) And (e1.LastName = e2.LastName)
End Function
```

Unfortunately, no keyword lets you reference the base class in a generic way, so you have to hard-code the name of the base class inside the source code of the derived class when calling a shared method of the base class.

Sealed and Virtual Classes

Visual Basic .NET provides a few additional keywords that let you decide whether other developers can or must inherit from your class and whether they have to override some of its members.

The NotInheritable Keyword

For security (or other) reasons, you might want to ensure that no one extends a class you created. You can achieve this by simply marking the class with the NotInheritable keyword:

```
' Ensure that no one can inherit from the Employee class.
NotInheritable Class Employee
    ⋮
End Class
```

Classes that can't be inherited from are also called *sealed classes*. In general, you rarely need to seal a class, but good candidates for the NotInheritable keyword are utility classes that expose functions as shared members. As you might expect, the Overridable keyword can't be used inside a sealed class.

The MustInherit Keyword

A situation that arises more frequently is that you want to prevent users from using your class as is and instead force them to inherit from it. In this case, the class is called a *virtual* or *abstract class* because you can use it only to derive new classes and can't instantiate it directly. The closest concept in Visual Basic 6 is the idea of abstract classes that you create to define an interface, with an important difference: you can reuse code inside Visual Basic .NET abstract classes, whereas you can't when you use a Visual Basic 6 class to define an interface.

To prevent direct usage of a class, you must flag it with the MustInherit keyword. You typically use this keyword when a class is meant to define a behavior or an archetypal object that never concretely exists. A typical example is the Animal class, which should be defined as virtual because you never instantiate a generic animal; rather, you create a specific animal—a cat, a dog, and so on, which derives some of its properties from the abstract Animal class.

Here's a more business-oriented example: your application deals with different types of documents—invoices, orders, payrolls, and so on—and all of them have some behaviors in common in that they can be stored, printed, displayed, or attached to an e-mail message. It makes sense to gather this common behavior in a Document class, but at the same time you want to be sure that no one mistakenly creates a generic Document object because your application doesn't know how to deal with it.

```
MustInherit Class Document
    ' Contents in RTF format
    Private m_RTFText As String

    Overridable Property RTFText() As String
        Get
            Return m_RTFText
        End Get
        Set(ByVal Value As String)
            m_RTFText = Value
        End Set
    End Property
```

(continued)

```
    ' Save RTF contents to file.
    Overridable Sub SaveToFile(ByVal fileName As String)
        ⋮
    End Sub

    ' Load RTF contents from file.
    Overridable Sub LoadFromFile(ByVal fileName As String)
        ⋮
    End Sub

    ' Print the RTF contents.
    Overridable Sub Print()
        ⋮
    End Sub

    ⋮
End Class
```

Now you can define other classes that inherit their behavior from the Document
virtual class:

```
Class PurchaseOrder
    Inherits Document

    ' Redefines how a PO is printed.
    Overrides Sub Print()
        ⋮
    End Sub
End Class
```

Note that you must explicitly use the Overridable keyword in the base class and
the Overrides keyword in the inherited class, even if the base class is marked
with MustInherit.

The MustOverride Keyword

In general, users of a virtual class aren't forced to override its properties and
methods. After all, the main benefit in defining a virtual class is that derived
classes can reuse the code in the base class. Sometimes, however, you want to
force inherited classes to provide a custom version of a given method.

   For example, consider this Shape virtual class, which defines a few properties and methods that all geometrical shapes have in common:

```
MustInherit Class Shape
    ' Position on the X-Y plane
    Public X, Y As Single
```

```
' Move the object on the X-Y plane.
Sub Offset(ByVal deltaX As Single, ByVal deltaY As Single)
    X = X + deltaX
    Y = Y + deltaY
    ' Redraw the shape at the new position.
    Display
End Sub

Sub Display()
    ' No implementation here
End Sub
End Class
```

The Shape virtual class must include the Display method—otherwise, the code in the Offset procedure won't compile—even though that method can't have any implementation because actual drawing statements depend on the specific class that will be inherited from Shape. Alas, the author of the derived class might forget to override the Display method, and no shape will be ever displayed.

In cases like this, you should use the MustOverride keyword to make it clear that the method is virtual and must be overridden in derived classes. When using the MustOverride keyword, you specify only the method's signature and must omit the End Property, End Sub, or End Function keyword:

```
MustInherit Class Shape
    ' ... (Other members as in previous code snippet) ...
    ⋮
    MustOverride Sub Display()
End Class
```

If a class has one or more virtual methods, the class itself is virtual and must be marked with the MustInherit keyword. The following Square class inherits from Shape and overrides the Display method:

```
Class Square
    Inherits Shape

    Public Side As Single

    Overrides Sub Display()
        ' Add here the statements that draw the square.
        ⋮
    End Sub
End Class
```

Scope

Visual Basic .NET accepts five different scope qualifiers: the three qualifiers available to Visual Basic 6 developers (Public, Friend, and Private) plus two new ones, Protected and Protected Friend. These two new qualifiers are related to inheritance, which explains why I have deferred their description until now. Before diving into a thorough discussion of scope, though, you must learn about one more Visual Basic .NET feature: nested classes.

Nested Classes

Unlike previous versions of the language, Visual Basic .NET lets you nest class definitions:

```
Class Outer
    ⋮
    Class Inner
        ⋮
    End Class
End Class
```

The code inside the Outer class can always create and use instances of the Inner class, regardless of the scope qualifier used for the Inner class. If the nested class is declared using a scope qualifier other than Private, the nested class is also visible to the outside of the Outer class, using the dot syntax:

```
Dim obj As New Outer.Inner
```

Nested classes serve a variety of purposes. First, they're useful for organizing all your classes in groups of related classes and for creating namespaces that help resolve name ambiguity. For example, you might have a Mouse class nested in an Animal class and another Mouse class nested inside a Peripheral class:

```
Class Animal
    ⋮
    ' This class can be referred to as Animal.Mouse.
    Class Mouse
        ⋮
    End Class
End Class

Class Peripheral
    ⋮
    ' This class can be referred to as Peripheral.Mouse.
    Class Mouse
        ⋮
    End Class
End Class
```

Code in the Animal class can refer to the inner Mouse class without using the dot syntax, and it can refer to the other mouse class using the Peripheral.Mouse syntax. Things become more complex when you have multiple nesting levels, as in the following code:

```
Class Peripheral
    Dim m As Mouse
    Dim kb As Keyboard
    Dim k As Keyboard.Key

    ⋮

    ' This class can be referred to as Peripheral.Mouse.
    Class Mouse
        Dim kb As Keyboard
        Dim k As Keyboard.Key
        ⋮
    End Class

    ' This class can be referred to as Peripheral.Keyboard.
    Class Keyboard
        Dim m As Mouse
        Dim k As Key

        ⋮

        ' This class can be referred to as Peripheral.Keyboard.Key.
        Class Key
            Dim m As Mouse
            Dim kb As Keyboard
            ⋮
        End Class
    End Class
End Class
```

Only classes nested immediately inside the outer class can be referenced without the dot syntax from inside the outer class (or its nested classes). For example, you need the dot syntax to refer to the Key class from any class other than Keyboard. However, the rule isn't symmetrical: you can refer to the Mouse class without the dot syntax from inside the Key class.

Another common use for nested classes is to encapsulate one or more auxiliary classes inside the class that uses them and to avoid making them visible to other parts of the application. In this case, the inner class should be marked with the Private scope qualifier. For example, you might create an XML-Parser class that parses an XML text and internally uses the Tag and Attribute classes to do the parsing. These classes aren't meant to be visible from the outside, so they're marked as private:

```
Class XMLParser
    ⋮
    ' These classes aren't visible from outside the XMLParser class.
    Private Class Tag
        ⋮
    End Class
    Private Class Attribute
        ⋮
    End Class
End Class
```

Inner classes have one peculiar feature: they can access private members in their container class if they're provided with a reference to an object of that container class. Consider these two classes:

```
Class Keyboard
    Dim m_Brand As String          ' A private member

    ReadOnly Property Brand() As String
        Get
            ' Code inside the outer class can access a private
            ' member without any reference. (Me is implicit.)
            Return m_Brand
        End Get
    End Property

    Class Key
        ' This public field is meant to be assigned when you're creating
        ' an instance of the Key class.
        Public ParentKeyboard As Keyboard

        ReadOnly Property Brand() As String
            Get
                ' Code inside the inner class can access a private member
                ' in the outer class but requires an object reference.
                Return ParentKeyboard.m_Brand
            End Get
        End Property
    End Class
End Class
```

You don't need an object reference to access a shared member in the outer class:

```
Class Keyboard
    ' This shared member is True if this class supports
    ' non-Latin keyboards.
```

```
Public Shared SupportsNonLatinKeyboards As Boolean

Class Key
    ReadOnly Property SupportsNonLatin() As Boolean
        Get
            ' You can access a shared member in the outer class
            ' without an object reference.
            Return SupportsNonLatinKeyboards
        End Get
    End Property
End Class
End Class
```

Note that the outer class can't expose a public field, property, or function that returns an instance of a private nested class:

```
Class Outer
    ' This public field is legal because it returns a Public inner class.
    Public Field1 As InnerPublic

    ' *** This public field isn't legal because you can't return
    '     a private inner class - you get a compilation error!
    Public Field2 As InnerPrivate

    ' This field is legal because it refers to a private nested class
    ' but the field is private.
    Dim Field3 As InnerPrivate

    Private Class InnerPrivate
        ⋮
    End Class
    Public Class InnerPublic
        ⋮
    End Class
End Class
```

Public, Private, and Friend Scope Qualifiers

As a Visual Basic 6 developer, you're already familiar with three of the five scope keywords in Visual Basic .NET.

The Public scope qualifier makes a class or one of its members visible outside the current assembly if the project is a library project. The meaning of Public scope is therefore the same as in Visual Basic 6.

The Private scope makes a class private and usable only inside its container. This container is usually the current application except in the case of nested classes. (As we've seen in the preceding section, a private nested class is usable only inside its container class.) A private member is usable only inside the class in which it's defined, and this includes any nested class defined in the same container. Leaving aside nested classes, the Private keyword has the same meaning as it does in Visual Basic 6.

The Friend scope qualifier makes a class or one of its members visible to the current assembly. So this keyword has almost the same meaning as under Visual Basic 6 if you replace the word *assembly* with *project*. Because most assemblies are made of just one project, for most practical purposes this keyword has retained its meaning in the transition to Visual Basic .NET. You can use the Friend keyword to make a nested class visible from outside its container without making it Public and visible also from outside the project. Note that Friend is the default scope for classes, unlike Visual Basic 6 classes, whose default scope is Public. To make a Visual Basic .NET class visible outside the assembly that contains it, you must explicitly flag the class with the Public keyword.

In general, no restriction applies to using and mixing these attributes unless the result would make no sense. For example, you can have a Private class that exposes a Public method, but a Public method in a Public class can't expose a Protected or Private member because Visual Basic .NET wouldn't know how to marshal it outside the current assembly. Similarly, you can't inherit a Friend class from a Private class, nor you can have a Public class that inherits from a Friend or Private class. The reason is that all the members in the base class should be visible to clients of the inherited class, so the scope of members in the base class can't be more limited than the scope of members in the derived class.

You can't use scope qualifiers to alter the scope of an overridden method. If a base class contains a Public method, for example, you can't override it with a Private or Friend method in the derived class. This rule ensures that if you assign a reference to a derived object to a base class variable, it's guaranteed that you can call all the overridden methods:

```
' If DerivedClass inherits from BaseClass,
' inheritance rules ensure that this assignment works.
Dim obj As BaseClass = New DerivedClass
' Because overridden methods can't have a narrower scope,
' the following statement is guaranteed to compile correctly.
obj.DoSomething
```

The Protected Scope Qualifier

Protected is a new scope qualifier that makes a member or a nested class visible inside the current class as well to all classes derived by the current class. Put another way, Protected members are private members that are also inherited by derived classes. Consider the following class, which has three Protected members and one Public method:

```
Class Customer
    ' This member is visible to this class and
    ' classes derived from this class.
    Protected AlwaysPaysOnTime As Boolean

    ' Compute the discount percentage on products.
    Protected Overridable Function ProductDiscount() As Single
        ' Offer an additional discount if the customer always pays on time.
        If AlwaysPaysOnTime Then
            ProductDiscount = 15
        Else
            ProductDiscount = 10
        End If
    End Function

    ' By default make no discount on shipment.
    Protected Overridable Function ShipmentDiscount() As Single
        Return 0
    End Function

    ' Compute the actual discount on an order, given the
    ' amount of products purchased and the amount of shipment.
    Function TotalOrderAmount(ByVal ProductAmount As Single, _
        ByVal ShipmentAmount As Single) As Single
        Return ProductAmount * (1 - ProductDiscount / 100) _
            + ShipmentAmount * (1 - ShipmentDiscount / 100)
    End Function
End Class
```

Unless you provide a way to modify the value of the AlwaysPaysOnTime field, the TotalOrderAmount method always evaluates the amount for an order by discounting it by 10 percent. You can implement a public method or property that lets clients modify the AlwaysPaysOnTime field, or you can create a new class that sets that field to True:

```
Class GoodCustomer
    Inherits Customer

    Sub New()
        ' Note that no MyBase.New is needed because the base
        ' class has no constructor with parameters.
        AlwaysPaysOnTime = True
    End Sub
End Class
```

The GoodCustomer class can access the AlwaysPaysOnTime protected field because the GoodCustomer class inherits from Customer. You can easily show that setting this field to True changes the way discounts are evaluated:

```
Sub TestProtectedScope()
    Dim c1 As New Customer()
    Dim c2 As New GoodCustomer()
    Console.WriteLine(c1.TotalOrderAmount(10000, 100))    ' => 9100
    Console.WriteLine(c2.TotalOrderAmount(10000, 100))    ' => 8600
End Sub
```

At the same time, you can verify that the AlwaysPaysOnTime field is private and can't be seen by regular clients:

```
' *** This statement doesn't compile.
c1.AlwaysPaysOnTime = True
```

Code inside the GoodCustomer class can invoke Protected methods defined in the Customer class, and a Protected property or method can be overridden to provide custom versions. For example, let's define a ForeignCustomer class that doesn't charge shipping fees to well-behaved foreign customers:

```
Class ForeignCustomer
    Inherits Customer

    ' A convenient constructor that lets us test well- and
    ' ill-behaved foreign customers
    Sub New(ByVal alwaysPaysOnTime As Boolean)
        Me.AlwaysPaysOnTime = alwaysPaysOnTime
    End Sub

    ' We don't charge shipping to well-behaved foreign customers.
    Protected Overrides Function ShipmentDiscount() As Single
        If AlwaysPaysOnTime Then ShipmentDiscount = 100
    End Function
End Class
```

The ShipmentDiscount function in the ForeignCustomer class redefines how shipping is charged and overrides the function defined in the base class (where it was conveniently marked with the Overridable keyword). Let's prove that this works as expected:

```
Sub TestProtectedScope2()
    Dim c3 As New ForeignCustomer(False)    ' Ill-behaved
    Dim c4 As New ForeignCustomer(True)     ' Well-behaved

    Console.WriteLine(c3.TotalOrderAmount(10000, 400))    ' => 9400
    Console.WriteLine(c4.TotalOrderAmount(10000, 400))    ' => 8500
End Sub
```

You can apply the Protected keyword to nested classes as well. You can use a nested Protected class only from inside the containing class and from inside derived classes, but not from elsewhere in the application. Here is an example:

```
Class Customer
    ⋮
    Protected Class OrderHistory
        Public Count As Integer
        Public TotalAmount As Single
        ⋮
    End Class
End Class

Class GoodCustomer
    Inherits Customer

    ' A derived class sees protected nested classes.
    Dim oh As Customer.OrderHistory
    ' Note that you don't even need the dot syntax.
    Dim oh2 As OrderHistory
    ⋮
End Class

' This class doesn't inherit from Customer.
Class AnotherClass
    ' *** This statement doesn't compile.
    Dim oh As Customer.OrderHistory
    ⋮
End Class
```

The Protected Friend Scope Qualifier

The fifth scope qualifier available in Visual Basic .NET is Protected Friend, which combines the features of the Friend and Protected keywords and therefore defines a member or a nested class that's visible to the entire assembly and to all inherited classes. This keyword seems to be redundant—you might think that Friend also comprises inherited classes—until you consider that Visual Basic .NET allows you to inherit classes from other assemblies. Let's rewrite the previous example, this time using the Protected Friend qualifier:

```
Class Customer
    ⋮
    Protected Friend Class OrderHistory
        Public Count As Integer
        Public TotalAmount As Single
        ⋮
    End Class
End Class
```

In this new version, the nested OrderHistory class is now fully visible to the assembly that hosts the Customer class *and* to all the classes inherited from Customer, regardless of whether they're defined inside or outside the current assembly.

Using Scope Qualifiers with Constructors

You might find it interesting to see what happens when you apply a scope qualifier other than Public to a constructor procedure. Using a Friend constructor makes the class creatable from inside the assembly but not from outside it: this is the closest equivalent of PublicNotCreatable classes in Visual Basic 6.

```
Public Class Widget
    ' This class can be created only from inside the current assembly.
    Friend Sub New()
        ⋮
    End Sub
End Class
```

You can define a Private Sub New method if you want to prevent clients—inside and outside the assembly—from instancing the class. This approach can be useful if the class contains only shared members, so there's no point in creating an instance of it:

```
Class Triangle
    ' This private constructor prevents clients from
    ' instancing this class.
    Private Sub New()
        ' No implementation code here.
    End Sub

    ' Add here all the shared members for this class.
    Shared Function GetArea( ... ) As Double
        ⋮
    End Function
    ⋮
End Class
```

Another use for Private constructors arises when you want clients to create instances through a shared member rather than with the usual New keyword, as in the following example:

```
Class Square
    Public Side As Double

    ' This private constructor prevents clients from
    ' instancing this class directly.
```

```
Private Sub New(ByVal side As Double)
    Me.Side = side
End Sub

' Clients can create a square only through this shared method.
Shared Function CreateSquare(ByVal side As Double) As Square
    Return New Square(side)
End Function
End Class
```

Clients can create a new Square object using this syntax:

```
Dim sq As Square = Square.CreateSquare(2.5)
```

Some classes in the .NET Framework expose this sort of constructor method, but in general you should stick to standard constructor methods because this alternative technique doesn't offer any clear advantage, except for the ability to run custom code before actually creating the instance.

The scope of the constructor has a far-reaching and somewhat surprising effect on the inheritance mechanism. To begin with, a class that has only Private constructors can't be used as a base class, even if it isn't flagged with the NotInheritable keyword. In fact, the derived class should have its own constructor (because the base class doesn't have a Public parameterless default constructor), but any attempt to call MyBase.New will fail because the Sub New procedure isn't visible outside the base class.

Along the same lines, a Public class that has one or more Friend Sub New methods can be used as a base class, but only if the derived class is defined in the same assembly. Any attempt to inherit that class from outside the assembly would fail because the inherited class can't call a constructor with a Friend scope. If clients outside the current assembly should be able to instantiate the base class, you can add a shared function that returns a new instance of the class:

```
' This class is visible from outside the assembly but can't
' be used as a base class for classes outside the assembly.
Public Class Widget
    ' This constructor can be called only from inside
    ' the current assembly.
    Friend Sub New()
        ⋮
    End Sub

    ' A pseudoconstructor method for clients located
    ' outside the current assembly.
    Public Shared Function CreateWidget() As Widget
        Return New Widget()
    End Function
End Class
```

Even if clients outside the current assembly shouldn't use the Widget class, you still have to mark it as Public (rather than Friend or Private) if you use Widget as the base class for other Public classes, as I explained in the preceding section.

If the constructor has Protected scope, the class can be used as a base class because the constructor of the derived class can always access this constructor, but the class can't be instantiated from inside or outside the current assembly. Finally, if the constructor has Protected Friend scope, the class can be used as a base class but can be instantiated only from inside the assembly it resides in and from inside derived classes.

Understanding from where you can instantiate a class and from where you can use it as a base class is made more complicated by the fact that nested classes can always access Private and Protected constructors. Table 7-1 can help you determine the effect of the scope of the constructor and the class itself.

Table 7-1   The Effect of Class Scope and Constructor Scope on a Class's Ability to Be Instantiated or Used as a Base Class

Class Scope*	Constructor Scope	Types That Can Instantiate This Class	Classes That Can Inherit from This Class
Private	Private	Nested types	Nested classes
	Protected	Nested types and inherited classes	Private classes defined in the same container
	Friend, Protected Friend, Public	Types defined in the same container	Private classes defined in the same container
Protected	Private	Nested types	Nested classes
	Protected	Nested types and inherited classes	Private/Protected classes defined in the same container
	Friend, Protected Friend, Public	Types defined in the same container and inherited classes	Private/Protected classes defined in the same container
Friend, Protected Friend	Private	Nested types	Nested classes
	Protected	Types defined in the same container and inherited classes	Classes defined in current assembly

Table 7-1 **The Effect of Class Scope and Constructor Scope on a Class's Ability to Be Instantiated or Used as a Base Class** *(continued)*

Class Scope*	Constructor Scope	Types That Can Instantiate This Class	Classes That Can Inherit from This Class
	Friend, Protected Friend, Public	Types defined in current assembly	Classes defined in current assembly
Public	Private	Nested types	Nested classes
	Protected	Nested types and inherited classes	All classes, inside or outside current assembly
	Friend	Types defined in current assembly	Classes defined in current assembly
	Protected Friend	Types defined in current assembly and inherited classes	All classes, inside or outside current assembly
	Public	All types, inside or outside current assembly	All classes, inside or outside current assembly

*   Note that you can have Private, Protected, and Protected Friend classes only inside a container type.

Redefining Events

You can't override events in the same way you override properties and methods, and in fact, you can't use the Overrides keyword on events. (However, you can use the Shadows keyword on events.)

Occasionally, you might want to redefine what happens when the base class raises an event. For example, the inherited class might need to perform some additional processing when an event is fired from inside the base class, or it might need to suppress some or all of the events that the base class raises. These two tasks require two different approaches.

If the derived class just needs to get a notification that an event is being raised from inside the base class, the simplest solution is to set up a WithEvents variable and assign it the Me reference. In other words, the derived class becomes a listener for its own events. Let's say that you have the following base class:

```
Class DataReader
    Event DataAvailable()
```

(continued)

```
    Sub GetNewData()
        RaiseEvent DataAvailable()
    End Sub
End Class
```

Next you create a derived FileDataReader class that inherits from DataReader but needs to get a notification whenever the DataAvailable event is fired to accomplish a noncritical task, such as incrementing a counter. The following implementation does the trick:

```
Class FileDataReader
    Inherits DataReader

    ' This variable will point to the object itself (Me).
    Dim WithEvents EventSink As FileDataReader
    ' This counter must be incremented after each event.
    Public EventCounter As Integer

    Sub New()
        MyBase.New()
        EventSink = Me
    End Sub

    Private Sub NotifyDataAvailable() Handles EventSink.DataAvailable
        ' Increment the counter.
        EventCounter += 1
    End Sub
End Class
```

This programming technique doesn't require that you change the base class in any way, but it has two serious shortcomings. First, the derived class has no control over the event itself, and it can't modify its arguments or prevent it from firing. Second, you aren't guaranteed that the event in the derived class fires before (or after) the event in clients, so different clients might see different values for the public EventCounter field during the event notification chain.

To solve both these problems, you must change the way the base class fires events—in other words, you must build the base class with inheritance in mind. Instead of using the RaiseEvent statement whenever you want to raise an event in the base class, you call an overridable method, which by convention is named OnEventName:

```
Class DataReader2
    Event DataAvailable()

    Sub GetNewData()
        OnDataAvailable()
    End Sub
```

```
' This procedure contains only the RaiseEvent statement.
Protected Overridable Sub OnDataAvailable()
    RaiseEvent DataAvailable()
End Sub
End Class
```

After this edit, the derived class can easily take control of how events are dispatched to clients and whether they are dispatched at all. For example, this new version raises no more than 10 events in clients:

```
Class FileDataReader2
    Inherits DataReader2

    ' This counter must be incremented after each event.
    Public EventCounter As Integer

    Protected Overrides Sub OnDataAvailable()
        ' Increment the counter.
        EventCounter += 1
        ' Raise only up to 10 events.
        If EventCounter <= 10 Then MyBase.OnDataAvailable()
    End Sub
End Class
```

Note that the derived class can't directly use the RaiseEvent statement to raise one of its own events if the event is defined in the base class. The only way to indirectly raise the event is by calling the OnDataAvailable method in the base class, as shown in the preceding code.

Inheritance is so central to Visual Basic .NET programming that you'll probably come back to this chapter to revisit these concepts more than once.

Part III

ADO.NET

Reading 8

ADO.NET

Introducing ADO.NET

ADO.NET is revolutionary by many measures. Nevertheless, if you're familiar with ADO it won't take much effort and time to learn ADO.NET and become as productive as you were using Visual Basic 6.

Major Changes from ADO

From an architectural perspective, the most important change from "classic" ADO is that ADO.NET doesn't rely on OLE DB providers and uses .NET managed providers instead. A .NET Data Provider works as a bridge between your application and the data source, so you see that it can be considered an evolution of the OLE DB provider concept. However, the inner implementation details are very different. ADO.NET and .NET managed data providers don't use COM at all, so a .NET application can access data without undergoing any performance penalty deriving from the switch from managed and unmanaged code. (Unfortunately, this isn't 100 percent true at the time of this writing because you still need COM to access any data source other than SQL Server, but this problem will be gone when new managed providers are released.)

From a programmer's perspective, the most important difference between ADO.NET and ADO is that dynamic and keyset server-side cursors aren't supported any longer. ADO.NET supports only forward-only, read-only resultsets (known as firehose cursors, even though they aren't really a type of cursor) and disconnected resultsets. Server-side cursors have been dumped because they consume resources on the server and create a large number of locks on database tables. Taken together, these two factors can hinder application scalability more than anything else.

Personally, I would have preferred a less drastic alteration because server-side cursors are easy to use and are useful in many cases—for example, I use

From *Programming Microsoft Visual Basic .NET* by Francesco Balena. pp. 999-1062, 1083-1986. (Redmond: Microsoft Press. 2002.) Copyright © 2002 by Francesco Balena.

server-side cursors for administrative tasks that run once in a while. But I agree that too many developers have used server-side cursors to create applications that perform poorly and don't scale well. Fortunately, ADO.NET uses an extensible architecture, and Microsoft has announced support for server-side cursors at a later time. In the meantime, you can still use server-side cursors through the ADO library, which you can access through the COM Interoperability layer of .NET. You go through an additional layer, and performance will be less than optimal, but this condition shouldn't be a serious problem because you would use these cursors only in exceptional cases.

✳✳✳

.NET Data Providers

.NET data providers play the same role that OLE DB providers play under ADO: they enable your application to read and write data stored in a data source. ADO.NET currently supports three providers:

- **The OLE DB .NET Data Provider** This provider lets you access a data source for which an OLE DB provider exists, although at the expense of a switch from managed to unmanaged code and the performance degradation that ensues.

- **The SQL Server .NET Data Provider** This provider has been specifically written to access SQL Server 7.0 or later versions using Tabular Data Stream (TDS) as the communication medium. TDS is SQL Server's native protocol, so you can expect this provider to give you better performance than the OLE DB Data Provider. Additionally, the SQL Server .NET Data Provider exposes SQL Server–specific features, such as named transactions and support for the FOR XML clause in SELECT queries.

- **The ODBC .NET Data Provider** This provider works as a bridge toward an ODBC source, so in theory you can use it to access any source for which an ODBC driver exists. However, as of this writing, this provider officially supports only the Access, SQL Server, and Oracle ODBC drivers, so there's no clear advantage in using it instead of the OLE DB .NET Data Provider. The convenience of this provider will be more evident when more ODBC drivers are added to the list of those officially supported.

✳✳✳

Database Independence with ADO.NET

Classic ADO promotes the reuse of data-related code from different data sources by having the Connection, Recordset, and Command objects work equally well with any data source. For example, the only point in code at which you must decide the actual data source you're using is when you build the connection string. Because all the ADO objects work with any data source, you're able to write programs that work with any data source for which an OLE DB provider exists just by providing a suitable connection string.

This approach works well in practice with small- or medium-size database applications. For example, I developed the source code of my VB-2-The-Max Web site (*www.vb2themax.com*) using Access because I wanted to take advantage of Access's ease of use and reporting capabilities. The real production site runs on SQL Server, however, and the only point at which the two versions differ is where the code defines the connection string.

When you turn to large-scale applications, however, ADO's database-agnostic approach shows its greatest limitation: you can't take advantage of the specific features of a given database. ADO partly copes with this limitation by having its main objects expose a Properties collection, which is filled with the dynamic properties that are specific to each provider. For example, you can use ADO's dynamic properties to decide how the ODBC driver behaves when login information isn't complete (the Prompt property) or to set an Access password (the Jet OLEDB:Database Password property). However, dynamic properties don't allow you to execute commands against the database, so you can't access all the peculiar features of a given database.

ADO.NET solves this problem in an ingenious way. On the one hand, each provider uses a different object to perform database-related tasks, so Microsoft (or the author of the data provider) can enhance each object with specific methods and properties that are meaningful only to that database. For example, the SqlConnection object has the PacketSize and ServerVersions properties (which are missing in the OleDbConnection object) and a BeginTransaction overloaded method that lets you create named transactions (which can't be used with the OLE DB .NET Data Provider).

On the other hand, because the objects in a specific .NET data provider must inherit from an ADO.NET base class or implement one of the IDb*xxxx* interfaces, you can create polymorphic code that works equally well with any provider. Here's a fragment of code that works well with either a SQL Server connection or a connection to an OLE DB source:

```
Dim cn As IDBConnection

' (UseSqlServerProvider is a Boolean defined and assigned elsewhere.)
If UseSqlServerProvider Then
    ' Create a connection using the SQL Server provider.
    ' (SqlPubsConnString is a string defined and initialized elsewhere.)
    cn = New SqlConnection(SqlPubsConnString)
Else
    ' Create a connection using the OLE DB provider.
    ' (BiblioConnString is a string defined and initialized elsewhere.)
    cn = New OleDbConnection(BiblioConnString)
End If


' (The following code works well with both providers.)
' Open the connection.
cn.Open
⋮
' Close the connection.
cn.Close
```

Even if the preceding code snippet is incomplete—for one thing, it doesn't show how to define the connection strings for the two providers—it should prove the point I want to make: ADO.NET lets you achieve database independence through common base classes and interfaces but without renouncing specific and more powerful features of each individual database engine. You pay for this extra flexibility in terms of the larger amount of code you have to write, however.

By comparison, ADO offers almost-free database-agnostic code and doesn't introduce any complexity into the code you write, but it prevents you from exploiting the best features of specific databases. Because the number of applications that really need to be database independent is relatively small, I believe that the ADO.NET approach is more reasonable because it delivers the best results in terms of performance and flexibility and adds complexity only to those few applications for which database independence is a requirement.

Even if you aren't writing a database-agnostic program but you often work with both providers, you might want to write procedures that you can easily reuse in different applications.

The Connection Object

Whether you work in connected or in disconnected mode, the first action you need to perform when working with a data source is to open a connection to it. In ADO.NET terms, this means that you create a Connection object that connects to the specific database.

The Connection object is similar to the ADO object of the same name, so you'll feel immediately at ease with the new ADO.NET object if you have any experience with ADO programming. Table 8-1 summarizes the properties, methods, and events of the ADO.NET Connection object and indicates the few members that are supported solely by either the OLE DB or the SQL Server .NET Data Provider.

Table 8-1   Properties, Methods, and Events of the Connection Object

Category	Name	Description
Properties	ConnectionString	The string used to connect to the data source.
	ConnectionTimeout	The number of seconds after which an unsuccessful connection times out. This property is read-only because you set this value in the ConnectionString property. (Default is 15 seconds.)
	Database	Returns the name of the database, as specified in the ConnectionString property (read-only).
	DataSource	Returns the name of the Data Source attribute, as specified in the ConnectionString property (read-only).
	ServerVersion	Returns the version of the connected server in the format *xx.yy.zzzz*, or an empty string if this information can't be retrieved. (The provider can also append a product-specific version string after the version number.)
	State	Returns the current state of the database. Can be an enumerated value in the following list: Closed, Connecting, Open, Executing, Fetching, and Broken.
(OleDb provider only)	Provider	Returns the value of the Provider attribute, as specified in the ConnectionString property (read-only).
(SQL Server provider only)	PacketSize	Returns the size in bytes of network packets used to communicate with SQL Server, as specified in the ConnectionString property. It can be any value in the range 512 to 32767. (Default is 8192.)

Table 8-1   **Properties, Methods, and Events of the Connection Object**   *(continued)*

Category	Name	Description
	WorkstationId	Returns a string that identifies the client, as specified by the Workstation ID attribute in the ConnectionString property.
Methods	Open	Opens the connection.
	Close	Closes the connection and releases all related resources.
	BeginTransaction	Begins a database transaction, using the isolation level specified in the optional argument.
	ChangeDatabase	Changes the name of the database for the current connection.
	CreateCommand	Creates a Command object related to the current connection.
(OleDb provider only)	GetOleDbSchemaTable	Returns the schema table and associated restriction columns of the schema whose GUID is passed as an argument.
	ReleaseObjectPool	A shared method that says the OLE DB connection pool can be released when the last connection is closed.
Events	StateChange	Fires when the State property changes.
	InfoMesssage	Fires when the database or the provider sends an informational or a warning message.

Setting the ConnectionString Property

The key property of the Connection object is ConnectionString, a string that defines the type of the database you're connecting to, its location, and other semicolon-delimited attributes. When you work with the OleDbConnection object, the connection string matches the connection string that you use with the ADO Connection object. Such a string typically contains the following information:

■   The Provider attribute, which specifies the name of the underlying OLE DB Provider used to connect to the data. As of this writing, the only valid values are SQLOLEDB (the OLE DB provider for Microsoft SQL Server), Microsoft.Jet.OLEDB.4.0 (the OLE DB provider for Microsoft Access), and MSDAORA (the OLE DB provider for Oracle).

- The Data Source attribute, which specifies where the database is. It can be the path to an Access database or the name of the machine on which the SQL Server or the Oracle database is located.

- The User ID and Password attributes, which specify the user name and the password of a valid account for the database.

- The Initial Catalog attribute, which specifies the name of the database when you're connecting to a SQL Server or an Oracle data source.

Once you've set the ConnectionString property correctly, you can open the connection by invoking the Open method:

```
Dim BiblioConnString As String = "Provider=Microsoft.Jet.OLEDB.4.0;" _
    & "Data Source=C:\Program Files\Microsoft Visual Studio\VB98\BIBLIO.MDB;"
' Open the Biblio.mdb database.
Dim cn As New OledbConnection()
cn.ConnectionString = BiblioConnString
cn.Open()
```

You can make your code more concise by passing the connection string to the Connection object's constructor method:

```
' Another, more concise, way to open the Biblio.mdb database.
Dim cn As New OledbConnection(BiblioConnString)
cn.Open()
```

The same description applies as well to the SqlConnection object, with just one difference: you must omit the Provider attribute from the connection string. In fact, you don't need this attribute in this case because you can connect only to a SQL Server database if you use the SQL Server .NET Data Provider. Also note that you can specify **(local)** as the Data Source attribute if you're connecting to the SQL Server on the local machine:

```
Dim SqlPubsConnString As String = "Data Source=(local); User ID=sa;" _
    & "Initial Catalog=pubs"
Dim cn As New SqlConnection(SqlPubsConnString)
cn.Open()
```

The connection string can include other attributes. For example, the Connection Timeout attribute sets the number of seconds after which the attempt to open the connection fails with an error. (The default value is 15 seconds.) After you open the connection, you can query the current value of this timeout with the ConnectionTimeout property:

```
' Specify a longer timeout when connecting to Pubs.
Dim cn As New SqlConnection("Data Source=(local); User ID=sa;" _
    & "Initial Catalog=pubs;Connection Timeout=30")
cn.Open()
Debug.WriteLine(cn.ConnectionTimeout)        ' => 30
```

Other values that you pass in the connection string depend on the specific OLE DB provider to which you're connecting. For example, the provider Microsoft.Jet.OLEDB.4.0 supports attributes for setting the database password or specifying the system database that contains information about groups and users.

When you're working with the SQL Server .NET Data Provider, you can specify two additional attributes in the connection string: Packet Size and Workstation ID. The former value sets the size of the network packet used to communicate with SQL Server; the latter is a string that can be later used to identify the client. (Read the description of the related PacketSize and WorkstationId properties in Table 8-1.) The Packet Size attribute is sometimes useful for optimizing the flux of data to and from SQL Server. For example, you might increase it if your application deals with large BLOB fields (such as images) or decrease it if you often query the server for a small amount of data.

```
' Optimize the connection for large BLOB fields.
Dim cn As New SqlConnection("Data Source=(local); User ID=sa;" _
    & "Initial Catalog=pubs;Packet Size=32767")
cn.Open()
Debug.WriteLine(cn.PacketSize)        ' => 32767
```

Note   All the code routines in this reading open a connection to either the Biblio.mdb database using the OLE DB .NET Data Provider (which comes with Visual Studio 6 and Access) or the Pubs database using the SQL Server .NET Data Provider (which is installed with any version of SQL Server). To keep code as concise as possible, the demo application defines these three connection strings at the module level:

```
' For Biblio.mdb using the OLE DB .NET Data Provider
Public BiblioConnString As String = "Provider=" _
    & "Microsoft.Jet.OLEDB.4.0;Data Source=" & _
    "C:\Program Files\Microsoft Visual Studio\VB98\Biblio.mdb"

' For SQL Server's Pubs using the OLE DB .NET Data Provider
Public OleDbPubsConnString As String = "Provider=" _
    & "SQLOLEDB.1;Data Source=.;" _
    & "Integrated Security=SSPI:Initial Catalog=Pubs"

' For Pubs using the SQL Server .NET Data Provider
Public SqlPubsConnString As String = "Data Source=.;" _
    & "Integrated Security=SSPI:Initial Catalog=Pubs"
```

Obviously, you should edit these connection strings to match your system's configuration. For example, you should change the Data Source value in BiblioConnString to assign it the actual path of Biblio.mdb.

Opening and Closing the Connection

You've already seen that the Open method takes no arguments, unlike the Open method of the ADO Connection object:

```
Dim cn As New OledbConnection(BiblioConnString)
cn.Open()
```

The State Property and the StateChange Event

The State property is a bit-coded field that indicates the current state of the database connection. It can be the combination of one or more of the following ConnectionState enumerated values: Closed, Connecting, Open, Executing, Fetching, and Broken. You typically check the State property to ensure that you're opening a closed connection or closing an open connection, as in this snippet:

```
' Close the connection only if it was opened.
If (cn.State And ConnectionState.Open) <> 0 Then
    cn.Close()
End If
```

Whenever the State property changes from Open to Close or vice versa, the Connection object fires a StateChange event:

```
Dim WithEvents cn As SqlConnection

Private Sub cn_StateChange(ByVal sender As Object, _
    ByVal e As System.Data.StateChangeEventArgs) Handles cn.StateChange
    ' Show the status of the connection in a Label control.
    If (e.CurrentState And ConnectionState.Open) <> 0 Then
        lblStatus.Text = "The connection has been opened"
    ElseIf e.CurrentState = ConnectionState.Closed Then
        lblStatus.Text = "The connection has been closed"
    End If
End Sub
```

Note that ConnectionState.Closed is equal to 0, so you can't use the And bitwise operator to test this state, unlike all the other values. Be careful not to throw an exception from inside this event handler because it would be returned to the code that issued the Open or Close method.

Although it's a good habit to test the state of the database before performing any operation on it, ADO.NET is much more forgiving than classic ADO in some cases. For example, you can execute the Close method of the Connection object (or any other ADO.NET object that exposes this method) without throwing any exception if the object is already closed:

```
' This statement never throws an exception.
cn.Close()
```

Dealing with Errors

As in ADO, you should protect your code from unexpected errors when attempting a connection to a database as well as while processing data coming from the database itself. However, when working with ADO.NET you have an added responsibility: because of the garbage collection mechanism intrinsic in .NET, the connection isn't automatically closed when the Connection object goes out of scope. In this case, in fact, the connection is closed in the Finalize protected method of the Connection object, and you know that the garbage collector might call this method several minutes after the object goes out of scope.

Because an error can occur virtually anywhere you're working in a database, you should protect your code with a Try block and ensure that you close the connection in the Finally section in an orderly way:

```
Dim cn As New SqlConnection(SqlPubsConnString)
Try
    cn.Open()
    ' Process the data here.
    ⋮
Catch ex As Exception
    MessageBox.Show(ex.Message)
Finally
    ' Ensure that the connection is closed.
    ' (It doesn't throw an exception even if the Open method failed.)
    cn.Close()
End Try
```

Most of the exceptions that you catch when working with the OLE DB .NET Data Provider are of class OleDbException. In addition to all the members it has in common with other exception classes, this class exposes the Errors collection that contains one or more OleDbError objects, each one describing how the original error in the database (for example, a violation of the referential integrity rules) has been reported to the many software layers that sit between the database and the application. (This concept is the same one on which the Errors collection of the ADO Connection object is based.) The following code shows how you can explore the OleDbException.Errors collection to show details about the caught exception:

```
' Run a query that references a table that doesn't exist.
Dim cmd As New OleDbCommand("UPDATE xyz SET id=1", cn)

Try
    cmd.ExecuteNonQuery()
Catch ex As OleDbException
    ' An OleDbException has occurred - display details.
    Dim i As Integer, msg As String
```

```
    For i = 0 To ex.errors.Count - 1
        Dim oledbErr As OleDbError = ex.Errors(i)
        msg = "Message = " & oledbErr.Message & ControlChars.CrLf
        msg &= "Source = " & oledbErr.Source & ControlChars.CrLf
        msg &= "NativeError = " & oledbErr.NativeError & ControlChars.CrLf
        msg &= "SQLState = " & oledbErr.SQLState & ControlChars.CrLf
    Next
    MessageBox.Show(msg)

Catch ex As Exception
    ' A generic exception has occurred.
    MessageBox.Show(ex.Message)
Finally
    ' Close the connection.
    cn.Close()
End Try
```

The SqlException object also exposes an Errors collection, containing one or more SqlError objects. The SqlError object doesn't support the NativeError and SQLState properties but exposes a few members that aren't in OleDbError:

- **Server**   The name of the SQL Server that generated the error

- **Procedure**   The name of the stored procedure or remote procedure call that generated the error

- **LineNumber**   The line number within the T-SQL batch or stored procedure where the error occurred

- **Number**   A number that identifies the type of error

- **Class**   The severity level of the error, in the range 1 through 25

Severity level values in the range 1 through 10 are informational and indicate problems deriving from mistakes in the information the user entered. Values in the range 11 through 16 are caused by the user and can be corrected by the user. Severity levels 17 and higher indicate serious software or hardware errors. In general, errors with severity levels equal to 20 or higher automatically close the connection. For this reason, you should always test the State property of the Connection object when an exception is thrown, regardless of the data provider you're working with.

Opening a Database Asynchronously

One of the great innovations of ADO was its ability to perform a few methods—most notably, the opening of a connection and the querying of data—in an asynchronous fashion, that is, without blocking the current application.

Asynchronous operations were pretty difficult to set up correctly, but they were a great tool in the hands of experienced programmers.

Don't look for asynchronous options in ADO.NET because you won't find any. Does this mean that ADO.NET is less capable than good old ADO? Of course not. It only means that asynchronous operation support is offered at the .NET Framework level through asynchronous delegates. Moving the support for asynchronous operations out of ADO.NET makes the object model cleaner and simpler, and even more flexible dealing with asynchronous operations. In fact, you can perform *any* ADO.NET operation, not just a few methods, while the main program does something else.

The following code snippet shows how you can open a connection asynchronously. You can use the same code pattern for any other database operation involving the Connection object or any other ADO.NET object:

```
Delegate Sub OpenMethod()

Sub OpenAsyncConnection()
    ' Define the Connection object.
    Dim cn As New OleDbConnection(BiblioConnString)
    ' Create a delegate that points to the Open method.
    Dim asyncOpen As New OpenMethod(AddressOf cn.Open)
    ' Call it asynchronously - pass the delegate as the cookie.
    Dim ar As IAsyncResult
    ar = asyncOpen.BeginInvoke(AddressOf OpenComplete, asyncOpen)
    ' Show a message in a Label control.
    lblStatus.Text = "Waiting ..."
    ' Do something else here.
    ⋮
End Sub

Sub OpenComplete(ByVal ar As IAsyncResult)
    ' Retrieve a reference to the delegate, passed in the cookie.
    Dim asyncOpen As OpenMethod = CType(ar.AsyncState, OpenMethod)

    Try
        ' Complete the operation.
        asyncOpen.EndInvoke(ar)
        ' Let the user know that the operation completed.
        MessageBox.Show("The connection has been opened")
    Catch ex As Exception
        ' Show an error message otherwise.
        MessageBox.Show(ex.Message)
    End Try
End Sub
```

Leveraging Connection Pooling

Connection pooling is a great feature of ADO.NET; it lets you transparently reuse a database connection when an application doesn't need it any longer. The mechanism works this way: when the first connection to the database is opened, a pool of identical connections is created, so subsequent requests don't have to wait to get a valid connection. When an application completes its database chores, it should explicitly close the Connection object so that it can be returned to the pool and made available for other applications. (Note that you must explicitly close the connection to return it to the pool.)

ADO.NET creates a number of connection pools equal to the number of distinct connection strings that your program uses, so the necessary condition for exploiting the connection pool is that you open all your database connections using *exactly* the same connection string. Even just an extra space or semicolon makes a connection string different, so pay attention.

This requirement means that you can't take advantage of connection pooling if you specify a different user name and password in the connection string. You're better off, therefore, using Windows integrated security instead of database security whenever it's feasible to do so:

```
Dim cn As New SqlConnection("Data Source=MyServer;" _
    & "Integrated Security=SSPI;Initial Catalog=pubs")
```

Another viable approach to reliable connection pooling is to encapsulate all the database access in a .NET component that logs in to the database using a special account and therefore uses the same connection string for all its open connections.

The OLE DB .NET Data Provider creates a connection pool based on the OLE DB session pooling. Connection pooling is enabled by default, but you can turn it off by specifying a special OLE DB Services value in the connection string:

```
Dim cn As New OleDbConnection("Provider=SQLOLEDB;" _
    & "Data Source=MyServer;Integrated Security=SSPI;OLE DB Services=-4")
```

The OleDbConnection object exposes a ReleaseObjectPool method that discards all unused connections from the pool. You might call it and then invoke the GC.Collect method to free as many resources as possible.

The SQL Server .NET Data Provider offers connection pooling based on Windows 2000 Component Services, using an implicit pooling model by default. This arrangement means that if the current thread has already opened a transaction using this provider, any new transaction opened will match the same transactional context. When the thread requests a connection, the pool is searched for a matching connection object. To be eligible for reuse, a connection in the pool must have exactly the same connection string, must have a matching transaction context (or not be associated with any transaction context), and must have a valid link to the specified server.

You can control the behavior of connection pooling under the SQL Server .NET Data Provider by using several values in the connection string. For example, you can disable automatic enlistment in the pooling by setting the Pooling attribute to False:

```
Dim cn As New SqlConnection("Data Source=MyServer;" _
    & "Integrated Security=SSPI;Initial Catalog=pubs;Pooling=false")
```

You can also avoid automatic enrollment in the current transaction if no transactions are required on the current connection, by setting the Enlist attribute to False:

```
Dim cn As New SqlConnection("Data Source=MyServer;" _
    & "Integrated Security=SSPI;Initial Catalog=pubs;Enlist=False")
```

You can set the minimum and maximum size of the pool by using the Min Pool Size and Max Pool Size attributes, whose default values are 0 and 100 respectively:

```
' If this is the first connection with this connection string, a
' pool with 10 identical connections is prepared.
Dim cn As New SqlConnection("Data Source=MyServer;" _
    & "Integrated Security=SSPI;Initial Catalog=pubs;" _
    & "Min Pool Size=10;Max Pool Size=120")
```

If the pool has reached its maximum size and all the connections are currently active and serving other applications, a request for an available connection is queued until another application releases one of the connections. If no connection is made available within the connection timeout period, an exception is thrown.

The Connection Lifetime attribute is useful in a clustered environment for taking advantage of any new server activated after the connection pool has already been created. As you know, all the connections in the pool link to the server on which they were originally opened. So by default they would never attempt to use any new server brought up after the pool has reached its maximum size. The Connection Lifetime sets the lifetime of a connection in the pool (in seconds). After this period, the connection is destroyed automatically; presumably, it will be replaced in the pool by a new connection that points to the server activated in the meantime.

```
' Destroy a connection in the pool after 2 minutes.
Dim cn As New SqlConnection("Data Source=MyServer;" _
    & "Integrated Security=SSPI;Initial Catalog=pubs;" _
    & "Connection Lifetime=120")
```

Connection pooling is a mixed blessing: on the one hand, it can dramatically improve the performance and scalability of your applications; on the other, it can give you headaches if you don't use it correctly. When you see that a database-intensive piece of code performs with suspicious sluggishness, you should double-check to see that it's using connection pooling correctly. To help you in this task, ADO.NET defines a few performance counters that you might want to monitor while searching for unexpected behaviors in the SQL Server .NET Data Provider. All the counters belong to the .NET CLR Data Performance object:

- **SqlClient: Current # connection pools**   Number of pools associated with the process

- **SqlClient: Current # pooled and nonpooled connections**   Number of connections, pooled or not

- **SqlClient: Current # pooled connections**   Number of connections in pools associated with the process

- **SqlClient: Peak # pooled connections**   Highest number of connections in all pools since the application started

- **SqlClient: Total # failed connects**   Number of connection attempts that failed for any reason

The .NET CLR Data Performance object exposes a sixth counter that isn't directly related to connection pooling but is useful in many other circumstances:

- **SqlClient: Total # failed commands**   Number of commands that failed for any reason

Working with Transactions

The way you work with transactions has changed in the transition from ADO to ADO.NET. The ADO Connection class exposes the BeginTrans, CommitTrans, and RollbackTrans methods, which let you start, commit, or abort a transaction. The isolation level of the transaction is determined by the current value of the IsolationLevel property.

Creating a Transaction Object

The ADO.NET Connection object exposes only the BeginTransaction method, which takes an optional argument that specifies the isolation level of the transaction being started. As in ADO, the isolation level is an enumerated value that tells how locks are created and honored during the transaction. In a difference from ADO, the BeginTransaction method is a function that returns a Transaction object: more precisely, it returns either an OleDbTransaction or a SqlTransaction object, depending on the .NET provider you're using:

```
' Opening a transaction with the OLE DB .NET Data Provider
Dim cn As New OleDbConnection(BiblioConnString)
Dim tr As OleDbTransaction = cn.BeginTransaction(IsolationLevel.Serializable)

' Opening a transaction with the SQL Server .NET Data Provider
Dim cn2 As New SqlConnection(SqlPubsConnString)
Dim tr2 As SqlTransaction = cn2.BeginTransaction(IsolationLevel.Serializable)
```

You then use the Transaction object to control the outcome of the transaction: you invoke the Commit method to confirm all the changes in the transaction and the Rollback method to cancel them:

```
Dim tr As OleDbTransaction
Try
    ' Start a transaction.
    tr = cn.BeginTransaction(IsolationLevel.Serializable)
    ' Insert here database processing code.
    ⋮
    ' If we get here, we can confirm all changes.
    tr.Commit()
Catch ex As Exception
    ' Display an error message, and roll back all changes.
    MessageBox.Show(ex.Message)
    tr.Rollback()
End Try
```

Selecting the Isolation Level

The IsolationLevel property returns an enumerated value that specifies the level of the current transaction and that's equal to the value passed to the Begin-Transaction method, as you can see in the preceding code example. Here's a brief description of the isolation levels that ADO.NET supports:

■ **Chaos**   The pending changes from the more highly isolated transactions can't be overridden. SQL Server doesn't support this isolation level.

■ **ReadUncommitted**   No shared (read) locks are issued, and no exclusive (write) locks are honored, which means that an application can read data that has been written from inside a transaction but not committed yet. If the transaction is then rolled back, the data that was read doesn't correspond to the data now in the database, a phenomenon known as *dirty reads*.

- **ReadCommitted (default)**   Shared (read) locks are issued, and exclusive (write) locks are honored; this isolation level avoids dirty reads, but an application isn't guaranteed to retrieve a given row if the same query is reexecuted (a problem known as *nonrepeatable reads*). Moreover, a reexecuted query might find additional rows because in the meantime the code running in another transaction has inserted one or more records (*phantom rows*).

- **RepeatableRead**   Exclusive locks are placed on all the rows being read so that code running in a transaction can't even read the data being read from inside another transaction. This isolation level degrades the scalability of the application but prevents the nonrepeatable reads problem. Phantom rows are still possible, however.

- **Serializable**   This level is similar to the RepeatableRead level, but an exclusive lock is issued on the entire range, and therefore code running in another transaction can't even add a new record in the same range. This isolation level is the least efficient one, but it also solves the phantom row problem: each transaction truly runs in complete isolation.

For more information about the implications of each isolation level, you should read a good database book. If you work primarily with SQL Server, I highly recommend *Inside SQL Server 2000*, by Kalen Delaney (Microsoft Press).

It should be noted that transactions offer a way to implement pessimistic concurrency in ADO.NET, even though ADO.NET doesn't directly support this type of concurrency, unlike classic ADO. While a transaction is held open, no other user can read the data you have modified (if the transaction level is ReadCommitted) or just read (if the transaction is RepeatableRead or Serializable). Transactions are often the only way you have to ensure that the read and write operations work in a consistent way, but misused transactions can quickly degrade the overall performance and scalability of entire applications. So it's your responsibility to commit or roll back the transaction as soon as possible.

Nesting Transactions

The OleDbTransaction object exposes a Begin method, which lets you start a transaction that's nested in the current transaction. The Begin method takes an optional isolation level and returns another OleDbTransaction object:

```
' Open an OLE DB connection.
Dim cn As New OleDbConnection(BiblioConnString)
cn.Open()
```

```
' Open the first (outer) transaction.
Dim tr As OleDbTransaction = cn.BeginTransaction(IsolationLevel.ReadCommitted)
' Do some work here.
  ⋮
' Open a nested (inner) transaction.
Dim tr2 As OleDbTransaction = tr.Begin(IsolationLevel.ReadUncommitted)
  ⋮
' Roll back the inner transaction.
tr2.Rollback()
  ⋮
' Commit the outer transaction.
tr.Commit()
' Close the connection.
cn.Close()
```

Not all databases support nested transactions. For example, Access supports them, but SQL Server doesn't. In fact, if you run the preceding code on a connection opened using the SQLOLEDB provider, you get the following error:

```
Cannot start more transactions on this session.
```

Working with Named Transactions

SQL Server doesn't support true nested transactions—that is, transactions that can be rolled back or committed independently of outer (pending) transactions—and for this reason, the SqlTransaction object doesn't expose the Begin method. However, SQL Server supports named transactions. A *named transaction* is a sort of bookmark that remembers the state of the database at a given moment so that you can restore that state by using a named rollback command. You can create as many bookmarks as you need with the SQL Server SAVE TRAN command. Here's a fragment of a T-SQL routine that shows how to work with named transactions:

```
BEGIN TRAN MainTran
-- Insert, delete, or modify rows here.
  ⋮
SAVE TRAN EndOfFirstPart
-- Do some more work here.
  ⋮
-- Restore the database contents as they were before the second SAVE TRAN.
ROLLBACK TRAN EndOfFirstPart
  ⋮
-- Commit all changes.
COMMIT TRAN
```

To support named transactions, the BeginTransaction method of the SqlConnection object takes an optional transaction name. In addition, the SqlTransaction object exposes a Save method: both this method and the Rollback method can take an optional transaction name. Here's a Visual Basic .NET snippet that performs the same task as the preceding T-SQL fragment:

```
Dim cn As New SqlConnection(SqlPubsConnString)
cn.Open()

' Open a transaction named MainTran.
Dim tr As SqlTransaction = _
    cn.BeginTransaction(IsolationLevel.ReadCommitted, "MainTran")
' Insert, delete, or modify rows here.
⋮
' Create a named save point.
tr.Save("EndOfFirstPart")
' Do some more work here.
⋮
' Restore the database contents as they were before the second SAVE TRAN.
tr.Rollback("EndOfFirstPart")
⋮
' Commit all changes.
tr.Commit()
```

The Command Object

After you've opened a connection, you can decide whether you want to work in connected or disconnected mode. In the former case, you typically create a Command object that contains a select query (to read data from the database) or an action query (to update data) and then run one of its Execute*xxxx* methods, for which the exact name depends on the type of query.

Table 8-2 summarizes all the main properties and methods of the Command object. Except for the Disposed event inherited from the Component class, the Command object has no events.

Table 8-2   Properties and Methods of the Command Object

Category	Name	Description
Properties	CommandText	The SQL text of the query.
	CommandType	An enumerated value that specifies the type of the query: Text, StoredProcedure, or TableDirect. (The last value is supported only by the OLE DB .NET Data Provider when working with Microsoft Access.)
	Connection	The Connection object associated with this command.

(continued)

Table 8-2 **Properties and Methods of the Command Object** *(continued)*

Category	Name	Description
	Transaction	The Transaction object corresponding to the transaction in which this command is executing.
	CommandTimeout	The number of seconds after which the query times out; default is 30 seconds. The value 0 means an infinite timeout and should be avoided.
	Parameters	The collection of parameters associated with this command.
	UpdatedRowSource	Specifies how command results are applied to the DataRow object. It's meaningful only when Command is associated with a DataAdapter object that performs an Update method.
Methods	ExecuteNonQuery	Executes the action query specified by CommandText and returns the number of rows affected.
	ExecuteReader	Executes the select query specified by CommandText and returns the DataReader object that lets you access the resultset. This method can take an optional CommandBehavior bit-coded value that further specifies how the command works—for example, whether it returns a single row or whether the connection should be closed when the method returns.
	ExecuteScalar	Executes the select query specified by CommandText and returns the scalar value in the first column of the first row, ignoring all other values.
	Cancel	Cancels the execution of the Command object; no error occurs if the command isn't running.
	CreateParameter	Creates a Parameter object connected to this parameterized command.
	ResetCommandTimeout	Resets the CommandTimeout property to its default value (30 seconds).
	Prepare	Creates a compiled version of the command on the data source; it can work only if CommandType is StoredProcedure, even though it might have no effect.
(SQL Server provider only)	ExecuteXmlReader	Performs that select query specified by CommandText (usually a SELECT FOR XML query) and returns an XmlReader object that lets you read the values in the resultset.

Creating a Command Object

The key properties of the Command object are CommandText (the SQL text of the action or select query) and Connection (the connection on which the query should run). You can set these properties individually, as in the following code snippet:

```
' Open a connection.
Dim cn As New OleDbConnection(BiblioConnString)
cn.Open()

' Define the command to insert a new record in the Authors table.
Dim sql As String = _
    "INSERT INTO Authors (Author, [Year Born]) VALUES ('Joe Doe', 1955)"

' Create an action command on that connection.
Dim cmd As New OleDbCommand()
cmd.Connection = cn
cmd.CommandText = sql

' Run the query; get the number of affected records.
Dim records As Integer = cmd.ExecuteNonQuery()
Debug.WriteLine(records)                        ' => 1

' Close the connection.
cn.Close()
```

Or you can pass these two values to the Command object's constructor, which makes for more concise code:

```
Dim cmd As New OleDbCommand(sql, cn)
```

If you've opened a transaction on the connection, you must enlist the command in the transaction by assigning the Transaction object to the property with the same name or you must pass this object to the Command's constructor:

```
' (This code assumes that you've opened a connection and defined a query.)
' Begin a transaction.
Dim tr As OleDbTransaction = cn.BeginTransaction
' Create an action command, and enlist it in the transaction.
Dim cmd As New OleDbCommand(sql, cn, tr)
' Run the query; get the number of affected records.
Dim records As Integer = cmd.ExecuteNonQuery()
' Commit (or roll back) the transaction.
tr.Commit()
```

You get an error if you don't enlist the Command object in the existing transaction (more precisely, the most nested transaction being opened on that connection). Therefore, you can't help passing the Transaction object to the constructor method or to the Transaction property. This operation could be performed implicitly by ADO.NET when the Command object is associated with the connection, so you might wonder why you have to do it manually. The only reasonable explanation for this behavior I can think of is that in the future it might be possible to associate the command with a transaction obtained in some other way—for example, a distributed transaction created by the Microsoft Distributed Transaction Coordinator (MS DTC). At this time, however, nothing in the documentation confirms or rejects this hypothesis.

Issuing Database Commands

As you've seen in the preceding code snippets, you can perform insert, update, and delete operations through a Command object by means of the Execute-NonQuery method, which returns the number of records that were affected by the statement:

```
Dim sql As String = _
    "INSERT INTO Authors (Author, [Year Born]) VALUES ('Joe Doe', 1955)"
Dim cmd As New OleDbCommand(sql, cn)
' Run the query; get the number of affected records.
Dim records As Integer = cmd.ExecuteNonQuery()
```

Of course, you can update existing records by using the UPDATE SQL statement and delete existing records with the DELETE statement. There isn't much else to say about this method except that—as with all database operations—you should protect it with a Try block:

```
Try
    ' Run the query; get the number of affected records.
    Dim records As Integer = cmd.ExecuteNonQuery()
Catch ex As Exception
    ' Process the error here.
    ⋮
Finally
    ' Always close the connection.
    cn.Close()
End Try
```

Reading Data

You can read data from a data source in three ways: by using the ExecuteReader method and the DataReader object to read complete resultsets; by using the Exe-cuteScalar method to read individual values; or by using the ExecuteXmlReader method and the XmlReader object to read the results of a FOR XML query on a SQL Server 2000 data source.

Using the ExecuteReader Method

The most common way to query the database in connected mode is through the ExecuteReader method of the Command object. This method returns a DataReader object, which you then use to read the resultset one row at a time, as you'd do with a forward-only, read-only Recordset under classic ADO. There are actually two versions of this object, OleDbDataReader and SqlDataReader.

```
' Create a query command on the connection.
Dim cmd As New OleDbCommand("SELECT * FROM Publishers", cn)
' Run the query; get the DataReader object.
Dim dr As OleDbDataReader = cmd.ExecuteReader()
' Read the names of all the publishers in the resultsets.
Do While dr.Read()
    Debug.WriteLine(dr.Item("Name"))
Loop
' Close the DataReader.
dr.Close
```

I discuss the DataReader object and its methods in greater detail in the section "The DataReader Object" later in this reading. For now, let me focus on how you can affect the query by passing an optional CommandBehavior bit-coded value to the ExecuteReader method. The available values for this argument are

■ **CloseConnection**   The connection should be closed immediately after the DataReader object is closed.

■ **SingleRow**   The SQL statement is expected to return a single row of data. The OLE DB .NET Data Provider uses this information to optimize the data retrieval operation.

■ **SingleResult**   The SQL statement is expected to return a single scalar value. (In this case, however, you should use the ExecuteScalar method instead of ExecuteReader, as I explain in the next section.)

■ **KeyInfo**   The query returns column and primary key information and is executed without locking the selected rows. In this case, the SQL Server .NET Data Provider appends a FOR BROWSE clause to the SQL statement, which requires that the table have a time-stamp field and a unique index. (See SQL Server Books Online for additional information.)

■ **SequentialAccess**   The query results are read sequentially at the column level instead of being returned as a whole block to the caller. You should use this option when the table contains very large text and binary fields that you read in chunks using the GetChars and

GetBytes methods of the DataReader object. In these circumstances, this option can improve the performance of your read operations significantly.

■ **SchemaOnly**   The query returns column information only and doesn't affect the database state.

Here's an example that uses the CloseConnection value:

```
' Run the query; get the DataReader object.
Dim dr As OleDbDataReader = cmd.ExecuteReader(CommandBehavior.CloseConnection)
' Process the data.
⋮
' Close the DataReader and (implicitly) the connection.
dr.Close()
```

The SingleRow option is useful when you're absolutely sure that the resultset contains only one row. This is often the case when the WHERE clause of the query filters a single record by its primary key, as in this example:

```
' Read a single line from the Publishers table.
Dim sql As String = "SELECT * FROM Publishers WHERE PubID=1"
Dim cmd As New OleDbCommand(sql, cn)
' Open a DataReader that contains one single row.
Dim dr As OleDbDataReader = cmd.ExecuteReader(CommandBehavior.SingleRow)
' Show name and city of this publisher.
dr.Read()
Debug.WriteLine(dr("Name") & " - " & dr ("City"))
dr.Close
```

Note that the argument is bit-coded, so you can combine multiple values using the Or operator:

```
Dim dr As OleDbDataReader = cmd.ExecuteReader(CommandBehavior.SingleRow _
    Or CommandBehavior.CloseConnection)
```

Using the ExecuteScalar Method

The ExecuteScalar method lets you perform a database query that returns a single scalar value in a more efficient way because it doesn't go through the overhead to build a resultset:

```
' Define the command to read a single scalar value
Dim sql As String = "SELECT Name FROM Publishers WHERE PubID=1"
' Create a command on that connection.
Dim cmd As New OleDbCommand(sql, cn)
' Read the value.
Dim pubName As String = cmd.ExecuteScalar().ToString
```

Another good occasion to use the ExecuteScalar method is for reading the result of aggregate functions, as in this code snippet:

```
' Read the number of records in the Publishers table.
Dim cmd As New OleDbCommand("SELECT COUNT(*) FROM Publishers", cn)
Dim recCount As Integer = CInt(cmd.ExecuteScalar())
```

Remember that the ExecuteScalar method works with *any* SQL query, and in all cases it returns the first field of the first row without raising an error if the query returns multiple columns or multiple rows.

Using the ExecuteXmlReader Method

SQL Server 2000 is able to process FOR XML queries and return data in XML format. If you connect to the database by using the SQL Server .NET Data Provider, you can leverage this capability with the ExecuteXmlReader of the SqlCommand object, which returns a System.Xml.XmlReader object that lets you walk through the resultset. Here's a code example that uses this feature:

```
' Open a connection to SQL Server 2000.
Dim cn As New SqlConnection(SqlPubsConnString)
cn.Open()
' Prepare a FOR XML command.
Dim sql As String = "SELECT pub_name FROM Publishers FOR XML AUTO, ELEMENTS"
Dim cmd As New SqlCommand(sql, cn)
' Create the XmlReader.
Dim reader As System.Xml.XmlReader = cmd.ExecuteXmlReader()
' Display XML data in a TextBox control.
Do While reader.Read
    txtOut.AppendText(reader.Value & ControlChars.CrLf)
Loop
' Close the XmlReader and the connection.
reader.Close()
cn.Close()
```

As you see, the XmlReader works similarly to the DataReader object, with a Read method that returns True if there are more elements and False when you arrive at the end of the resultset.

Working with Parameters and Stored Procedures

The SQL command that you pass to a Command object can contain parameters, an especially useful feature when you're working with stored procedures. The exact syntax you can use in the SQL command depends on which data provider you're working with, so we'll examine the two providers separately.

Parameterized Commands

A common misconception is that parameters are useful only when you're work-ing with stored procedures. But in fact, you can define a parameterized SQL command that contains one or more question marks as placeholders, as in this line of code:

```
SELECT * FROM Titles WHERE PubId=? AND [Year Published]=?
```

When you use this syntax—which is valid only with the OLE DB .NET Data Provider—you must manually create one or more Parameter objects and add them to the Command object's Parameters collection in the exact order in which the parameter appears in the SQL command. You can choose from three ways of creating a Parameter object: you can use the Parameter's constructor, use the Command's CreateParameter method, or invoke the Add method of the Parameters collection:

```
' First method: the Parameter's constructor
Dim par As New OleDbParameter("PubId", OleDbType.Integer)
par.Value = 156               ' Set the parameter's value.
cmd.Parameters.Add(par)       ' Add to the collection of parameters.
Dim par2 As New OleDbParameter("YearPub", OleDbType.SmallInt)
par2.Value = 1992
cmd.Parameters.Add(par2)


' Second method: the Command's CreateParameter method
Dim par As OleDbParameter = cmd.CreateParameter
' Note that setting the name and the type isn't mandatory.
par.Value = 156
cmd.Parameters.Add(par)
par = cmd.CreateParameter      ' Reuse the same variable.
par.Value = 1992
cmd.Parameters.Add(par)


' Third method: passing name and value to the Parameters.Add method
cmd.Parameters.Add("PubId", 156)
cmd.Parameters.Add("YearPub", 1992)
```

(The Parameters collection implements the IList interface, so it exposes all the usual methods for adding, inserting, and removing elements.) The syntax with the SQL Server .NET Data Provider is different: it doesn't support question marks in queries and requires you to use @ parameters, as in this line of code:

```
SELECT * FROM Titles WHERE title_id=@TitleId
```

The code for creating the Parameters collection is similar, but of course you must use a SqlParameter object instead:

```
' First method: the Parameter's constructor
Dim par As New SqlParameter("TitleId", SqlDbType.VarChar)
par.Value = "BU1032"                ' Set the parameter's value.
cmd.Parameters.Add(par)             ' Add to the collection of parameters.

' Second method: the Command's CreateParameter method
Dim par As SqlParameter = cmd.CreateParameter
par.Value = "BU1032"
cmd.Parameters.Add(par)

' Third method: passing name and value to the Parameters.Add method
cmd.Parameters.Add("TitleId", "BU1032")
```

After the Parameters collection is set up, you can call the ExecuteReader method to retrieve the resultset as usual, or the ExecuteNonQuery method if it is an action query that doesn't return data rows. Parameterized commands are useful when you must perform the same type of query more than once, each time with different parameter values. The following example shows how you can extract different rows from the same table without having to create a different Command object:

```
' Create a SQL command with one parameter.
Dim sql As String = "SELECT * FROM Publishers WHERE PubID=?"
Dim cmd As New OleDbCommand(sql, cn)
' Define the first (and only) parameter, and assign its value.
cmd.Parameters.Add("PubID", 156)

' Read the result.
Dim dr As OleDbDataReader = cmd.ExecuteReader()
' No need to loop because we know there is only one row.
dr.Read()
Debug.WriteLine(dr("Name"))
dr.Close()

' Change the parameter's value, and reexecute the query.
cmd.Parameters(0).Value = 10
dr = cmd.ExecuteReader
dr.Read()
Debug.WriteLine(dr("Name"))
dr.Close()
```

Stored Procedures

The substantial difference between executing a simple parameterized SQL command and calling a stored procedure is that in the latter case, you just specify the name of the stored procedure in the command text and set the Command-Type property to StoredProcedure:

```
' Run the byroyalty stored procedure in SQL Server's Pubs database.
Dim cmd As New SqlCommand("byroyalty", cn)
cmd.CommandType = CommandType.StoredProcedure
' Create the first parameter, and assign it the value 100.
' (Note that the parameter name must match the name used in the procedure.)
cmd.Parameters.Add("@percentage", 100)
' Read the result.
Dim dr As SqlDataReader = cmd.ExecuteReader()
```

You can execute a SQL Server stored procedure by using either the OLE DB .NET Data Provider or the SQL Server .NET Data Provider, the only difference being that the former provider doesn't require that the name you use for a parameter match the parameter's name as defined in the stored procedure itself.

In another difference from parameterized commands, when you're working with stored procedures you must account for the type and the direction of each parameter. In general, the type of each Parameter must match the type of the argument that the stored procedure accepts; if this doesn't happen, you might have problems passing and retrieving a value from that stored procedure. You can pass the type as the second argument to the Parameter's constructor by using an enumerated OleDbType value, which is similar to the data types that ADO supports:

```
' Create a Parameter of type Single.
Dim param1 As New OleDbParameter("param1", OleDbType.Single)
```

When working with strings, you can also specify a size:

```
Dim param2 As New OleDbParameter("param2", OleDbType.VarChar, 100)
```

The same syntax applies to SqlParameter objects, except that you specify the type by using a SqlDbType enumeration value. In some cases, the name of this value differs from its OLE DB counterpart:

```
' Create a Single parameter for SQL Server.
Dim param3 As New SqlParameter("param3", SqlDbType.Float)
```

By default, all parameters are created as input parameters. If you're calling a stored procedure that returns a value through an argument, you must set the Direction property to either InputOutput or Output. If the stored procedure returns a value, you must define an additional parameter; the name of this parameter doesn't matter as long as it's the first parameter appended to the Parameters collection and its Direction property is set to ReturnValue.

To test how to work with output parameters and return values, you can define a new byroyalty2 stored procedure in SQL Server's Pubs database by running this script in SQL Server's Query Analyzer:

```
CREATE PROCEDURE byroyalty2 @percentage int, @avgprice float output
AS
-- Return the average price for all titles in the second argument.
SELECT @avgprice= AVG(Price) FROM Titles
-- Return a resultset.
SELECT au_id FROM titleauthor
    WHERE titleauthor.royaltyper = @percentage
-- Return the number of titles in the second argument.
DECLARE @numtitles Int
SELECT @numtitles=COUNT(*) FROM titles
RETURN @numtitles
```

Here's the complete source code of a routine that invokes the byroyalty2 stored procedure and displays its results in a multiline TextBox control:

```
Dim cn As New SqlConnection(SqlPubsConnString)
cn.Open()

Dim sql As String = "byroyalty2"
Dim cmd As New SqlCommand(sql, cn)
cmd.CommandType = CommandType.StoredProcedure

' Define the return value parameter.
cmd.Parameters.Add("@numtitles", OleDbType.Integer)
cmd.Parameters(0).Direction = ParameterDirection.ReturnValue
' Define the first (input) parameter, and assign its value.
cmd.Parameters.Add("@percentage", 100)

' Define the second (output) parameter, and set its direction.
' (A better method for setting the direction and other properties.)
With cmd.Parameters.Add("@avgprice", SqlDbType.Float)
    .Direction = ParameterDirection.Output
End With

' Read the result.
Dim dr As SqlDataReader = cmd.ExecuteReader()
Do While dr.Read
    txtOut.AppendText(dr(0).ToString & ControlChars.CrLf)
Loop
dr.Close()

' You can read the return value and output argument only after
' closing the DataReader object.
txtOut.AppendText("Number of titles = " & _
    cmd.Parameters("@numtitles").Value.ToString & ControlChars.CrLf)
txtOut.AppendText("Average price = " & _
    cmd.Parameters("@avgprice").Value.ToString & ControlChars.CrLf)
' Close the connection.
cn.Close()
```

As a remark in the preceding code snippet explains, you can read output arguments and return values only after you've closed the DataReader object. This is a known problem of SQL Server and doesn't depend on ADO.NET. (As a matter of fact, you have the same problem also when calling a SQL Server stored procedure from ADO.)

When invoking a SQL Server stored procedure that doesn't have output parameters or a return value, you can take the following shortcut: just create an EXEC statement that contains the name of the stored procedure followed by all its input parameters, as in this code snippet:

```
Dim sql As String = "EXEC byroyalty 100"
Dim cmd As New SqlCommand(sql, cn)
cmd.CommandType = CommandType.Text
```

Note that in this case you don't have to set the CommandType property to StoredProcedure because from the perspective of ADO.NET, you're executing a regular SQL command.

Automatic Population of the Parameters Collection

When working with stored procedures, you can save some time by having ADO.NET populate the Parameters collection of the Command object automatically by means of the DeriveParameters shared method of the OleDbCommand-Builder or SqlCommandBuilder class:

```
' Get the parameters for the byroyalty stored procedure in Pubs.
Dim cmd As New SqlCommand("byroyalty", cn)
cmd.CommandType = CommandType.StoredProcedure

' Let the CommandBuilder object populate the Parameters collection.
SqlCommandBuilder.DeriveParameters(cmd)

' Show number and names of parameters.
Debug.WriteLine(cmd.Parameters.Count & " parameters")    ' => 2 parameters
Debug.WriteLine(cmd.Parameters(0).ParameterName)          ' => @RETURN_VALUE
Debug.WriteLine(cmd.Parameters(1).ParameterName)          ' => @percentage
```

ADO supports a similar technique based on the Parameters.Refresh method, but Microsoft initially decided not to make this technique available to ADO.NET developers because of its horrible performance. In fact, both ADO's Refresh method and the ADO.NET DeriveParameters method require a round-trip to the SQL Server database to acquire the metadata needed to fill the Parameters collection. Because the signature of a stored procedure rarely changes after the application is deployed, it makes sense that you burn the names and the type of the parameters in code to speed up execution.

Even if you don't count performance problems, filling the Parameters collection automatically isn't usually a good idea. For example, the preceding code snippet shows that the DeriveParameters method incorrectly detects a return value parameter, even when the stored procedure doesn't really have a return value. In some circumstances, this method isn't smart enough to read the exact type and direction of parameters. For example, if you run the DeriveParameters method on the byroyalty2 stored procedure that we've defined in the preceding section, you'll see that the @avgprice output parameter is incorrectly retrieved as an input/output parameter. You can remedy this problem either by manually adjusting the Direction property to Output or by assigning a dummy value to the @avgprice parameter before calling the stored procedure, even if this value will never be used. If you fail to take either of these steps, the ExecuteReader method will throw an exception.

Despite its defects, the DeriveParameters method fits the bill during the prototyping phase, but be prepared to replace it with code that populates the Parameters collection manually before you ship the application. Here's a tip: you should always reference your parameters by their names rather than by their indexes in the Parameters collection so that you don't have to change your code if you switch from automatic to manual creation of the Parameters collection. And don't include the return value parameter (if the stored procedure doesn't have one).

```
' This statement works regardless of how you fill the Parameters collection.
cmd.Parameters("@percentage").Value = 100
```

The DeriveParameters method works in a slightly different way in the two .NET data providers. As you've seen, the parameter names that the SQL Server .NET Data Provider retrieves have a leading @ character and match their definitions in the stored procedure. This character is missing when you retrieve the collection of parameters using the OLE DB .NET Data Provider. (The present or missing @ character is an issue only if you want to change the provider during the development phase.)

> **Note**   The DeriveParameters method was added rather late in the beta process, which explains why earlier articles and books on ADO.NET don't cover it. I suspect that the main reason for its introduction was the disappointed feedback from earlier adopters who would have liked to have a mechanism similar to the ADO Parameters.Refresh method. However, remember that you should use the DeriveParameters method only during the testing step, and you should populate the Parameters collection manually in the definitive version of your application to avoid an unnecessary round-trip to the server.

The DataReader Object

I summarize the most important properties and methods of the DataReader object in Table 8-3. The most important of these members are described in the following sections.

Iterating over Individual Rows

Using the DataReader object couldn't be simpler: you invoke its Read method to advance to the next row in the resultset and check its return value to see whether you have more results (if True) or are at the end of the resultset (if False). Because of this double function, you can create tight loops based on the DataReader object:

```
Do While dr.Read()
    ' Process the current row here.
    :
Loop
dr.Close()
```

It's important that you close the DataReader object when you don't have to process any more rows, to release resources on both the client and the server and make the connection available again for other commands. In fact, you can't issue any other command on a connection while a DataReader object is active on that connection. The only command you can perform on a connection actively serving a DataReader is the Close method.

You can check whether a connection is available by using its State property. The DataReader object doesn't expose this property, but you can check whether it has been closed by means of its IsClosed property.

Table 8-3   Properties and Methods of the DataReader Object

Category	Name	Description
Properties	IsClosed	Returns True if the DataReader is closed.
	FieldCount	Returns the number of columns in the current row.
	Item	Returns the value of the column with the specified index or name.
	RecordsAffected	Returns the number of rows inserted, deleted, or updated by the SQL statement.
	Depth	Returns the depth of nesting of the current row. (The outermost table has a depth of 0.)

Table 8-3   Properties and Methods of the DataReader Object *(continued)*

Category	Name	Description
Methods	Read	Advances to the next row and returns True if there are more rows, False if the end of the resultset has been found.
	Close	Closes the DataReader object, releases all the resources allocated to it, and makes the connection available for other commands.
	NextResult	Advances to the next resultset and returns True if there is another resultset. Use this method to process multiple resultset results, such as those returned by batch SQL statements and stored procedures.
	GetName	Returns the name of the column with the specified index.
	GetOrdinal	Returns the index of a column corresponding to the field name passed as an argument.
	IsDBNull	Returns True if the column at the specified index contains a DBNull value.
	GetValue	Returns the value of a column at the specified index in its native format.
	GetValues	Takes an Object array and fills it with the values from all the columns in the resultset; returns the number of Object instances in the array.
	GetBoolean, GetByte, GetChar, GetDateTime, GetDecimal, GetDouble, GetFloat, GetGuid, GetInt16, GetInt32, GetInt64, GetString, GetTimeSpan	Retrieves the strongly typed value of the field at the specified column index. (GetTimeSpan isn't supported by the SQL Server .NET Data Provider.)
	GetBytes	Fills a Byte array (or a portion thereof) with the contents of a binary field; returns the number of bytes read.
	GetChars	Fills a Char array (or a portion thereof) with the contents of a long text field; returns the number of characters read.
	GetFieldType	Returns the System.Type object that describes the type of the field at a given index.

(continued)

Table 8-3   **Properties and Methods of the DataReader Object**   *(continued)*

Category	Name	Description
	GetDataTypeName	Returns the name of the source data type for the column whose index is passed as an argument.
	GetSchemaTable	Returns a DataTable that describes the column metadata.
(SQL Server provider only)	GetSqlBinary, GetSql-Boolean, GetSqlByte, GetSqlDateTime, GetSqlDecimal, GetSql-Double, GetSqlGuid, GetInt16, GetInt32, GetInt64, GetSqlMoney, GetSqlSingle, GetSql-String	Retrieve the strongly typed value of the field at the specified column index as one of the Sql-Types.Sql*xxxx* data types.
	GetSqlValue	Gets an Object that's a representation of the underlying Data.SqlDbTypeVariant value.
	GetSqlValues	Takes an Object array and fills it with the value from all the columns in the resultset; returns the number of Object instances in the array.

Reading Column Values

A quick look at Table 8-3 shows that the DataReader object provides many properties and methods that let you read the value of the columns in the resultset.

The Item read-only property gives you a means to access any field by either its name or its (zero-based) column index in a way that resembles the kind of access you perform with the Fields collection of the ADO Recordset:

```
' Read the result into a DataReader object.
Dim dr As OleDbDataReader = cmd.ExecuteReader(CommandBehavior.CloseConnection)

' Display the names of all publishers.
Do While dr.Read()
    Dim res As String = String.Format("{0} - {1}", _
        dr.Item("Name"), dr.Item("City"))
    ' Append the result to the current contents of a TextBox control.
    txtOut.AppendText(res & ControlChars.CrLf)
Loop
' Close the DataReader and the connection.
dr.Close()
```

Item is the default member, so you can make your code more concise by omitting it:

```
Dim res As String = String.Format("{0} - {1}", dr("Name"), dr("City"))
```

You can iterate over all the columns in the resultset by using an index that goes from 0 to FieldCount <−1; then you can use the GetName method to retrieve the name of the field and the GetValue method (or the Item property) to read the field's value. If you're dealing with a nullable field, however, you should protect your code from exceptions by checking a field with the IsDB-Null method:

```
' Read the result into a DataReader object.
Dim dr As OleDbDataReader = cmd.ExecuteReader(CommandBehavior.CloseConnection)

' Display the value of all fields.
Do While dr.Read
    ' Prepare the buffer for the values of this row.
    Dim res As String = ""
    Dim i As Integer

    ' Iterate over all fields.
    For i = 0 To dr.FieldCount - 1
        ' Insert a comma if necessary.
        If res.Length > 0 Then res &= ", "
        ' Append field name and value.
        res &= dr.GetName(i) & "="
        ' Protect the code from null values.
        If dr.IsDBNull(i) Then
            res &= "<NULL>"
        Else
            res &= dr.GetValue(i).ToString
        End If
    Next
    ' Append to the result text box.
    txtOut.AppendText(res & ControlChars.CrLf)
Loop
' Close the DataReader and the Connection.
dr.Close()
```

When you read all the fields in the current row, you can optimize your code by using the GetValues method, which returns all the fields' values in an Object array. The following code snippet uses this method and makes the code even faster by retrieving the names of all fields once and for all outside the main loop and by using a StringBuilder object instead of a regular String. After the value has been moved to an element of the Object array, you must test it using the IsDBNull function instead of the DataReader's IsDBNull method:

```
' Run the query; get the DataReader object.
Dim dr As OleDbDataReader = cmd.ExecuteReader(CommandBehavior.CloseConnection)

' Build the array of all fields.
Dim fldNames(dr.FieldCount - 1) As String
Dim i As Integer
For i = 0 To dr.FieldCount - 1
    fldNames(i) = dr.GetName(i)
Next

' Display all fields.
Do While dr.Read
    Dim res As New System.Text.StringBuilder(256)
    ' Get all the values in one shot.
    Dim values(dr.FieldCount - 1) As Object
    dr.GetValues(values)

    ' Iterate over all fields.
    For i = 0 To dr.FieldCount - 1
        ' Insert a comma if necessary.
        If res.Length > 0 Then res.Append(", ")
        ' Append field name and equal sign.
        res.Append(fldNames(i))
        res.Append("=")
        ' Append the field value, or <NULL>.
        If IsDBNull(values(i)) Then
            res.Append("<NULL>")
        Else
            res.Append(values(i).ToString)
        End If
    Next
    ' Append to the result text box.
    res.Append(ControlChars.CrLf)
    txtOut.AppendText(res.ToString)
Loop
' Close the DataReader and the Connection.
dr.Close()
```

The OLE DB .NET Data Provider offers several Get*xxxx* methods to retrieve field values in their native format, saving you the overhead of going through a more generic Object variable. Compare how you can retrieve an integer value with the generic GetValue method and the more specific GetInt32 method:

```
' The generic GetValue method requires type casting.
Dim res As Integer = CInt(dr.GetValue(0))
' The specific GetInt32 method does not.
Dim res2 As Integer = dr.GetInt32(0)
```

Using Specific SQL Server Types

The SQL Server .NET Data Provider also provides the same Get*xxxx* methods as the OLE DB provider, with one glaring exception: it doesn't support the Get-TimeSpan method. On the other hand, the SQL Server provider supports more specific GetSql*xxxx* methods, which behave much like their Get*xxxx* counterparts except that they return specific SQL Server types defined in the System.Data.SqlTypes namespace:

```
' This code assumes that dr is a SqlDataReader object.
Dim res As Integer = dr.GetSqlInt32(0)
```

When you're working with the SQL Server .NET Data Provider, you should always use these more specific types because they prevent conversion errors caused by loss of precision and provide faster code as well. This advice is especially important to follow with the SqlDecimal data type, which provides a precision of 38 digits instead of the 28 digits that the .NET Decimal type provides.

Table 8-4 summarizes the data types in the System.Data.SqlTypes namespace and aligns them with the corresponding SQL Server type and with the corresponding value of the enumerated SqlDbType (defined in System.Data). As you see, some of the SqlTypes correspond to more than one native SQL Server type.

Table 8-4   SqlTypes and the Corresponding Native SQL Server Types and SqlDbType Enumerated Values

SqlTypes	Native SQL Server	SqlDbType Enumerated Value
SqlBoolean	bit	Bit
SqlByte	tinyint	TinyInt
SqlInt16	smallint	SmallInt
SqlInt32	int	Int
SqlInt64	bigint	BigInt
SqlSingle	real	Real
SqlDouble	float	Float
SqlDecimal	decimal	Decimal
SqlDateTime	datetime	DateTime
	smalldatetime	SmallDateTime

(continued)

Table 8-4 **SqlTypes and the Corresponding Native SQL Server Types and SqlDbType Enumerated Values** *(continued)*

SqlTypes	Native SQL Server	SqlDbType Enumerated Value
SqlMoney	money	Money
	smallmoney	SmallMoney
SqlString	char	Char
	nchar	NChar
	ntext	NText
	nvarchar	NVarChar
	sysname	VarChar
	text	Text
	varchar	VarChar
SqlBinary	binary	Binary
	varbinary	VarBinary
	image	Image
	timestamp	TimeStamp
SqlGuid	uniqueindentifier	UniqueIdentifier
Object	sql_variant	Variant

Reading Multiple Resultsets

Some databases support multiple statements in one query. For example, you can send multiple commands to SQL Server, using the semicolon as a separator:

```
SELECT Name FROM Publishers WHERE PubId=10;
SELECT Name FROM Publishers WHERE PubId=12
```

Multiple queries let you create batch commands, which minimize the number of round-trips to the server and network traffic. (One batch command uses a single network packet to carry multiple queries that would otherwise require multiple packets.) The DataReader object supports multiple resultsets by means of the NextResult method, which returns True if there is one more resultset and False otherwise. The following code snippet shows how to use this method with any number of resultsets:

```
' Open a connection to the Pubs database on SQL Server.
Dim cn As New SqlConnection(SqlPubsConnString)
cn.Open()

' Define a SQL statement with multiple queries.
```

```
Dim sql As String = "SELECT pub_name FROM Publishers;SELECT Title FROM titles"
Dim cmd As New SqlCommand(sql, cn)
Dim dr As SqlDataReader = cmd.ExecuteReader()

Dim resCount As Integer
Do
    ' Process the next resultset.
    resCount += 1
    txtOut.AppendText("RESULTSET #" & resCount.ToString)
    txtOut.AppendText(ControlChars.CrLf)

    ' Process all the rows in the current resultset.
    Do While dr.Read
        txtOut.AppendText(dr(0).ToString)
        txtOut.AppendText(ControlChars.CrLf)
    Loop
    txtOut.AppendText(ControlChars.CrLf)
Loop While dr.NextResult
' Close the DataReader and the connection.
dr.Close()
cn.Close()
```

Figure 8-1 shows the outcome of this code.

If the SQL statement contains action queries—such as an INSERT, a DELETE, or an UPDATE statement—they're correctly ignored by the NextResult method because they don't return any resultsets. (Under the same circumstances, the NextResultset method of the ADO Recordset object returned a closed Recordset, so you had to write additional code to handle this special case.)

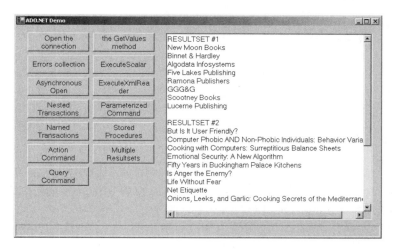

Figure 8-1. The demo program lets you test several features of the DataReader object.

✳✳✳

The DataSet Object

Because ADO.NET (and .NET in general) is all about scalability and performance, the disconnected mode is the preferred way to code client/server applications. Instead of a simple disconnected recordset, ADO.NET gives you the DataSet object, which is much like a small relational database held in memory on the client. As such, it provides you with the ability to create multiple tables, fill them with data coming from different sources, enforce relationships between pairs of tables, and more.

Even with all its great features, however, the DataSet isn't always the best answer to all database programming problems. For example, the DataSet object is great for traditional client/server applications—for example, a Windows Forms application that queries a database on a networked server—but is almost always a bad choice in ASP.NET applications and, more generally, in all stateless environments. An ASP.NET page lives only a short lifetime, just for the time necessary to reply to a browser's request, so it rarely makes sense to use a DataSet to read data from a database, then send the data to the user through HTML, and destroy the DataSet immediately afterward. (Yes, you might save the DataSet in a Session variable, but this technique takes memory on the server and might create server affinity, two problems that impede scalability.)

Exploring the DataSet Object Model

The DataSet is the root and the most important object in the object hierarchy that includes almost all the objects in the System.Data namespace. Figure 8-2 shows the most important classes in this hierarchy, with the name of the property that returns each object.

An important feature of the DataSet class is its ability to define relationships between its DataTable objects, much like what you do in a real database. For example, you can create a relationship between the Publishers and the Titles DataTable objects by using the PubId DataColumn that they have in common. After you define a DataRelation object, you can navigate from one table to another, using the DataTable's ChildRelations and ParentRelations properties.

A DataSet object consists of one or more DataTable objects, each one containing data coming from a database query, an XML stream, or code added programmatically. Table 8-5 summarizes the most important members of the DataSet class.

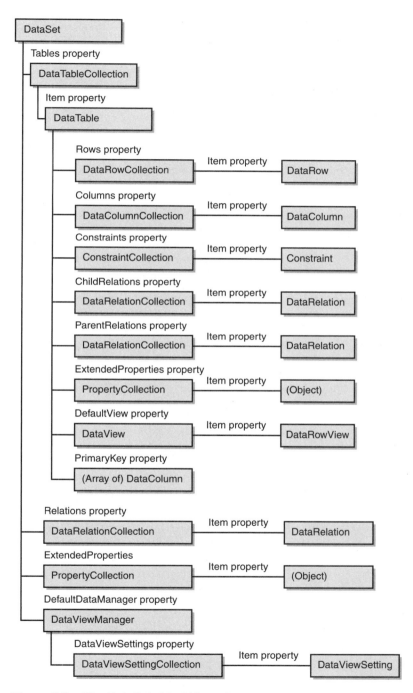

Figure 8-2.   The DataSet object hierarchy.

Table 8-5 Main Properties, Methods, and Events of the DataSet Class

Category	Name	Description
Properties	DataSetName	The name of this DataSet object.
	Namespace	The namespace for this DataSet, used when importing or exporting XML data.
	Prefix	The XML prefix for the DataSet namespace.
	CaseSensitive	True if string comparisons in this DataSet are case sensitive.
	Locale	The CultureInfo object containing the locale information used to compare strings in the DataSet (read/write).
	HasErrors	Returns True if there are errors in any of the DataTable objects in this DataSet.
	EnforceConstraints	True if constraint rules are enforced when attempting an update operation.
	Tables	Returns the collection of child DataTable objects.
	Relations	Returns the collection of DataRelation objects.
	ExtendedProperties	Returns the PropertyCollection object used to store custom information about the DataSet.
	DefaultViewManager	Returns a DataViewManager object that allows you to create custom search and filter settings for the DataTable objects in the DataSet.
Methods	AcceptChanges	Commits all changes to this DataSet after it was loaded or since the most recent AcceptChanges method.
	RejectChanges	Rejects all changes to this DataSet after it was loaded or since the most recent AcceptChanges method.
	HasChanges	Returns True if the DataSet has changed. It takes an optional DataRowState argument that lets you check for modified, inserted, or deleted rows only.
	Merge	Merges the current DataSet with another DataSet, a DataTable, or a DataRow array.
	Reset	Resets the DataSet to its original state.
	Clone	Creates a cloned DataSet that contains the identical structure, tables, and relationships as the current one.
	Copy	Creates a DataSet that has both the same structure and the same data as the current one.

Table 8-5   Main Properties, Methods, and Events of the DataSet Class *(continued)*

Category	Name	Description
	Clear	Clears all the data in the DataSet.
	GetChanges	Gets a DataSet that contains all the changes made to the current one since it was loaded or since the most recent AcceptChanges method, optionally filtered using the DataRowState argument.
	ReadXml	Reads an XML schema and data into the DataSet.
	ReadXmlSchema	Reads an XML schema into the DataSet.
	GetXml	Returns the XML representation of the contents of the DataSet.
	InferXmlSchema	Infers the XML schema from the TextReader or from the file into the DataSet.
	WriteXml	Writes the XML schema and data from the current DataSet.
	WriteXmlSchema	Writes the current DataSet's structure as an XML schema.
Events	MergeFailed	Fires when two DataSet objects being merged have the same primary key value and the EnforceConstraints property is True.

✳✳✳

Creating a DataTable Object

The code that follows creates a DataSet object that contains an Employees table:

```
' This is at the form level, to be shared among all procedures.
Dim ds As New DataSet()

Sub CreateEmployeesTable()
    ' Create a table; set its initial capacity and case sensitivity.
    Dim dtEmp As New DataTable("Employees")
    dtEmp.MinimumCapacity = 100
    dtEmp.CaseSensitive = False

    ' Create all columns.
    ' You can create a DataColumn and then add it to the Columns collection.
    Dim dcFName As New DataColumn("FirstName", GetType(String))
    dtEmp.Columns.Add(dcFName)
    ' Or you can create an implicit DataColumn with the Columns.Add method.
    dtEmp.Columns.Add("LastName", GetType(String))
    dtEmp.Columns.Add("BirthDate", GetType(Date))

    ' When you have to set additional properties, you can use an explicit
    ' DataColumn object, or you can use a With block.
```

(continued)

```
With dtEmp.Columns.Add("HomeAddress", GetType(String))
    .MaxLength = 100
End With
' (When you must set only one property, you can be more concise,
'  even though the result isn't very readable.)
dtEmp.Columns.Add("City", GetType(String)).MaxLength = 20

' Create a calculated column by setting the Expression
' property or passing it as the third argument to the Add method.
dtEmp.Columns.Add("CompleteName", GetType(String), _
    "FirstName + ' ' + LastName")

' Create an ID column.
Dim dcEmpId As New DataColumn("EmpId", GetType(Integer))
dcEmpId.AutoIncrement = True        ' Make it auto-increment.
dcEmpId.AutoIncrementSeed = 1
dcEmpId.AllowDBNull = False          ' Default is True.
dcEmpId.Unique = True                ' All key columns should be unique.
dtEmp.Columns.Add(dcEmpId)           ' Add to Columns collection.

' Make it the primary key.
Dim pkCols() As DataColumn = {dcEmpId}
dtEmp.PrimaryKey = pkCols
' You can also use a more concise syntax, as follows:
dtEmp.PrimaryKey = New DataColumn() {dcEmpId}

' This is a foreign key, but we haven't created the other table yet.
dtEmp.Columns.Add("DeptId", GetType(Integer))

' Add the DataTable to the DataSet.
ds.Tables.Add(dtEmp)
End Sub
```

The MinimumCapacity property offers an opportunity to optimize the performance of the application: the first rows that you create—up to the number defined by this property—won't require any additional memory allocation and therefore will be added more quickly.

As you see in the listing, you define the type of a DataColumn by using a System.Type object. So most of the time you'll use the Visual Basic GetType function for common data types such as String, Integer, and Date. The many remarks explain the several syntax variations that you might adopt when you're adding a new column to the table's schema.

Some columns might require that you set additional properties. For example, you should set the AllowDBNull property to False to reject null values, set the Unique property to True to ensure that all values in the column are unique, or set the MaxLength property for String columns. You can create auto-incrementing columns (which are often used as key columns) by setting the AutoIncrement property to True and optionally setting the AutoIncrementSeed and AutoIncrementStep properties:

```
' Create an ID column.
   Dim dcEmpId As New DataColumn("EmpId", GetType(Integer))
   dcEmpId.AutoIncrement = True          ' Make it auto-increment.
   dcEmpId.AutoIncrementSeed = 1
   dcEmpId.AllowDBNull = False           ' Default is True.
   dcEmpId.Unique = True                 ' All key columns should be unique.
```

You can set the primary key by assigning a DataColumn array to the PrimaryKey property of the DataTable object. In most cases, this array contains just one element, but you can create compound keys made up of multiple columns if necessary:

```
' Create a primary key on the FirstName and LastName columns.
' (Create the DataColumn arrays on the fly.)
dtEmp.PrimaryKey = New DataColumn() _
   {dtEmp.Columns("FirstName"), dtEmp.Columns("LastName")}
```

The DataTable built in the CreateEmployeesTable procedure also contains a calculated column, CompleteName, evaluated as the concatenation of the FirstName and LastName columns. You can assign this expression to the Expression property or pass it as the third argument of the Add method. The "Working with Expressions" section later in this chapter describes which operators and functions you can use in an expression.

> **Note** Interestingly, you can store any type of object in a DataSet, including forms, controls, and your custom objects. When using a column to store an object, you should specify the column type with GetType(Object). If the object is serializable, it will be restored correctly when you write the DataSet to a file and read it back. (If the object isn't serializable, you get an error when you attempt to serialize the DataSet.) Note that the object state isn't rendered correctly as XML when you issue the WriteXml method, however.

✳✳✳

The DataAdapter Class

You can create a DataSet object, load it with data produced by your application (or read from a text file), create constraints and relationships, and define calculated fields. In other words, you can use the DataSet as a sort of scaled-down, client-side database that your code defines and fills with data. While this functionality can be very useful in many scenarios, the majority of .NET applications have to process data coming from a real database, such as Access, SQL Server, or Oracle.

The key to using the DataSet in this way is the DataAdapter object, which works as a connector between the DataSet and the actual data source. The DataAdapter is in charge of filling one or more DataTable objects with data taken from the database so that the application can then close the connection and work in a completely disconnected mode. After the end user has performed all his or her editing chores, the application can reopen the connection and reuse the same DataAdapter object to send changes to the database.

Admittedly, the disconnected nature of the DataSet makes life for us developers more complex, but it greatly improves its versatility, in my opinion. You can now fill a DataTable with data taken from any data source—whether it's SQL Server, a text file, or a mainframe—and process it with the same routines, regardless of its origin. The decoupled architecture based on the DataSet and the DataAdapter makes it possible to read data from one source and send updates to another source, should it be necessary. You have a lot more freedom when working with ADO.NET but also many more responsibilities.

All the code samples that follow assume that a proper connection string has been defined previously and stored in one of the following global variables:

```
' Connection string to Biblio.mdb using the OLE DB .NET Data Provider
Public BiblioConnString As String = "Provider=Microsoft.Jet.OLEDB.4.0;" _
    & "Data Source=C:\Program Files\Microsoft Visual Studio\VB98\Biblio.mdb"
' Connection string to SQL Server's Pubs using the OLE DB .NET Data Provider
Public OledbPubsConnString As String = "Provider=SQLOLEDB.1;Data Source=.;" _
    & "Integrated Security=SSPI:Initial Catalog=Pubs"
' Connection string to Pubs using the SQL Server .NET Data Provider
Public SqlPubsConnString As String = "Data Source=.;" _
    & "Integrated Security=SSPI:Initial Catalog=Pubs"
```

Introducing the DataAdapter

The first thing you need to know about the DataAdapter is that there's actually one DataAdapter class for each .NET data provider, so you have the OleDbDataAdapter and the SqlDataAdapter classes. All DataProvider objects expose the same set of properties and methods because they inherit from the DbDataAdapter abstract class. All the .NET data providers that are to be released in the future will include their own DataAdapter because the DataAdapter must know how to read from and update a specific data source. Except for their names and a few other details—such as how they deal with parameters—you use the OleDbDataAdapter and the SqlDataAdapter in exactly the same way. (See Table 8-6 for their main properties, methods, and events.)

Table 8-6   Main Properties, Methods, and Events of the OleDbDataAdapter and SqlDataAdapter Classes

Category	Name	Description
Properties	SelectCommand	The SQL statement used to read the data source.
	DeleteCommand	The SQL statement used to delete rows in the data source.
	InsertCommand	The SQL statement used to insert rows in the data source.
	UpdateCommand	The SQL statement used to update rows in the data source.
	TableMappings	The collection of table mappings, which maintain the correspondence between columns and tables in the data source and columns and tables in the DataSet.
	MissingMappingAction	The action to take when incoming data doesn't have a matching table or column.
	MissingSchemaAction	The action to take when an existing DataSet schema doesn't match incoming data.
	AcceptChangesDuringFill	Determines whether the AcceptChanges method is called after a DataRow has been added to the DataTable.
Methods	Fill	Adds or refreshes rows in a DataSet with data coming from a DataAdapter or an ADO Recordset.
	FillSchema	Adds a DataTable to the DataSet and configures the schema of the new table based on schema in the data source.
	Update	Updates the data source with the appropriate insert, update, and delete SQL statements.
	GetFillParameters	Gets the parameters set by the user when executing a SQL SELECT statement.
Events	RowUpdating	Fires before sending a SQL command that updates the data source.
	RowUpdated	Fires after sending a SQL command that updates the data source.
	FillError	Fires when an error occurs during a Fill operation.

Reading Data from a Database

The DataAdapter's constructor is overloaded to take zero, one, or two arguments. In its most complete form, you pass to it a SQL SELECT statement (or an ADO.NET Command object containing a SQL SELECT statement) and a Connection object, as in this code snippet:

```
Dim cn As New OleDbConnection(BiblioConnString)
cn.Open()

' Create a DataAdapter that reads and writes the Publishers table.
Dim sql As String = "SELECT * FROM Publishers"
Dim da As New OleDbDataAdapter(sql, cn)
```

Or you can create a DataAdapter and then assign an ADO.NET Command object to its SelectCommand property:

```
da = New OleDbDataAdapter()
da.SelectCommand = New OleDbCommand(sql, cn)
```

✳✳✳

Adding a DataAdapter Object to Our Program

The DataAdapter is the object that connects to the database to fill the memory resident DataSet. Then the DataAdapter connects to the database again to update the data on the basis of the operations performed while the DataSet held the data.

In the past, data processing has been primarily connection-based. Now, in an effort to make multitiered applications more efficient, data processing is turning to a message-based approach that revolves around chunks of information. At the center of this approach is the DataAdapter, which provides a link between a DataSet and its data source that's used to retrieve and save data. It accomplishes these processes by means of requests to the appropriate SQL commands made against the data source.

1. In the toolbox, double-click the SqlDataAdapter control to add a SqlDataAdapter to our program. When the SqlDataAdapter is added, the Data Adapter Configuration Wizard is displayed, as shown in Figure 8-3. Click Next, and follow the steps to configure the new SqlDataAdapter.

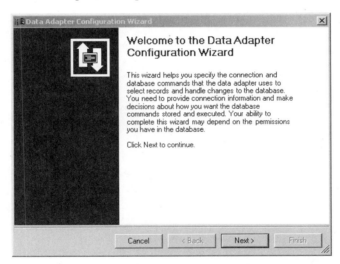

Figure 8-3   The opening screen for the Data Adapter Configuration Wizard.

From *Coding Techniques for Microsoft Visual Basic .NET* by John Connell. pp. 414-421. (Redmond: Microsoft Press. 2002.) Copyright © 2002 by John Connell.

2. Select the database connection to the Northwind database we just built, as shown in Figure 8-4. (Notice that at this point you can still create a new connection by clicking New Connection.) Click Next.

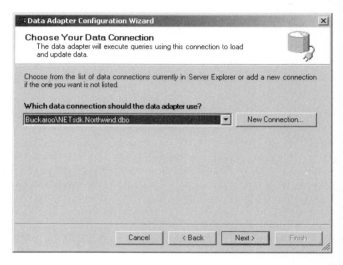

Figure 8-4   Selecting our database connection in the wizard.

Remember when I mentioned that the SQLClient DataAdapter is a bit trickier to set up than the OleDB DataAdapter? This is where the wizard earns its pay. We'll let the wizard add the SQL statements by selecting the Use SQL Statements option, shown in Figure 8-5. Click Next to continue.

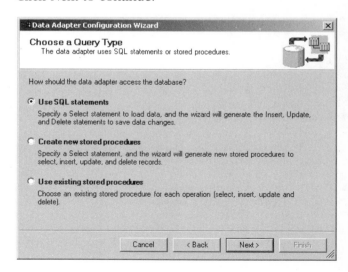

Figure 8-5   Letting the wizard do the work.

3. The next screen, shown in Figure 8-6, lets us use a standard SQL statement to select the data we want the DataAdapter to retrieve from the database. In this case, type in the SELECT statement shown in Figure 8-6, which selects all the records and all the fields from the Customers table in the Northwind database.

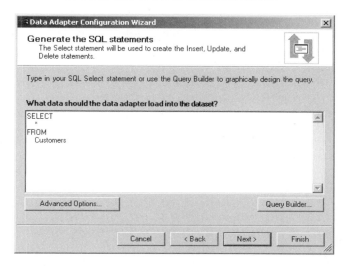

Figure 8-6   Selecting the data we want to retrieve.

4. Click the Advanced Options button. You'll see the Advanced SQL Generation Options dialog box, shown in Figure 8-7. Leave the three options checked by default. You can see that the wizard will generate all the SQL statements for us and also take care of the details of detecting changes between the data in the database and our data set.

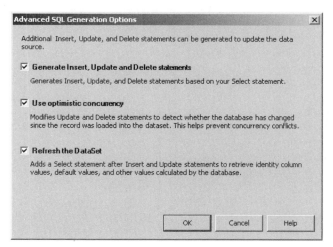

Figure 8-7   Advanced options in the wizard.

5. Click OK to close the Advanced SQL Generation Options dialog box. Now click the Query Builder button to display the Query Builder, shown in Figure 8-8. You can see that all columns for all records are selected. If you wanted to modify the conditions for retrieving data from the database, you would do that here. Let's keep things simple for our first example and leave the SELECT statement as is.

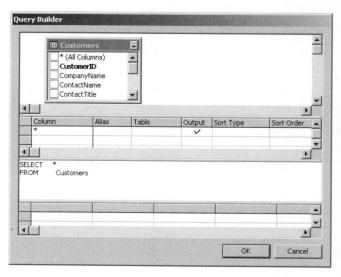

Figure 8-8   The Query Builder.

6. Click OK to close the Query Builder dialog box, and then click Next in the configuration wizard. Using our instructions, the wizard now goes to work constructing the underpinnings of the SQL connection and commands.

7. Click Finish to dismiss the wizard, whose work is now done. We'll soon see that the work was not trivial.

I described the SqlDataAdapter as a bridge between the data source and the memory-resident data set. The wizard added the commands for that bridge, which are illustrated in Figure 8-9.

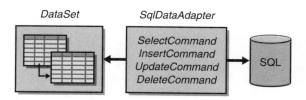

Figure 8-9   The wizard builds its bridge.

Finishing the User Interface

Before we look at the data and the program's code in more detail, let's finish the interface for our form. Add a DataGrid component and two command buttons from the Windows Forms tab of the toolbox to the form. Set the properties for the controls as listed in Table 8-7. Your form should now look something like Figure 8-10.

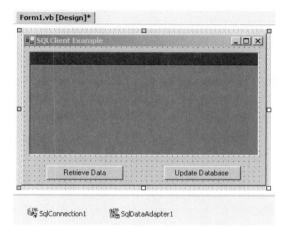

Figure 8-10   Adding interface controls to our form.

> **Tip**   Take a moment and bring up the properties sheet for the Data-Grid control. Click the AutoFormat hyperlink displayed under the list of properties. An Auto Format dialog box will be displayed. Click a few of the formats to get an idea of how you can display your data. When you've finished exploring the various built-in formats, click Cancel to stick with the default view. When you start writing your own .NET database programs for production, you can add a lot of eye candy options for free.

Table 8-7   Properties for the SQLDataGrid Form

Object	Property	Value
Form	Text	SQLClient Example
DataGrid		Defaults
Button	Text	&Retrieve Data
	Name	btnRetrieve
Button	Text	&Update Database
	Name	btnUpdate

A Sneak Preview of Our Data from the DataAdapter

Let's take a quick look at the data that we'll retrieve. Right-click on the form, and then select Preview Data. You can see the data that will be displayed when our program comes to life.

1. In the Data Adapter Preview dialog box, be sure that SqlDataAdapter1 is selected in the Data Adapters list, as shown in Figure 8-11, and then click the Fill Dataset button. This dialog box provides all sorts of information, including how large the data set will be in bytes.

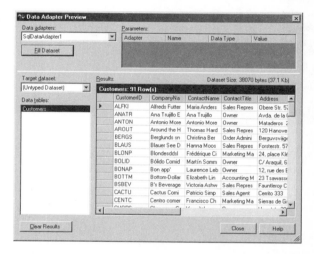

Figure 8-11 Previewing our data in the Data Adapter Preview dialog box.

2. Close the Data Adapter Preview dialog box, right-click the form again, and select Generate Dataset to display the Generate Dataset dialog box, shown in Figure 8-12. Accept the defaults, and then click OK.

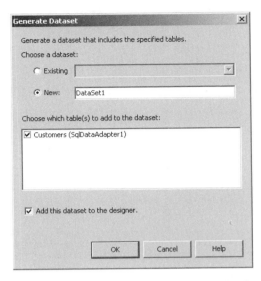

Figure 8-12   The Generate Dataset dialog box.

When you dismiss the Generate Dataset dialog box, a new DataSet object will be added to your program. Right-click on the DataSet object to display its properties dialog box, shown in Figure 8-13.

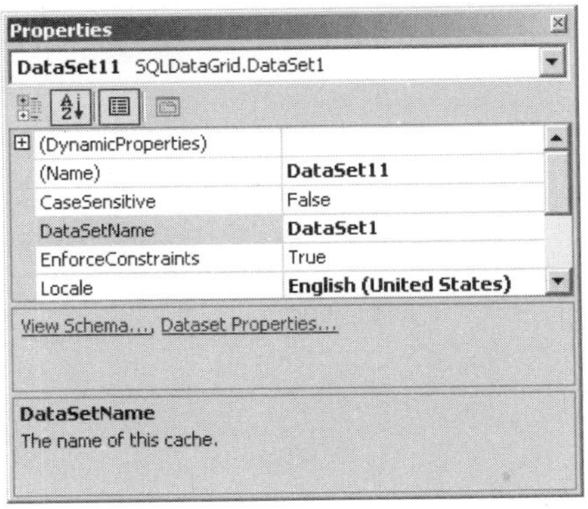

Figure 8-13   The properties dialog box for the new DataSet object.

Notice the two hyperlinks at the bottom of the properties dialog box. One leads you to a view of the database schema; the other shows a view of the data set properties.

3. Click the View Schema hyperlink. You'll see the database schema, which is the template of the table our data adapter will use to pull the records from the database. The schema is shown in Figure 8-14.

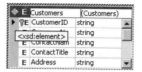

Figure 8-14   The database schema.

Part IV

ASP.NET

Reading 9

ASP.NET and Web Services

We're now going to look at how we can use Visual Basic .NET to render Web pages, using the same techniques we've learned when building a Windows Forms application. I'll also describe Web services, which are used to communicate with interfaces of remote components. If the use of Web services sounds strange, hang on until you reach the second part of the reading. Web services are going to become the next big thing on the Internet, and Microsoft .NET is poised to make this happen.

Web Forms (the controls and classes .NET provides for building Web pages) and Web services (programmable application logic accessible by standard Internet protocols) are part of the framework for Internet functionality included in Visual Basic .NET and are known by the umbrella term ASP.NET. If you have previously worked with Active Server Pages (ASP), you will be surprised at how much different and more efficient ASP.NET is. ASP.NET encompasses a completely new programming object model. It replaces the Visual Basic 6 WebClasses and DHTML pages. Not only that, but the ASP.NET programming model is also more consistent and easier to use.

A Look Back at ASP

ASP is a powerful model and is the right tool for most jobs. The information systems department I manage has written and is running more than 100 ASP pages that clients (internal and external) use to access various pieces of functionality within our organization. But if you've had the chance to work with ASP, you know that it has some drawbacks. You know that you have to write code to

From *Coding Techniques for Microsoft Visual Basic .NET* by John Connell. pp. 497-548. (Redmond: Microsoft Press. 2002.) Copyright © 2002 by John Connell.

perform any operation, and you quickly notice that you are dealing with spaghetti code. The unstructured nature of ASP code—where everything is placed in an ASP page—often offends purists. Yes, you can use *include* statements, but doing that requires more work. You usually find ASP logic script code mixed with HTML tags for presentation. This mix, of course, does not help readability or debugging, and because ASP uses interpreted script, performance problems arise in some cases. But in spite of the difficulties, ASP has evolved to become the foremost tool in the Windows-oriented Web programmer's toolbox.

One thing that always bites Web developers is the need for multiple browser support. When we design ASP pages for external clients, we must either program to the lowest common denominator of browser or write extra classes to support each browser the clients might use. Not only that, but no state management is available unless the programmer writes acres of code to persist values from page to page. Of course, ASP has the *Application* and *Session* objects, but there are two potential problems with these. First, they make scaling a high-volume site difficult. Second, because they are run on the server, if the host has a server farm, you can't be sure that the next page won't be served from a completely different machine. Luckily, ASP.NET solves these thorny problems.

Why ASP.NET?

The compelling nature of ASP.NET will draw Web programmers toward its orbit for the following reasons:

- **Language independence.** ASP.NET allows you to use compiled languages, providing better performance and cross-language compatibility.

- **Simplified development.** ASP.NET makes even the richest pages straightforward and easy to write.

- **Separation of code and content.** Each Web Form has a code module with the same name but with the extension .vb. This so-called *code behind the page* contains the program logic code, while the Web Form contains the visual components.

- **Improved scalability.** New session-state features make it easy to create Web Forms that work on Web server farms (multiple servers).

- **Support for multiple clients.** ASP.NET controls can automatically detect the client and optimize themselves for a consistent look and feel. You no longer have to write separate code for different browsers.

- **New Web Forms controls.** The new controls can output HTML 3.2 for down-level browsers while taking advantage of the runtime libraries for enhanced interactivity on richer clients. Our programs can now output to a whole new range of platforms such as wireless phones, palm pilots, and handheld pagers and devices.

- **Server-side processing.** ASP.NET changes each page into a server-side object. More properties, methods, and events can be used with your code to create content dynamically. The *runat="server"* attribute converts the HTML element into a server-side control that is visible and therefore programmable within ASP.NET on the server. Events raised by Web Form controls are detected, and the appropriate code is executed on the server in response to these events.

> **Note**   ASP.NET is written entirely in the new C# language. All ASP.NET pages have the .aspx file extension, which allows both .asp and .aspx files to be run on the same machine under the existing ASP runtime.

Getting from There to Here

In some ways, everything you've learned in this book up to now has poised us to write ASP.NET programs. You will soon see how similar that is to creating Windows Forms programs in .NET. You drag and drop controls and set properties in the same manner you do with Windows Forms. You use the technologies you've learned about so far—the .NET Framework; object-oriented programming; events, properties, and methods; ADO.NET; and XML—and put them together in Web Forms.

When I hire a new programmer, I'm amazed at how many applicants are proud to say they understand Visual Basic. The applicants describe how they know various esoteric uses of items such as control arrays or undocumented memory pointers. What they fail to realize is that I'm looking for someone that understands database design, n-tier architecture, ActiveX Data Objects (ADO), XML, HTML, Dynamic HTML (DHTML), object-oriented programming, Transmission Control Protocol/Internet Protocol (TCP/IP), the Open Systems Interconnection (OSI) protocol stack, custom ActiveX control construction, network security, firewalls, and so

(continued)

Getting from There to Here   *(continued)*

---

on. Many of these technologies and concepts are implemented in Visual Basic. Learning the language is only the first part—not the be-all and end-all, but rather a beginning.

While it's easy to find people who know Visual Basic, it's difficult to find people who understand the gestalt of how programs operate in a distributed environment. And if you look back at how much ground we've covered in this book to get to this point, you might be pleasantly surprised at how most of what you've learned will be directly applicable to writing ASP.NET programs.

Several years ago, when graphical tools such as Visual Basic came on the scene, many software developers were concerned that programming would become so easy that they would be out of a job. After all, even accountants could drag buttons to a form and set properties. However, quite the opposite has happened. Programming has become exponentially more abstract. It turns out that we need the graphical capabilities so that we can concentrate on application design and fitting the pieces together. A Visual Basic .NET program has many moving parts—especially programs running on the Internet. Luckily, Visual Basic .NET provides some very powerful graphical tools that help get Web sites up and running quickly.

Our First Web Form

To give you an immediate sense of how powerful Web Forms are, we'll create a simple program that uses the new calendar control. The program will display a calendar from which the user must select a date before submitting the page. If a date is not selected, a field validator will notify the user and the page won't be sent.

Start a new ASP.NET Web application project with the name WebForms, as shown in Figure 9-1. Notice that the location of the file will be the local host. If you are running Internet Information Services (IIS) or Personal Web Server on the same machine as Visual Studio .NET, the local host will usually be C:\Inetpub\wwwroot.

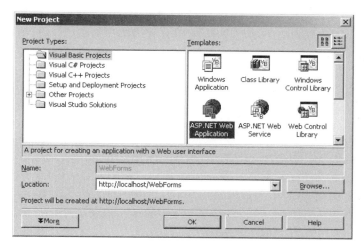

Figure 9-1   Create an ASP.NET Web application named WebForms.

The default workspace for an ASP.NET Web application, shown in Figure 9-2, looks a bit different from what we're used to seeing. The toolbars are slightly different, and the design surface is white, but the overall feel is the same. (The message you see on the form is not part of our application; it's simply a note from Visual Basic .NET telling us which layout mode is being used.)

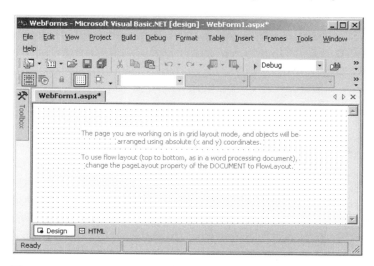

Figure 9-2   The default ASP.NET Web application workspace.

Tip   To change the layout of the ASP.NET Web application workspace, right-click on the display area and select Properties. When the Document Property Pages dialog box appears, you can change the page layout. The page layout options you use will be primarily a matter of preference. The FlowLayout setting allows the user to add text and hard paragraph breaks to the page, which is converted into HTML code. When the default GridLayout setting is selected, the controls are placed on the surface of the page but are not interspersed with HTML code, as happens in FlowLayout. If you have ever used Microsoft FrontPage, you are familiar with the WYSIWYG style, which is a huge improvement over earlier designs.

The Solution Explorer reveals that a few more files are required when developing Web Forms rather than Windows Forms, as you can see in Figure 9-3. The classes that include the visual components are located in the *System.Web* namespace. Table 9-1 lists and describes the files in our Web-Forms project.

Figure 9-3   Web Forms applications have more files than Windows Forms applications.

Table 9-1   The Files in Our WebForms Project

File	Description
AssemblyInfo.vb	An optional project information file that contains metadata about the assemblies in a project, such as name, version, and culture information.
Web.config	An XML-based file that contains configuration information for ASP.NET resources.
Global.asax	An optional file for handling application-level events. This file resides in the root directory of an ASP.NET application. When deployed, this project's WebService1.dll file will contain the "code-behind" file associated with the .asax file. I'll be covering code-behind files shortly.
WebForms.vsdisco	An optional XML-based file that contains links (URLs) to resources providing discovery information for a Web service.
WebForm1.aspx	The user interface file we are now working with.

New Server Controls

If you take a look at the Web Forms tab in the toolbox, shown in Figure 9-4, you can see the names of quite a few new controls. These controls are referred to as *server controls* and are similar to the Windows Forms controls we've been working with. Each control provides a consistent set of properties and methods. In addition, these controls manage state, can be manipulated in code, and provide a limited set of events to which we can add our program logic.

Figure 9-4   Web Forms server controls.

Another set of controls available for Web Forms appears on the HTML tab, shown in Figure 9-5. These controls are referred to as *HTML server controls*. Each of these controls is basically a one-to-one match for the HTML controls found on current Web pages. These controls are not sophisticated and have no intelligence for handling how they appear with various browsers. HTML server controls were provided to update existing pages to the new server controls. Unless you are updating pages already created, I'd suggest you stick with the server controls on the Web Forms tab.

Figure 9-5   HTML server controls.

ASP.NET server controls are incredibly powerful. They have a more consistent and flexible object model than the ASP object model that is familiar to classic Visual Basic programmers. When a control is served to the client, it is rendered in HTML automatically. Server controls contain automatic browser detection logic and can customize and optimize their output. The new controls can also perform data binding.

In addition to the HTML server controls and the Web Forms server controls, we also have new validation controls. Field validation has always been the bane of ASP developers. Addressing the problem required a few more acres of code, but that's no longer the case. The validation controls are wired to a control such as a text box, and they take care of our needs, such as constraints on numeric-only or required fields.

Let's go ahead and add controls from the Web Forms tab to our designer. Add a text box, a calendar, a button, and a RequiredFieldValidator. Position the controls roughly as shown in Figure 9-6.

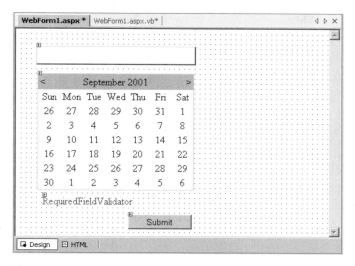

Figure 9-6   Add the controls shown here.

The HTML Presentation Template

Notice the Design and HTML options at the bottom of the designer window. A Web Form consists of two pieces: an HTML-based template that contains the layout of the page, and a code module that contains the code behind the page. Click the HTML tab to see the following code that will be sent to a browser. The code will look familiar to those of you who have worked with ASP. You really don't need to know how to read HTML, but this code provides insight into how Web Forms do their magic.

```
<%@ Page Language="vb" AutoEventWireup="false"
  Codebehind="WebForm1.aspx.vb" Inherits="WebForms.WebForm1"%>
<!DOCTYPE HTML PUBLIC "-//W3C//DTD HTML 4.0 Transitional//EN">
<HTML>
  <HEAD>
    <title></title>
    <meta name="GENERATOR" content=
      "Microsoft Visual Studio.NET 7.0">
    <meta name="CODE_LANGUAGE" content="Visual Basic 7.0">
    <meta name="vs_defaultClientScript" content="JavaScript">
    <meta name="vs_targetSchema"
      content="http://schemas.microsoft.com/intellisense/ie5">
  </HEAD>
  <body MS_POSITIONING="GridLayout">
    <form id="Form1" method="post" runat="server">
      <asp:TextBox id="TextBox1" style="Z-INDEX: 101;
```

(continued)

```
        LEFT: 32px; POSITION: absolute; TOP: 27px"
        runat="server" Width="233px"></asp:TextBox>
      <asp:Calendar id="Calendar1" style="Z-INDEX: 102;
        LEFT: 35px; POSITION: absolute; TOP: 61px"
        runat="server" Width="233px"></asp:Calendar>
      <asp:RequiredFieldValidator id="RequiredFieldValidator1"
        style="Z-INDEX: 103; LEFT: 44px; POSITION: absolute;
        TOP: 263px" runat="server"
        ErrorMessage="RequiredFieldValidator">
      </asp:RequiredFieldValidator>
      <asp:Button id="Button1" style="Z-INDEX: 104;
        LEFT: 150px; POSITION: absolute; TOP: 295px"
        runat="server" Width="112px" Text="Submit"></asp:Button>
    </form>
  </body>
</HTML>
```

The Structure of a Web Form

Visual Basic .NET Web Forms are based on a Microsoft ASP.NET technology in which code that runs on the server dynamically generates Web page output to the client browser. Take a look at the first line with the *@Page* directive.

```
<%@ Page Language="vb" AutoEventWireup="false"
  Codebehind="WebForm1.aspx.vb" Inherits="WebForms.WebForm1"%>
```

Web Forms pages are built on the ASP.NET Page framework, which means that each Web Forms page is an object that derives from the ASP.NET *Page* class. *Page* objects are compiled and automatically cached.

A *Page* object also acts as a container for the various controls. When a user requests a Web Forms page from a server, the Page framework runs the Web Forms *Page* object and all the individual controls on it. It then converts the output of the *Page* class and of the controls to HTML that can be rendered in a browser. In addition, the Page framework supports controls that can be programmed for user interaction with your Web Forms pages. User actions in a form are captured and processed by the Page framework in a way that lets you treat them as standard events.

The *@Page* directive tag also defines characteristics of the page. First of all, the directive indicates that the language will be Visual Basic (instead of C#, for example). *AutoEventWireUp* determines whether the *Page_Load* event handler is automatically wired to the *OnPageLoad* event. Setting the value to False means that we need to provide our own code for this handler if required.

The next statement is the rather cryptic *Codebehind = "WebForm.aspx.vb"*. This statement is necessary because the code that drives the page is actually placed in another file. This file is the code behind the interface defined in WebForm1.aspx. I'll examine that file in detail shortly, but briefly, it contains a class definition that is used as the base class for the Web Forms page. This particular base class will be used in conjunction with code in this file to generate the HTML that reaches the user. Web Forms essentially separate the user interface (WebForm.aspx) from the code that implements it (Web-Form.aspx.vb). The Web Forms Page framework and the relationships between these files are shown in Figure 9-7.

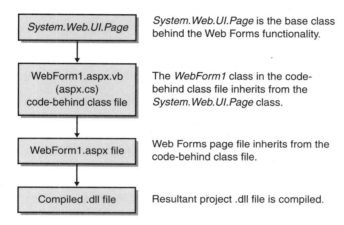

Figure 9-7   The relationships between the Web Forms Page framework files.

Within the ASP.NET *Page* class model, the entire Web Forms page is really an executable program that generates output that is then sent to the browser. The ASP.NET *Page* class model makes developing a Web Forms application identical to developing a Windows Forms application, and it is a quantum leap in functionality for ASP developers. Separating our class, WebForm1.aspx.vb, as the code-behind file is not only easier to debug (trust me on this one), but you can now let the designers work on the user interface for a Web page while the programmers work on the code behind it all.

Our code-behind class *WebForm1* inherits from the *Page* class that lives in the *System.Web.UI* namespace. The *Page* class contains the properties, methods, and events in the Web Forms page framework.

```
Public Class WebForm1
    Inherits System.Web.UI.Page
```

Our user interface file, WebForm1.aspx, inherits from the code-behind class.

```
<%@ Page Language="vb" AutoEventWireup="false"
  Codebehind="WebForm1.aspx.vb" Inherits="WebForms.WebForm1"%>
```

Both files are then compiled into a DLL that is run from the server.

The Controls

Web Forms server controls are referenced with the syntax *<asp:ControlName>*. All of the properties of the control are set within the *<asp:ControlName ....>* and *</asp:ControlName>* tags. The calendar control is given an ID of Calendar1, the default name of the calendar when it's drawn on the form. Then some style and location properties are set. Finally the critical *runat="server"* attribute is provided, which makes all of this code work.

```
<asp:Calendar id="Calendar1" style="Z-INDEX: 102;
  LEFT: 35px; POSITION: absolute; TOP: 61px"
  runat="server" Width="233px"></asp:Calendar>
```

If the *runat="server"* attribute is left out, we are effectively providing client-side code, which will fail miserably if the control uses any server-side style coding. Note that the syntax for controls is based on XML, so you'll get an error if you inadvertently omit the closing tags.

The beauty of Web Forms server controls is that we have full access to their properties and events through the Properties window (just as we do with their Windows Forms brethren) and can receive instant feedback in the code or design environment whenever we make changes.

Viewing the Code-Behind File

Return to Design mode and choose Code from the View menu to display the code-behind file, WebForm1.aspx.vb. This file is where the Visual Basic .NET code we use to handle the logic for the page lives. By now you should be quite familiar with this code, so I won't spend time on it here.

```
Public Class WebForm1
    Inherits System.Web.UI.Page
    Protected WithEvents Calendar1 As _
        System.Web.UI.WebControls.Calendar
    Protected WithEvents TextBox1 As _
        System.Web.UI.WebControls.TextBox
    Protected WithEvents Button1 As _
        System.Web.UI.WebControls.Button
    Protected WithEvents RequiredFieldValidator1 As _
        System.Web.UI.WebControls.RequiredFieldValidator

#Region " Web Form Designer Generated Code "

    'This call is required by the Web Form Designer
    <System.Diagnostics.DebuggerStepThrough()> _
    Private Sub InitializeComponent()

    End Sub
```

(continued)

```
Private Sub Page_Init(ByVal sender As System.Object, _
    ByVal e As System.EventArgs) Handles MyBase.Init
    'CODEGEN: This method call is required by the
    ' Web Form Designer.
    'Do not modify it using the code editor.
    InitializeComponent()
End Sub

#End Region

Private Sub Page_Load(ByVal sender As System.Object, _
    ByVal e As System.EventArgs) Handles MyBase.Load
    'Put user code to initialize the page here
End Sub
End Class
```

Setting the Properties on Our Web Page

Return to the design WebForm1.aspx form, and right-click the calendar control. Select Auto Format to bring up the Calendar Auto Format dialog box, shown in Figure 9-8. Select the Professional 1 scheme, and then click OK. Setting this property will make our page look pretty sophisticated.

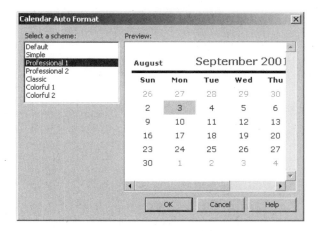

Figure 9-8   The Professional 1 scheme provides a sophisticated look for a Web page.

Arrange the controls as shown in Figure 9-9, and then set the properties for the controls as listed in Table 9-2.

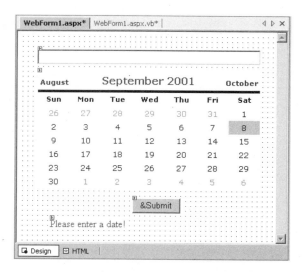

Figure 9-9 Arrange the controls as shown here.

Table 9-2 Properties for the WebForm Controls

Object	Property	Value
Text box	*ID* (like *Name* in Windows)	tbDate
Calendar	Keep defaults	
Button	*ID*	btnSubmit
	Text	&Submit
RequiredFieldValidator1	*ControlToValidate*	tbDate (from the drop-down list)
	ErrorMessage	"Please enter a date!"

Adding the Calendar Control Code

Double-click the calendar control. The template for the *SelectionChanged* event handler will be created automatically. Add a single line of code that will take the date the user selects and display it in the text box. Notice that several built-in formats are available for us. In this example, we'll use the *ToLongDateString* format.

```
Private Sub Calendar1_SelectionChanged( _
    ByVal sender As System.Object,_
    ByVal e As System.EventArgs) _
```

(continued)

```
Handles Calendar1.SelectionChanged

    tbDate.Text = Calendar1.SelectedDate.ToLongDateString

End Sub
```

Running the Web Form

Go ahead and run the Web Form by pressing F5. The browser is invoked, and your page is displayed, as you can see in Figure 9-10. Click the Submit button without selecting a date. Notice that the RequiredFieldValidator becomes visible and displays our error message. No code was required to accomplish this, which will make any grizzled ASP programmer smile. We were able to display this page—with a sophisticated calendar, text box, button, and field validation control—with only a single line of code. This is nothing short of amazing.

Figure 9-10   The WebForms application in action.

When the Submit button is clicked, the date is submitted back to the server. By default, a button control on a Web Form application is a submit button that posts data back to the server. You can provide an event handler for the *Click* event to programmatically control the actions performed when a submit button is clicked. In our case, we didn't write any code for the button. Still, when it is pressed, it attempts to post data back to the server. It couldn't here because the required field *tbDate* is empty.

Now select a date from the calendar, and click the Submit button once more. This time we are successful. The date is displayed in the text box in the long date format, as you can see in Figure 9-11.

Figure 9-11 The text box shows dates in the long date format.

Examining the HTML Sent to the Browser

Run the WebForms application again, but before you select a date, click the View Source menu option from Internet Explorer. I mentioned that ASP.NET pages and controls can remember their state between calls to the server. Let's see how this magic is accomplished. Examine the first few lines of the HTML our program sent to the browser.

```
<!DOCTYPE HTML PUBLIC "-//W3C//DTD HTML 4.0 Transitional//EN">
<HTML>
  <HEAD>
    <title></title>
      <meta name="GENERATOR" content="Microsoft Visual
        Studio.NET 7.0">
      <meta name="CODE_LANGUAGE" content="Visual Basic 7.0">
      <meta name="vs_defaultClientScript"
        content="JavaScript">
      <meta name="vs_targetSchema"
        content="http://schemas.microsoft.com/intellisense/ie5">
  </HEAD>
  <body MS_POSITIONING="GridLayout">
    <form name="Form1" method="post" action="WebForm1.aspx"
      language="javascript" onsubmit="ValidatorOnSubmit();"
      id="Form1">
<input type="hidden" name="__VIEWSTATE" value="dDwtMzQ0NzE0MzI40zs" />
```

Notice the text string in the hidden input field with the name _VIEWSTATE_. It is the hidden _VIEWSTATE_ field that encapsulates the state of the form. This information is used when the form is posted back to the server to re-create the user interface, keep track of changes, and so on. Essentially it holds the state of the form and controls.

Click a date on the calendar, and examine the source code from the browser again. Notice that the _VIEWSTATE_ string has grown quite a bit. It contains the selected date, changes to the calendar, and other information. As you can imagine, on sophisticated Web forms, this string can grow quite large.

```
<input type="hidden" name="__VIEWSTATE" value="dDwtMzQ0NzE0M
zI403Q802w8aTwxPjs+02w8dDw7bDxpPDM+0z47bDx0PEAwPHA8cDxsPFNEO
z47bDxsPFN5c3R1bS5EYXR1VG1tZSwgbXNjb3JsaWIsIFZ1cnNppb249MS4wL
jI0MTEuMCwgQ3VsdHVyZT1uZXV0cmFsLCBQdWJsaWNLZX1Ub2t1bj1iNzdhN
WM1NjE5MzR1MDg5PDIwMDEtMDktMjY+0z47Pj47Pjs70zs70zs70zs+0zs+0
z4+0z4+0z4=" />
```

The _VIEWSTATE_ string will remember the form's state and thus any values that have been submitted. It's important to keep in mind that the server has nothing to do with maintaining this state information. Remembering the values is performed entirely by the _VIEWSTATE_ string. The server requires no resources to maintain the form's state and absolutely no state is being stored on the server. Instead, the values are posted to the server using standard methods. When the server posts back to the page, the _VIEWSTATE_ string prepopulates the form with the previous values.

The _VIEWSTATE_ string is an elegant method of storing a Web page's state. Because HTTP is a stateless protocol, Web pages are created from scratch each and every time a round trip between the server and the client occurs. After a Web page is served, the server is finished with the page and no further connection with the client is maintained. Web pages are stateless, and no values from Web page variables are maintained on the server. Not only that, but also in a Web server environment in which a user might get one page from one server and the next page from a totally different server (because of load balancing), using _VIEWSTATE_ permits the page to hold its own state. ASP.NET gets around this serious limitation and behaves as though the server remembers each and every detail of each page.

The Web Form state information is tokenized, which means it is translated into a compressed form. And because HTTP does not permit binary objects to be sent, the tokens are all text based. Preliminary tests at Microsoft have revealed that even with very long _VIEWSTATE_ strings, performance is comparable to other more complex state management techniques.

> **Note** ASP.NET does not support Visual Basic Scripting Edition. The default language is Visual Basic. ASP.NET code is compiled into intermediate language and then executed by the common language runtime.

If you look at the rest of the source code that's sent to the browser, you'll notice that each of our Web Forms controls is converted to HTML for display in the browser. We drew the text box on the Web Form, but the ASP.NET run-time engine did all the coding for us.

```
<input name="tbDate" type="text" readonly="readonly"
  id="tbDate" style="border-style:Outset;height:26px;
  width:350px;LEFT: 38px; POSITION: absolute; TOP: 34px" />
```

For the sake of brevity, I'll show only a portion of the HTML used to generate the calendar. We are several levels of abstraction removed from having to provide all this code ourselves. We can now program a consistent object model of a graphical control, yet the ASP.NET run-time engine will take our graphical calendar control and convert it to HTML 3.2 to ensure that it can be consistently displayed on even older browsers. We can draw a calendar control on our Web Form, and that control is converted to HTML for us. Cool.

```
<table id="Calendar1" cellspacing="0" cellpadding="2"
  bordercolor="White" border="0" style="color:Black;
  background-color:White;border-color:White;border-width:1px;
  border-style:solid;font-family:Verdana;font-size:9pt;
  height:190px;width:350px;border-collapse:collapse;LEFT: 34px;
  POSITION: absolute; TOP: 72px">
<tr><td colspan="7" style="background-color:White;
  border-color:Black;border-width:4px;border-style:solid;">
  <table cellspacing="0" border="0" style="color:#333399;
  font-family:Verdana;font-size:12pt;font-weight:bold;
  width:100%;border-collapse:collapse;">
    <tr><td valign="Bottom" style="color:#333333;font-size:8pt;
      font-weight:bold;width:15%;">
```

Building a Loan Payment Calculator

Where I work, we've built a Web-based loan origination system. Clients can enter various parameters and see which loan products they qualify for. Then we pass some XML files to Fannie Mae for credit analysis and receive our response in XML. This data is parsed, and an e-mail message is sent back to the client. We then use Simple Object Access Protocol (SOAP) to pass e-mail messages around to the various internal departments. This system reduces the time it takes to return an acknowledgment to the user from days to a few minutes. Best of all, this system is available 24 hours a day, 7 days a week.

Let's build a very simple online calculator that includes user interaction. The program will let users enter the amount they want to borrow, an interest rate, and the term (in months) over which they want to repay the loan. The finished product is shown in Figure 9-12.

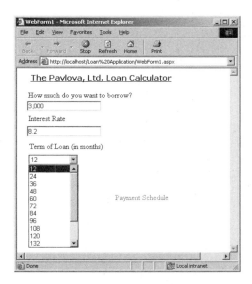

Figure 9-12 The finished online calculator application.

We will have to write some validation code to ensure the information the user enters is valid. We will also add a hyperlink control to enable navigation to another page, one that displays the loan payment schedule. The hyperlink will be disabled until legitimate information is entered and a monthly payment is calculated. When the user clicks the Calculate button and the payment is calculated, the Payment Schedule hyperlink is enabled and the user can navigate to another page, as shown in Figure 9-13.

Notice in Figure 9-14 that on the loan payment schedule page, the values from the first page are retained and are used to populate a Web Forms data grid. We can show some useful information such as how much of the payment goes to principal and how much to interest. The PrincipalRemaining and PaidToDate columns provide a good roadmap of how much of the loan is left to be paid. We will build a table from scratch, populate it with the loan information, and bind it to the data grid. This program will also demonstrate how to navigate from page to page as well as how to cache variables from one page to use on another.

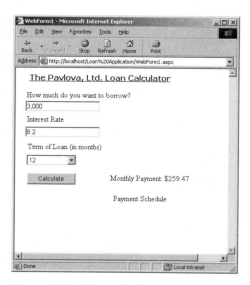

Figure 9-13   The calculator application enables the Payment Schedule hyperlink after it calculates a payment.

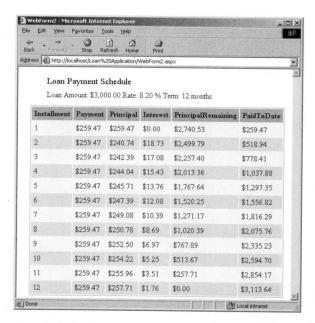

Figure 9-14   The calculated values populate a Web Forms data grid.

Building Our Loan Application Project

Start a new Web Forms project and call it Loan Application. On the default form, add the controls listed in Table 9-3 and set their properties as described. The form should look something like Figure 9-15.

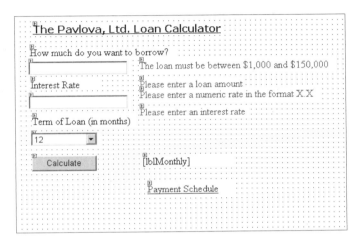

Figure 9-15   Your form should look similar to this.

Table 9-3   **Properties for the Loan Application Controls**

Object	Property	Value
Label	*Name*	lblTitle
	Font	Verdana
	Bold	True
	Underlined	True
	Text	The Pavlova, Ltd. Loan Calculator
Label	*Name*	lblAmount
	Text	How much do you want to borrow?
Text box	*Name*	tbAmount
	Text	""
Label	*Name*	lblRate
	Text	Interest Rate
Text box	*Name*	tbRate
	Text	""

(continued)

Table 9-3 Properties for the Loan Application Controls *(continued)*

Object	Property	Value
Label	*Name*	lblTerm
	Text	Term of Loan (in months)
Drop-down list	*Name*	ddlTerm
Button	*Name*	btnCalculate
	Text	Calculate
Label	*Name*	lblMonthly
	Text	""
Range validator	*ID*	rvAmount
	ControlToValidate	tbAmount
	MaximumValue	150000
	MinimumValue	1000
	ErrorMessage	The loan must be between $1,000 and $150,000
	Type	Currency
Required field validator	*ID*	rfvAmount
	ControlToValidate	tbAmount
	ErrorMessage	Please enter a loan amount
Regular expression validator	*ID*	revRate
	ControlToValidate	tbRate
	ErrorMessage	Please enter a numeric rate in the format X.X
	ValidationExpression	\d*[.]{0,1}\d*
Required field validator	*ID*	rfvRate
	ControlToValidate	tbRate
	ErrorMessage	Please enter an interest rate
Hyperlink	*ID*	hlSchedule
	Text	Payment Schedule

We want to add the months in which to repay the loan to the drop-down list. Right-click the drop-down list, and then select Properties. Select the Items property box and then click the ellipsis to display the ListItem Collection Editor dialog box. Add the numbers shown in Figure 9-16, representing 15 years—from 12 through 180 months.

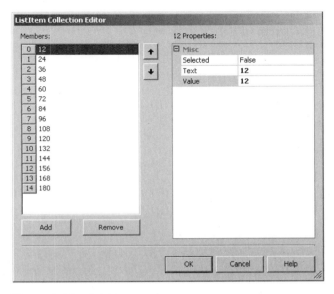

Figure 9-16   Add these values.

Adding Code to the Code-Behind Form

Right-click on the designer surface and select View Code to open the file WebForm1.aspx.vb, which is our code-behind form. Each .aspx Web Form that we create has its associated .aspx.vb code module behind it. This module contains our business logic. The relationship between the two forms is shown in Figure 9-17.

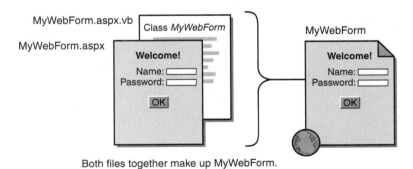

Both files together make up MyWebForm.

Figure 9-17   The relationship between a Web Form and its code-behind form.

WebForm1.aspx.vb contains the code that responds to events fired from the Web Form. Add these two *Imports* statements before the WebForm1 class statement.

```
Imports System.Math
Imports System.Web.Caching

Public Class WebForm1
    Inherits System.Web.UI.Page
```

Now add the following code to the *Page_Load* event handler. This code simply initializes our drop-down list and disables the hyperlink.

```
Private Sub Page_Load(ByVal sender As System.Object, _
    ByVal e As System.EventArgs) Handles MyBase.Load

    'Put user code to initialize the page here

    If Not IsPostBack Then
        ddlTerm.SelectedIndex = 0
        hlSchedule.Enabled = False
    End If
End Sub

Private Sub btnCalculate_Click(ByVal sender As System.Object, _
    ByVal e As System.EventArgs) Handles btnCalculate.Click

    calculatePayment()
    hlSchedule.Enabled = True
End Sub

Private Sub calculatePayment()
    Dim iLoanAmount As Integer = CInt(tbAmount.Text)
    Dim sRate As Single = (CSng(tbRate.Text) / 100)
    Dim iterm As Integer = CInt(ddlTerm.SelectedItem.Value)

    Dim sPayment As Single = Pmt(sRate / 12, iterm, _
        -iLoanAmount, 0, DueDate.BegOfPeriod)

    lblMonthly.Text = "Monthly Payment: " & _
        Math.Round(sPayment, 2).ToString("C")

    Cache("LoanAmount") = iLoanAmount
    Cache("Rate") = sRate
    Cache("Term") = iterm
    Cache("Payment") = Math.Round(sPayment, 2)
End Sub
```

The Life of a Web Form

A Web Form has four basic states in its life cycle—initialization, loading the page, event handling, and clearing up resources.

- **Page initialization.** The *Page_Init* event is fired when a page is initialized. At this point, controls perform all initialization required to create and set up each instance.

- **Page load.** The *Page_Load* event occurs after initialization. Here the page checks to see whether it is being loaded for the first time. It also performs data binding, reads and updates control properties, and restores the state saved from a previous client request.

- **Event handling.** Every action on a Web Form fires an event that goes to the server. Essentially there are two views of a Web Form—client view and server view. All processing of data is performed on the server. When an event is fired, the event goes to the server and returns the corresponding data.

- **Cleanup.** This stage is the last one to occur when a form is ready to be discarded. The *Page_Unload* event fires and does such cleanup work as closing files, closing database connections, and discarding objects.

How Our Program Works

When the *Page_Load* event fires, all the controls have been instantiated. There are tasks (such as initializing controls) that we want to perform only when the page first loads. Using the *Page* class's *IsPostBack* property, we can do just that. *IsPostBack* gets a value indicating whether the page is being loaded in response to a client postback or whether it is being loaded and accessed for the first time. If the page load is not in response to a client postback, we know that the page is being loaded for the first time. Here we simply select the first item in our drop-down list (so that we have a current value) and disable the hyperlink control.

```
Private Sub Page_Load(ByVal sender As System.Object, _
    ByVal e As System.EventArgs) Handles MyBase.Load

    'Put user code to initialize the page here

    If Not IsPostBack Then
        ddlTerm.SelectedIndex = 0
        hlSchedule.Enabled = False
    End If
End Sub
```

When the user clicks the Calculate button, our validation controls perk up their ears. If any field is empty or contains an invalid value, the user is prompted to fix whatever is wrong and the code in the button's *Click* event does not fire. When all the validation criteria are met, the routine *calculatePayment* is called. We know that when this routine is called, we will receive a solid value because we validated each of the fields.

I like to use controls such as drop-down lists with predefined values. The man-machine interface is the most difficult to program because users can do anything imaginable—and many things unimaginable. But by populating a drop-down list with valid data, users can select only a valid value.

```
Private Sub btnCalculate_Click(ByVal sender As System.Object, _
    ByVal e As System.EventArgs) Handles btnCalculate.Click

        calculatePayment()
        hlSchedule.Enabled = True
End Sub
```

The *calculatePayment* routine does the heavy lifting. We can initialize the first three variables based on values in the form's controls. Remember, these variables are stored as text values, so we simply cast them as the correct numeric values of integer or single. The rate must be divided by 100 because a rate of 8.2 is really 0.082 when used in calculations.

```
Private Sub calculatePayment()
    Dim iLoanAmount As Integer = CInt(tbAmount.Text)
    Dim sRate As Single = (CSng(tbRate.Text) / 100)
    Dim iterm As Integer = CInt(ddlTerm.SelectedItem.Value)
```

Determining the payment is simple because Visual Basic .NET has a built-in financial function named *Pmt*. This function returns a *Double* value (we use a *Single* in our code) specifying the payment for an annuity on the basis of periodic, fixed payments and a fixed interest rate. We pass in the value of the variables taken from the Web Form and place them as parameters to the *Pmt* function. The loan amount is given a negative sign because it returns a negative amount, so we make it positive. There is no future value so that value is 0.

```
PMT(RATE, Number of Periods, Loan Amount, _
    Future Value, Due Date)
```

We again take advantage of the new Visual Basic .NET feature of dimming and initializing this variable on the same line.

```
Dim sPayment As Single = Pmt(sRate / 12, iterm, _
    -iLoanAmount, 0, DueDate.BegOfPeriod)
```

We imported the Math library because we wanted the *Round* method that it includes. This method will display our value with only two decimal values instead of 10, which would normally be shown. Rounding values like this is an added touch that separates professional software from the rest.

```
lblMonthly.Text = "Monthly Payment: " & _
    Math.Round(sPayment, 2).ToString("C")
```

It's necessary to retain the values we got from this form and pass them to another form that will display the payment schedule. That bit of work is simple with the *Cache* class, which implements the cache for a Web Forms application. One instance of this class is created per application domain, and it remains valid as long as the application domain remains active. As long as our program is running, its *Cache* object remains intact. We simply add to the *Cache* with the following syntax:

```
Cache("Key") = value
```

Here's the relevant code from our program:

```
Cache("LoanAmount") = iLoanAmount
Cache("Rate") = sRate
Cache("Term") = iterm
Cache("Payment") = Math.Round(sPayment, 2)
```

You can improve your application's performance by storing your objects and values in the cache. The cache is global to the ASP.NET application, is thread safe, and implements automatic locking so that it is safe for you to access your cached objects and values concurrently from more than one page.

Taking a Closer Look at Our Drop-Down List

Take a look at the HTML code behind our WebForm1.aspx file by clicking HTML in the lower left side of the designer. You can see that the drop-down list control has the *asp:* directive along with various attributes that deal with its size and position.

```
<asp:dropdownlist id="ddlTerm" style="Z-INDEX: 107;
  LEFT: 24px; POSITION: absolute; TOP: 188px"
  runat="server" Height="22px" Width="104px">
    <asp:ListItem Value="12">12</asp:ListItem>
    <asp:ListItem Value="24">24</asp:ListItem>
    <asp:ListItem Value="36">36</asp:ListItem>
    <asp:ListItem Value="48">48</asp:ListItem>
    ⋮
</asp:dropdownlist>
```

Remember that when the form is run, we programmatically select the first element in the drop-down list to ensure that we have a valid value. If you look at the HTML source within the browser as your page is displayed, you can see that the item is selected in the HTML code.

```
<option selected="selected" value="12">12</option>
<option value="24">24</option>
<option value="36">36</option>
<option value="48">48</option>
```

Then, when the user selects a value from the drop-down list and clicks the Calculate button and a postback occurs, the code is changed to show that the user selected a new value.

```
<option value="12">12</option>
<option value="24">24</option>
<option value="36">36</option>
<option value="48">48</option>
<option selected="selected" value="60">60</option>
<option value="72">72</option>
```

Adding the Payment Schedule Page

Now it's time to add another Web Form to our program. This page will hold the payment schedule. After we have this page set up, we can set the hyperlink property for our control on the input page so that it will navigate to the payment schedule page. Click Project | Add Web Form, select the Web Form template, and keep the default name WebForm2.aspx, as shown in Figure 9-18.

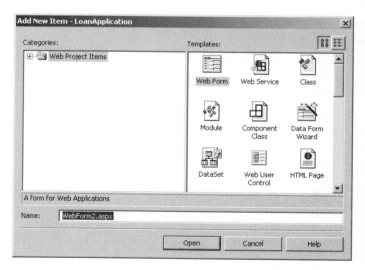

Figure 9-18 Add another Web Form to the program.

Return to the WebForm1 main page to complete our remaining task—assigning the *NavigateURL* property of our hyperlink control. Right-click on the control and select Properties. Click the ellipsis next to NavigateURL to display the Select URL dialog box, shown in Figure 9-19. Select WebForm2.aspx.

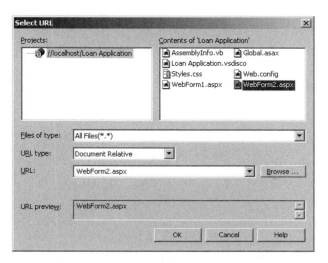

Figure 9-19 Select WebForm2.aspx in the Select URL dialog box.

Return to the payment schedule form (WebForm2.aspx), and add two labels and a data grid. We want to change the default look of the form to something a bit more interesting. Right-click on the data grid, and select Auto Format. Select the Colorful 5 scheme. Our form is shown in Figure 9-20.

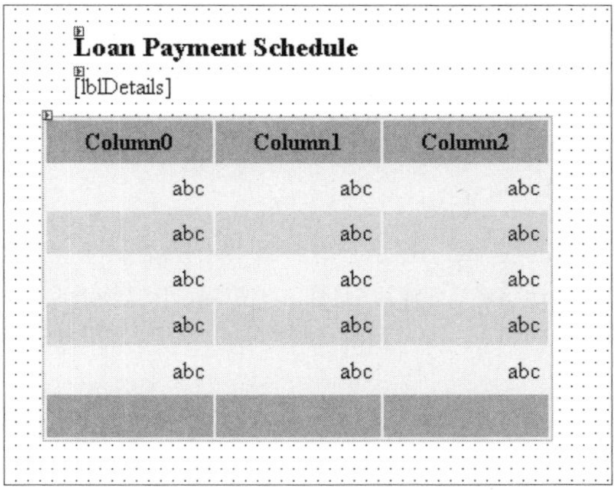

Figure 9-20 Add two labels and a data grid.

Set the properties of the labels and data grid as shown in Table 9-4.

Table 9-4 Properties for the WebForm2.aspx Controls

Object	Property	Value
Label	*ID*	lblTitle
	Font/Size	Larger
	Text	Loan Payment Schedule
Label	*ID*	lblDetails
	Text	""
Data grid	*ID*	dgSchedule
	CellPadding	5
	CellSpacing	2

Right-click on the designer, and then select View Code. The second code-behind form, this one named WebForm2.aspx.vb, is added to your project.

Adding Our Class Code

Add the following two *Imports* statements at the top of the class:

```
Imports Loan_Application.WebForm1

Imports System.Web.Caching

Public Class WebForm2
    Inherits System.Web.UI.Page
    Protected WithEvents dgSchedule As _
        System.Web.UI.WebControls.DataGrid
    Protected WithEvents lblTitle As _
        System.Web.UI.WebControls.Label
    Protected WithEvents lblDetails As _
        System.Web.UI.WebControls.Label
```

After the class and control definitions, add the following variables and routines. We will be using some of these variables in more than one location, so place them in the class-level area so that they can be seen throughout the entire class.

```
Dim dsSchedule As DataSet
Dim tblTable As DataTable
Dim iLoanAmount As Integer
Dim sRate As Single
Dim iTerm As Integer
Dim sPayment As Single
```

```vb
Dim colColumn1 As DataColumn
Dim colColumn2 As DataColumn
Dim colColumn3 As DataColumn
Dim colColumn4 As DataColumn
Dim colColumn5 As DataColumn
Dim colColumn6 As DataColumn


Private Sub Page_Load(ByVal sender As System.Object, _
    ByVal e As System.EventArgs) Handles MyBase.Load
    'Put user code to initialize the page here

    iLoanAmount = Cache("LoanAmount")
    sRate = Cache("Rate")
    iTerm = Cache("Term")
    sPayment = Cache("Payment")
    lblDetails.Text = "Loan Amount: " & _
        iLoanAmount.ToString("C") & "    Rate:  " & _
        sRate.ToString("P") & "    Term:  " & _
        iTerm.ToString & " months."
    'Build the dataset and table
    constructTable()
    calculateSchedule()
End Sub


Private Sub calculateSchedule()

    Dim iInstallment As Integer
    Dim drDataRow As DataRow
    Dim sPrincipal As Single
    Dim sPaidToDate As Single = 0
    Dim sTotalPrincipal As Single = iLoanAmount

    For iInstallment = 1 To iTerm
        drDataRow = dsSchedule.Tables("Schedule").NewRow
        dsSchedule.Tables("Schedule").Rows.Add(drDataRow)
        drDataRow("Installment") = iInstallment
        drDataRow("Payment") = sPayment.ToString("C")

        sPrincipal = PPmt(sRate / 12, iInstallment, iTerm, _
            -iLoanAmount, 0, DueDate.BegOfPeriod)
        drDataRow("Principal") = Math.Round(sPrincipal, _
            2).ToString("C")

        drDataRow("Interest") = (sPayment - _
            sPrincipal).ToString("C")

        sTotalPrincipal -= sPrincipal
```

(continued)

```vb
            drDataRow("PrincipalRemaining") = _
                sTotalPrincipal.ToString("C")

            sPaidToDate += sPayment
            drDataRow("PaidToDate") = sPaidToDate.ToString("C")

            dsSchedule.AcceptChanges()
        Next

        With dgSchedule
            .PageSize = iTerm
            .DataSource = _
                New DataView(dsSchedule.Tables("Schedule"))
            .DataBind()
        End With
    End Sub

    Private Sub constructTable()
        'Instantiate the dataset and table
        dsSchedule = New DataSet("PaymentSchedule")
        tblTable = New DataTable("Schedule")
        dsSchedule.Tables.Add(tblTable)

        colColumn1 = New DataColumn("Installment")
        colColumn1.DataType = System.Type.GetType("System.Int32")

        colColumn2 = New DataColumn("Payment")
        colColumn2.DataType = System.Type.GetType("System.String")

        colColumn3 = New DataColumn("Principal")
        colColumn3.DataType = System.Type.GetType("System.String")

        colColumn4 = New DataColumn("Interest")
        colColumn4.DataType = System.Type.GetType("System.String")

        colColumn5 = New DataColumn("PrincipalRemaining")
        colColumn5.DataType = System.Type.GetType("System.String")

        colColumn6 = New DataColumn("PaidToDate")
        colColumn6.DataType = System.Type.GetType("System.String")

        With tblTable.Columns
            .Add(colColumn1)
            .Add(colColumn2)
            .Add(colColumn3)
            .Add(colColumn4)
            .Add(colColumn5)
            .Add(colColumn6)
        End With
    End Sub
```

How the Calculator Works

When the page loads, we read the values we stuffed in the cache and assign them to our class-level variables. The details of the loan are displayed in the lbl-Details label. Note that we can use the formatting method of the *ToString* method to quickly and painlessly format our output.

```
Private Sub Page_Load(ByVal sender As System.Object, _
    ByVal e As System.EventArgs) Handles MyBase.Load
    'Put user code to initialize the page here

    iLoanAmount = Cache("LoanAmount")
    sRate = Cache("Rate")
    iTerm = Cache("Term")
    sPayment = Cache("Payment")
    lblDetails.Text = "Loan Amount: " & _
        iLoanAmount.ToString("C") & "    Rate:  " & _
        sRate.ToString("P") & "    Term:   " & _
        iTerm.ToString & " months."
    'Build the dataset and table
    constructTable()
    calculateSchedule()
End Sub
```

In our *constructTable* routine, a *DataSet* object and table are instantiated. The table is then added to the new data set. Six columns are created and given names that will be shown as the column titles. The first column will hold an integer because this column will display the payment number. However, we want to format the rest of the fields and display them as currency, so they are all made to hold the *String* data type. Finally, each of the six columns are added to the table columns collection.

```
Private Sub constructTable()
    'Instantiate the dataset and table
    dsSchedule = New DataSet("PaymentSchedule")
    tblTable = New DataTable("Schedule")
    dsSchedule.Tables.Add(tblTable)

    colColumn1 = New DataColumn("Installment")
    colColumn1.DataType = System.Type.GetType("System.Int32")

    colColumn2 = New DataColumn("Payment")
    colColumn2.DataType = System.Type.GetType("System.String")

    colColumn3 = New DataColumn("Principal")
    colColumn3.DataType = System.Type.GetType("System.String")

    colColumn4 = New DataColumn("Interest")
    colColumn4.DataType = System.Type.GetType("System.String")
```

(continued)

```
        colColumn5 = New DataColumn("PrincipalRemaining")
        colColumn5.DataType = System.Type.GetType("System.String")

        colColumn6 = New DataColumn("PaidToDate")
        colColumn6.DataType = System.Type.GetType("System.String")

        With tblTable.Columns
            .Add(colColumn1)
            .Add(colColumn2)
            .Add(colColumn3)
            .Add(colColumn4)
            .Add(colColumn5)
            .Add(colColumn6)
        End With
    End Sub
```

Now that the table has been dynamically created and added to the data set, it can be populated. The procedure-level variables are dimmed—no surprises here.

```
Private Sub calculateSchedule()

        Dim iInstallment As Integer
        Dim drDataRow As DataRow
        Dim sPrincipal As Single
        Dim sPaidToDate As Single = 0
        Dim sTotalPrincipal As Single = iLoanAmount
```

Essentially, we loop through from 1 to the number of months, perform calculations, and then bind the information to the data grid. For each iteration of the loop, a new *DataRow* object is added, created from the Schedule table in the data set. That new empty row is then added to the Schedule table. Recall that we gave each of the columns names such as "Installment" and "Payment" when we created the table. Now that we have a new data row, we can easily access the columns in the row by their names. The Installment column will contain the number of months from 1 to the term of the loan. The Payment column will always contain the same value—the fixed payment each month—so we simply add that value. Again, notice that we format the value by converting it to "C", for currency.

```
For iInstallment = 1 To iTerm
    drDataRow = dsSchedule.Tables("Schedule").NewRow
    dsSchedule.Tables("Schedule").Rows.Add(drDataRow)
    drDataRow("Installment") = iInstallment
    drDataRow("Payment") = sPayment.ToString("C")
```

Visual Basic has another handy built-in financial function, *PPmt*. This function returns a value specifying the principal payment for a given period of an annuity based on periodic, fixed payments and a fixed interest rate. By passing in the rate (divided by 12 to represent a single month), the payment, the term of the loan, the amount, 0, and whether the payment is due at the beginning or end of the period, we get the principal amount. That amount is then rounded, formatted, and placed in the Principal column of that row.

```
sPrincipal = PPmt(sRate / 12, iInstallment, iTerm, _
    -iLoanAmount, 0, DueDate.BegOfPeriod)
drDataRow("Principal") = Math.Round(sPrincipal, _
    2).ToString("C")
```

We can easily deduce how much of the payment goes toward interest by simply subtracting the principal from the payment.

```
drDataRow("Interest") = (sPayment - _
    sPrincipal).ToString("C")
```

The total principal to be paid (that is, the loan amount) is decremented by the principal paid for this single payment. The amount is formatted and added to the remaining principal column of the row.

```
sTotalPrincipal -= sPrincipal
drDataRow("PrincipalRemaining") = _
    sTotalPrincipal.ToString("C")
```

We initialize how much we have paid to date to 0 at the beginning of the routine and then increment it for each payment made. The user can then see how much he or she has paid into the loan for each payment. That value is then added to the correct column of the row. Finally we add the changes to the data set for that new row.

```
sPaidToDate += sPayment
drDataRow("PaidToDate") = sPaidToDate.ToString("C")

dsSchedule.AcceptChanges()
```

We wrap up the routine by setting how many rows the data grid displays to the number of months of the loan. A *DataView* object that contains the Schedule table with all the new rows is assigned to the *DataSource* property of the data grid. Finally we bind the *DataView* object to the data grid and it is displayed.

```
With dgSchedule
    .PageSize = iTerm
    .DataSource = New _
        DataView(dsSchedule.Tables("Schedule"))
    .DataBind()
End With
```

After all this, you should make an important note. All this code is for logic processing and none for displaying the data on the Web Form. On our Web Forms, we used the same object models for the controls that we used in Windows Forms. And the code behind is just like Windows Forms code. This is a milestone in Web development. Programming for the Web is nearly identical to programming for Windows!

Tracing Our Program

A useful way to find out what is happening in our program is to enable tracing. In the HTML section of the WebForm1.aspx form, add the attribute *Trace="True"* to the first line.

```
<%@ Page Language="vb"  AutoEventWireup="false"
  Codebehind = "WebForm1.aspx.vb" Trace="True"
  Inherits = "Loan_Application.WebForm1"%>
```

By adding this attribute, you can get some handy information about the page, including its Session ID and the timing information to display the page. This information is shown in Figure 9-21. (The *Visible* property of each control on the page was temporarily set to False to capture the figure.)

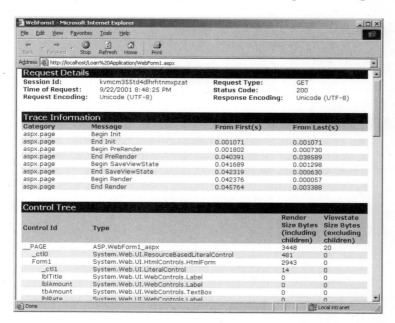

Figure 9-21 Enable tracing to get a wealth of information about the page.

Web Services: The New Marketplace

As we all know, the Internet represents both value and reach for businesses of all sizes by providing opportunities to find new customers, streamline supply chains, provide new services, and secure financial gain. A major impediment has held back the enormous potential of the Internet marketplace to open up trade worldwide. This roadblock is not only in the way of those already conducting business-to-business (B2B) e-commerce but also in the way of businesses that are not yet players in the digital economy. This roadblock is one of design. Most Internet services currently in place take divergent paths to connect buyers, suppliers, marketplaces, and service providers, which means that without large investments in their technology infrastructure, a furniture manufacturer in North Carolina might have a difficult time working with a specialized fittings supplier in Borneo. Also, the furniture manufacturer can only work with global trading partners it knows about, so there has to be a mechanism for the supplier to make its presence widely known. E-commerce participants have not yet agreed on one standard or backbone on which to communicate their services, which makes finding and working with potential trading partners severely limited. This situation, however, is rapidly changing.

What Are Web Services?

In very general terms, ASP.NET pages are for human interaction with a Web server, and Web services are for programmatic interaction with a Web server. Web services are a general model for building applications that can be implemented for any operation that supports communication over the Internet. Web services combine both component-based development models and the Web. Of course, component-based object models such as Distributed Component Object Model (DCOM), Remote Method Invocation (RMI), and Internet Inter-Orb Protocol (IIOP) have been around for some time. The down side of these models is that they depend on a protocol that's particular to the object model. Web services, on the other hand, extend these models a bit further to communicate using SOAP and XML, which essentially eradicates the object model–specific protocol barrier. The nature of a Web service is shown in Figure 9-22.

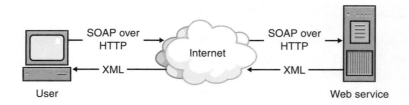

Figure 9-22   High-level view of the Web service model.

As you can see in the illustration, SOAP calls are remote function calls that invoke code-method executions on Web services components. The output from these methods is rendered as XML and passed back to the user. This magic can be accomplished because Web services basically use text-based HTTP and SOAP to make business data available on the Web. A Web service exposes business objects (such as COM objects, Java Beans, and so on) to SOAP calls over HTTP and then executes remote function calls on their receipt. Consumers of Web services can easily invoke method calls on remote objects using SOAP and HTTP and have their data returned via text-based XML. This is an elegant and compelling scenario.

OK, Now How Do We Communicate?

Let's say that the North Carolina–based furniture manufacturer wants to communicate with the Borneo-based fittings supplier. How does the furniture manufacturer become aware of the semantics required to actually use the fittings supplier's Web service?

This question is easily answered—by conforming to a common standard. A few of these standards are the Service Description Language (SDL), SOAP Contract Language (SCL), and Network Accessible Service Specification Language (NASSL), which are XML-like languages built to facilitate communication between a client and a server. IBM and Microsoft, however, recently agreed on the Web Services Description Language (WSDL) as a Web service standard. Therefore, in order to dynamically communicate, each Web service exposes the structure of its components using WSDL.

WSDL is a general-purpose XML language for describing the interface, protocol bindings, and deployment details of network services. WSDL defines XML grammar for describing network services as collections of communication endpoints capable of exchanging messages. WSDL service definitions provide documentation for distributed systems and automate the details involved in communications between applications. Like XML, WSDL is extensible to allow the description of endpoints and their messages, regardless of what message formats or network protocols are used to communicate. WSDL can be used to design specifications to invoke and operate Web services on the Internet and to access and invoke remote applications and databases.

Visual Basic .NET makes it easy to create Web services with components that communicate using HTTP GET, HTTP POST, and SOAP. Consumers of a Web service don't need to know anything about the platform, object model, or programming language used to implement the service. Consumers only need to understand how to send and receive SOAP messages (HTTP and XML).

The decentralized nature of Web services enables both the client and the Web service to function as autonomous units. This provides limitless ways to consume a Web service—for example, a call to a Web service that might be included in your Web application, or from a middleware component, or even from another Web service, as in our furniture supplier example.

Finding Out Who Is Offering What in the Global Marketplace

To address the problems of finding what Web services are out there and how to communicate with them, a group of technology and business leaders have come together to develop the Universal Discovery, Description, and Integration (UDDI) specification. The UDDI service is an industry-wide effort to bring a common standard to B2B integration. It defines a set of standard interfaces for accessing a database of Web services. This initiative creates a platform-independent, open framework to enable businesses to accomplish several goals at once. The UDDI data structure provides a framework for the description of basic business and service information and also architects an extensible mechanism to provide detailed service access information:

- Businesses can discover each other.

- The definition of how businesses interact over the Internet is defined.

- Businesses can easily share information in a global registry.

UDDI is the name of a group of Web-based registries that expose information about a business or other entity and its technical interfaces (APIs). This way, UDDI provides a way for businesses to publish information about their own services as well as find services they need from other businesses.

The UDDI specifications take advantage of World Wide Web Consortium (W3C) and Internet Engineering Task Force (IETF) standards such as XML, HTTP, and Domain Name System (DNS) protocols. Also, cross-platform programming features are addressed by adopting early versions of the SOAP messaging specifications found at the W3C Web site. There are three steps in how the UDDI works:

1. Software companies, standards bodies, and programmers populate the registry with descriptions of different types of services they support.

2. The UDDI Business Registry assigns a programmatically unique identifier to each service and business registration.

3. Marketplaces, search engines, and business applications query the registry to discover services at other companies.

Conceptually, the information provided in a UDDI business registration consists of three components. There are the "white pages," which include the business address, contact, and known identifiers. Next are the "yellow pages," which include industrial categorizations. And finally there are the "green pages," which contain technical information about services that are exposed by the business.

As you might guess, it's the green pages that allow us to automatically discover how to use the service because they include references to specifications for the Web services as well as support for pointers to various file and URL-based discovery mechanisms, if required.

Once a Web service is found, there must be a mechanism to determine exactly what methods (essentially that service's API) it exposes. For example, a client needs to know that the service has a method named *getProductDescription* that takes a long and returns a string. The client can accomplish this task using the WSDL, which is conceptually similar to a COM type library. Using WSDL, a C++ or Java client can understand the parameters of the *getProductDescription* API and build the correct SOAP message to invoke the service. Essentially, WSDL is a specification for using XML schemas to fully describe the service's API.

The third Web service standard is the use of XML schema definition language (XSD). XSD defines a pretty large set of data types that should cover most applications' needs. The standard data types ensure that the data passed between service and client, such as integers and dates, are interpreted and laid out in memory the same way on each side. However, if absolutely necessary, XSD permits you to define your own data types when required. Since XSD is used, both the client and the service can agree on what is a string, a long, and so on.

The vocabulary surrounding Web services is that a Web service *provides* services by exposing its API while a client *consumes* those services, as shown in

Figure 9-23. So a client first finds out about a service from UDDI, then uses WSDL to determine how to communicate with the service, and then contacts the service.

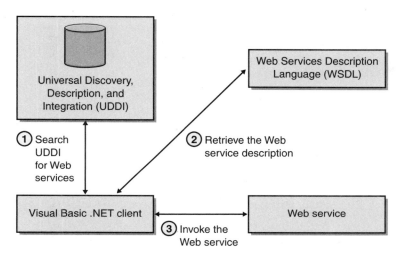

SOAP messages—standard encoding using XSD data types

Figure 9-23   How a client discovers and communicates with a Web service.

Where Are Web Services Going?

Web services are quickly becoming the programmatic backbone for electronic commerce. The future looks bright for Web service technology developed with Visual Basic .NET. However, Microsoft is not alone in the race for Web services technology. Both Sun and IBM are also very interested. In addition, SOAP toolkits are available for Apache and Java Web servers. Although the discovery process is still in the embryonic stages, Web services have the potential to introduce new concepts to the Internet. For example, it would be easy to construct Web sites that generate revenue for each request serviced to a user. This micro-billing would charge by use, not by a flat monthly fee. It's easy to see how searches on sites for periodical publications might charge $1.50 to view any article over 5 years old.

I'm sure you're aware of federations of Web services—situations in which one Web service might call on another Web service to provide value. For example, if my Web service sends foreign denominated wire transfers, behind the scenes I might call on one Web service to validate the user and another to provide the real-time currency exchange rates. By using others' services, my service can concentrate on formatting the instructions correctly and efficiently to send the wire instruction to the Federal Reserve or S.W.I.F.T. When looked at in this light, Web services can be described as the "plug and play" building blocks of B2B Web solutions.

Building a Web Service

With all the daily decisions Visual Basic .NET programmers have to make, wouldn't it be helpful if there were an oracle of sorts we could turn to for sage development advice? If there were a Web service we could query for answers to our thorny problems, life would be so much simpler. So, let's create such a Web service for the betterment of all.

Start a new project and select ASP.NET Web Service. Name the project MagicEightBall. The New Project dialog box for our Web service is shown in Figure 9-24.

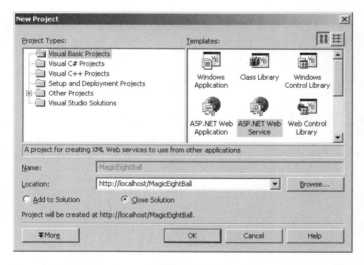

Figure 9-24   Create an ASP.NET Web Service project named MagicEightBall.

You'll be presented with a blank designer screen with the Service1.asmx.vb tab. Right-click the designer, and select Properties. Change the name from Service1 to Magic8Ball. This change will also change the name of the class in the code-behind from Service1 to Magic8Ball.

Bring up the Solution Explorer, and then right-click the Service1.asmx file. Rename the file Magic8.asmx. Right-click the designer again, and then select View Code to bring up the code window. Next change the URL to *http:// www.solidstatesoftware.com/webservices/* in the code before the class declaration. This statement provides a unique namespace for our Web service. The code should look like this:

```
<System.Web.Services.WebService(Namespace:= _
    "http://www.solidstatesoftware.com/webservices/")>
Public Class Magic8Ball
    Inherits System.Web.Services.WebService
```

Add the following code to the template:

```
Private possibleFutures() As String = _
    {"The answer is unclear", _
     "Uncertain at this time", _
     "I have no idea", _
     "Absolutely yes!", _
     "Ask again later", _
     "Emphatically No!", _
     "Buy Microsoft short"}

<WebMethod(Description:="Provides an answer")> _
Public Function getFuture() As String

    Dim rndRandom As System.Random = New System.Random()
    Dim iLower = possibleFutures.GetLowerBound(0)
    Dim iUpper = possibleFutures.GetUpperBound(0)

    Return possibleFutures(rndRandom.Next(iLower, iUpper))

End Function

<WebMethod(Description:="Ask me a question")> _
Public Function getAnswer(ByVal Question As String) As String

    Dim rndRandom As System.Random = New System.Random()
    Dim iLower = possibleFutures.GetLowerBound(0)
    Dim iUpper = possibleFutures.GetUpperBound(0)
    Dim sAnswer As String

    sAnswer = Question & "?  " & _
        possibleFutures(rndRandom.Next(iLower, iUpper))

    Return sAnswer
End Function
```

The first member is a class-level array of strings, named *possibleFutures*. This array is private so that it can't be seen from outside the Web service. Next are two Web methods, *getFuture* and *getAnswer*. By prefacing each with the *<WebMethod()>* directive, we expose both of these methods to the outside world. The templates for the Web methods will show *WebMethod()*. By adding the description, users querying your Web service can see a useful message showing what each method is used for. Also notice that we used *Question* as the parameter for the *getAnswer* method instead of *sQuestion*. We used this name because *Question* will show up when our service is queried, making it crystal clear what the purpose of the method is. We keep our Web service simple, but just simple enough to provide sage advice to anyone who cares to query for it.

The first Web method, *getFuture*, returns an answer. The second, *getAnswer*, takes a specific question from the user and appends the answer. As you can see, we generate a random number between 0 and the number of entries in the *possibleFutures* array. A random response will be returned to the client using our service. If you want any helper functions, simply make them private so that they can't be seen by the outside world. We won't spend any more time on these methods because they should be very familiar by now.

Run the Program

Web services have no visual interface; they simply expose methods. Without writing any additional code, the screen shot shown in Figure 9-25 is displayed, showing the name of the Web service and the two services it currently offers.

Figure 9-25   The MagicEightBall application in action.

Click on *getFuture* to see information about the method along with a button you can click to invoke the method, shown in Figure 9-26. In addition, a
sample SOAP request and response are provided.

Figure 9-26   Information about the *getFuture* method.

Click the Invoke button. A new browser window is displayed with the
XML formatted response from the Magic8Ball Web service. We can see that an
example answer is "Uncertain at this time." This text is what would be
returned to a program on the Internet that invoked the *getFuture* method of
our Web service.

```
<?xml version="1.0" encoding="utf-8" ?>
<string xmlns="http://www.solidstatesoftware.com/webservices/">
Uncertain at this time</string>
```

Close the second browser window, click the back button on the first
browser, and click *getAnswer*. This method requires a string to be entered, so
the name of the parameter, *Question*, is displayed as a prompt with a text
box to enter our query. Now you can see why we used *Question* instead of
the traditional *sQuestion* we would normally use when humans do not see
parameters. Even though most programmers are human, they don't count in
this context. Enter a question in the text box, and click Invoke, as shown in
Figure 9-27.

Figure 9-27 Type in a question before you invoke the *getAnswer* method.

Another browser window is opened, and our answer is provided in XML. The service works as advertised. The question is displayed along with the answer.

```
<?xml version="1.0" encoding="utf-8" ?>
<string xmlns="http://www.solidstatesoftware.com/webservices/">
Will Web services be the next big thing? Uncertain
 at this time</string>
```

Now close the second browser window, click the back button in the first browser window, and click Service Description. A small portion of the WSDL for our Web service is shown in Figure 9-28.

Figure 9-28   A small portion of the WSDL for our Web service.

This WSDL file will be used to build a proxy class in a client that consumes our Web service.

Consuming the MagicEightBall Web Service

Start a new Windows application project named ConsumeEightBall. To keep things simple while illustrating each of the important concepts in this topic, our client will exercise both exposed Web methods of the MagicEightBall Web service. One button will retrieve an answer, and a second button will accept a question in the text box and return the question and answer. Our client is shown in Figure 9-29.

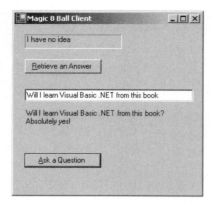

Figure 9-29   The ConsumeEightBall application in action.

One of the key questions you might have is, "Does a client actually execute methods on the Web service's Web server?" As you can imagine, doing that would be a serious security threat. Web masters don't want anyone to use their Web resources in a way that could do malicious damage to sensitive data, not to mention chewing up bandwidth. We also have to keep in mind that Web services are distributed applications. With distributed applications, we have to be concerned about the marshaling of data.

To get around these problems, we actually replicate the object behavior locally on the user's machine. In our example, we will replicate the MagicEight-Ball Web service functionality on the client's program. It sounds strange, but stay tuned. We do this replication by creating a proxy object to act on behalf of the original Web service. The proxy object has all the publicly available data interfaces that the original Web service does.

How do we get the publicly available data interface? Recall that we used the *<WebMethod()>* directive in our MagicEightBall service. Only Web methods will be replicated at the proxy object. This limitation protects our service from exposing sensitive business logic to malicious hackers at the client end. So we program to the proxy object in our program, and it takes care of sending the SOAP messages to and from the real Web service, as shown in Figure 9-30.

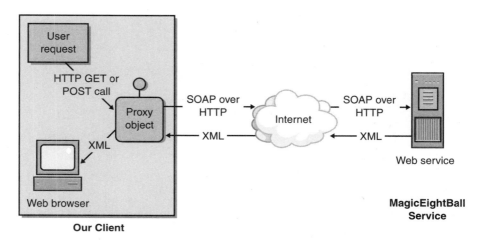

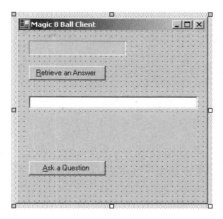

Figure 9-30   The proxy object takes care of sending the SOAP messages to and from the real Web service.

Building Our Web Services Client Program

Add two labels, two buttons, and a text box to the ConsumeEightBall default form, as shown in Figure 9-31.

Figure 9-31   Add these controls to the form.

Set the properties for each of the controls and the form as shown in Table 9-5.

Table 9-5 Properties for the ConsumeEightBall Controls

Object	Property	Value
Form1	*Text*	Magic 8 Ball Client
Label	*Name*	lblRetrieveAnswer
	BorderStyle	Fixed3D
	Text	""
Button	*Name*	btnRetrieve
	Text	&Retrieve an Answer
Text box	*Name*	txtQuestion
	Text	""
Label	*Name*	lblQuestion
	Text	""
Button	*Name*	btnAskQuestion
	Text	&Ask a Question

Adding a Proxy Class to Our Program

To access the MagicEightBall Web service, we have to add a proxy class. You can add a proxy through the command line with a program called Wsdl.exe, but this approach is pretty difficult. I won't cover it, but if you are interested, you can check out the online help. Instead, we will do it the easy way.

Choose Add Web Reference from the Project menu to bring up the Add Web Reference dialog box. Click Web References On Local Web Server to display all the .vsdisco files in the InetPub\wwwroot directories. Click the .vsdisco file for our MagicEightBall service, as shown in Figure 9-32.

Click View Contract at the right side of the Add Web Reference dialog box to examine the XML formatted .vsdisco discovery file. Click the Add Reference button to add this file to the project. Now take a look at the Solution Explorer. Notice in Figure 9-33 that the Web References folder contains the WSDL file of our Web service. This file is what's used to create the proxy that our program will use.

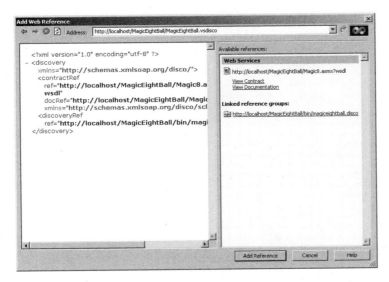

Figure 9-32   Click the .vsdisco file for our MagicEightBall service.

Figure 9-33   The Web References folder contains the WSDL file of our Web service.

Adding Code to Get Our Magic Eight Ball Answers

First right-click the form and choose View Code. Next add the *Imports* statement that will reference the local host folder in our Solution Explorer. This statement gives us the reference to the proxy class that was automatically built for us.

```
Imports ConsumeEightBall.localhost
```

Now add the code for the two buttons.

```
Private Sub btnRetrieve_Click(ByVal sender As System.Object, _
    ByVal e As System.EventArgs) Handles btnRetrieve.Click

    Dim Magic8 As New localhost.Magic8Ball()
    lblRetrieveAnswer.Text = Magic8.getFuture
End Sub

Private Sub btnAskQuestion_Click(ByVal sender As System.Object, _
    ByVal e As System.EventArgs) Handles btnAskQuestion.Click

    Dim Magic8 As New localhost.Magic8Ball()

    If (txtQuestion.Text.Length < 2) Then
        MessageBox.Show("Please enter a question to submit.", _
            "Magic 8 Ball Client", MessageBoxButtons.OK, _
            MessageBoxIcon.Question)
    Else
        lblQuestion.Text = Magic8.getAnswer(txtQuestion.Text)
    End If
End Sub
```

As you can see, all we have to do is create a reference to the *Magic8Ball* proxy that we just added. In both procedures, we created a local variable, *Magic8*, that is a new instance of the *Magic8Ball* proxy class. When the first button is clicked, we simply display the answer from the *getFuture* Web method, and when the second button is clicked, we pass in a question from the text box to the *getAnswer* Web method. As you can see, we simply have to get a reference to the proxy class *Magic8Ball*, as we would from any other class we might use from the .NET Framework or build ourselves. Then we can reference it. What could be easier?

Conclusion

To me, Web services are the most exciting offering of the entire .NET experience. In this reading alone, you've learned how to build sophisticated, multi-page, data-validated ASP.NET pages. You also learned how to both build and then consume Web services. That shows how easy these powerful technologies have become with Visual Basic .NET.

Index

Symbols
& (ampersand), as accelerator key, 140

A
abstract classes
   CollectionBase class, 105–7
   DictionaryBase class, 107–8
   ReadOnlyCollectionBase class, 103–4
accelerator key, ampersand (&) as, 140
AcceptChanges method, 236
AcceptChangesDuringFill property, 241
access keys, 128–29
accessibility-related properties, 118–19
AccessibleDefaultActionDescription property, 119
AccessibleDescription property, 118
AccessibleName property, 118
AccessibleRole property, 118
action queries, 233
ActivateControls method, 121
Active Server Pages. *See* ASP
ActiveX
   vs. .NET Framework, 21–22, 23
   and Visual Basic .NET Toolbox, 33–34
Adapter method, 95
Add method
   ArrayList object, 93
   IDictionary interface, 88
   IList interface, 87
   SortedList object, 101
AddHandle keyword, 38
AddRange method, 94
ADO (ActiveX Data Objects)
   vs. ADO.NET, 195–96, 197
   vs. DAO, 27–29
ADO.NET
   asynchronous operations, 205–6
   vs. classic ADO, 195–96, 197
   connection pooling, 207–9
   data independence feature, 197–98
   DataSet object, 234–39
   error handling, 204–5
   overview, 195–96
   transactions, 209–13
AllowDBNull property, 238

AllowDrop property, 119
ampersand (&), as accelerator key, 140
Anchor property, 117
And method, 89
AndAlso keyword, 38
Ansi keyword, 38
apartment threading, 30–31
App object, 23
appearance-related events, 124–25
appearance-related methods, 121–22
arithmetic operators, 11–12
Array object. *See also* arrays
   Clear method, 81
   Copy method, 81–83
   CreateInstance method, 77, 79
   GetLength method, 76
   GetLowerBound method, 76, 77
   GetUpperBound method, 76
   IndexOf method, 83–85
   LastIndexOf method, 84–85
   Length property, 76
   overview, 75–77
   Rank property, 76
   Reverse method, 80–81
   Sort method, 79–81
   syntax, 75
ArrayList object
   Adapter method, 95
   Add method, 93
   AddRange method, 94
   BinarySearch method, 95
   Capacity property, 92
   Clear method, 93
   CopyTo method, 94
   Count property, 92, 93
   IndexOf method, 95
   InsertRange method, 94
   LastIndexOf method, 95
   overview, 92–95
   Remove method, 93
   RemoveRange method, 94
   Repeat method, 92
   Reverse method, 95

ArrayList object
  Sort method, 95
  SortRange method, 95
  ToArray method, 94
arrays
  arrays of, 85–86
  clearing elements, 81
  copying, 78–79
  copying elements, 81–83
  creating, 75–78
  lower dimension, 41–42
  nonzero-based, 77–78
  searching values, 83–85
  sorting elements, 79–81
  zero-based lower bound, 41–42
ASP, 253–54
ASP.NET
  as basis for Web Forms, 262
  creating Web Forms, 256–70
  features, 254–55
  list of Web Form project files, 259
  Web Form structure, 262–63
  vs. Web services, 289
ASP.NET Web Service, 294–96
.aspx file extension, 255
AssemblyInfo.vb file, 259
asynchronous operations, ADO.NET, 205–6
attributes, in Visual Basic .NET, 12
Auto keyword, 38
AutoIncrement property, 238
AutoIncrementSeed property, 239
AutoIncrementStep property, 239

B

BackColor property, 118
background compilation, 17, 19
base classes, 144, 146, 149, 159–74
Begin method, 211–12
BeginTrans method, 209
BeginTransaction method, 200, 209–10, 212
Biblio.mdb database, 202
BinarySearch method, 95
BitArray object
  And method, 89
  CopyTo method, 89
  Count property, 89
  Get method, 89

Length property, 89
Not method, 89
Or method, 89
overview, 88–90
Set method, 89
SetAll method, 89
Xor method, 89
Bottom property, 117
Bounds property, 117
BringToFront method, 120
build errors, 63
button controls, 115, 260, 267, 274, 302
Byte data type, 14

C

C# language, 17–19, 255
Cache object, 279
Calendar Auto Format dialog box, 265–66
calendar control
  overview, 264
calendar control, Web Forms
  adding code, 266–67
  adding to designer, 260
  setting properties, 265
  viewing HTML code in Internet Explorer,
    268–70
Call keyword, 39
call stack, 61–63
CallWndProc method, 122
Cancel method, 214
CanFocus property, 119
CanSelect property, 119
Capacity property, 92, 100
Capture property, 119
CaseSensitive property, 236
Catch keyword, 39, 57. See also
    Try...Catch...Finally construct
CausesValidation property, 118
CChar keyword, 38
central exception handlers, 64–70
ChangeDatabase method, 200
ChangeUICues event, 123
Chaos isolation level, 210
CheckBox control, 115
CheckedListBox control, 115
child controls, methods common to, 121
ChildRelations property, 234

circular buffers, 91–92
Class keyword, 38
class library, 23, 45, 46–49
classes
  abstract, 103–8
  creating, 103
  methods and properties, 144
  nested, 178–81
  vs. objects, 138–39
  sealed, 174–77
  vs. structures, 50–52
  virtual, 174–77
Clear method
  Array object, 81
  ArrayList object, 93
  DataSet object, 237
  IDictionary interface, 88
  IList interface, 87
  SortedList object, 101
Click event, 123, 129
ClientRectangle property, 117
ClientSize property, 117
Clipboard object, 23
Clone method, 101, 236
Close method, 27, 200, 227
CloseConnection value, 217
CObj keyword, 38
code-behind files
  adding code, 275–76
  for loan payment calculator, 275–76
  overview, 262, 263
  viewing, 264–65
Collect method, 27
collection classes, 103
Collection object, 23
CollectionBase class, 105–7
ColorDialog control, 116
color-related properties, 118
ComboBox control, 115
Command object
  creating, 215–16
  list of methods, 214
  list of properties, 213–14
  overview, 213
  Parameters collection, 220–21, 224–25
CommandTimeout property, 214
CommandText property, 213, 215

CommandType property, 213, 221–22
Commit method, 210
CommitTrans method, 209
common language runtime (CLR), 23
CommonDialog control, 116
CompanyName property, 119
compiler, background, 17, 19
component model–related namespaces, 147
Component Services, 207
configuration-related namespaces, 147
Connection object
  list of events, 200
  list of methods, 200
  list of properties, 199–200
  overview, 199
  type identity and, 27
connection pooling, 207–9
Connection property, 213, 215
ConnectionString property, 199, 200–202
ConnectionTimeout property, 199, 201
constructors
  in derived classes, 163–65
  scope qualifiers and, 186–89
ConsumeEightBall project, 299–301
container controls, events common to, 125
ContainerControl class, 114
Contains method
  IDictionary interface, 88
  IList interface, 87
  Queue object, 92
  SortedList object, 101
  Stack object, 90
  Windows Forms control, 121
ContainsFocus method, 122
ContainsKey method, 101
ContainsValues method, 101
context menus, 129–30
ContextMenu control, 115
ContextMenu property, 119
Control class, 113–14
ControlAdded event, 125
ControlRemoved event, 125
controls, Web Forms, 259, 260, 265–66
controls, Windows Forms
  accessibility-related properties, 118–19
  appearance-related events, 124–25
  appearance-related methods, 121–22

controls, Windows Forms
 color and graphics–related properties, 118
 creation-related properties, 119
 design only, 119
 drag and drop–related events, 124
 events for container controls, 125
 extender provider, 116
 focus-related events, 123
 focus-related methods, 122
 on forms, 112
 keyboard and mouse–related events, 123–24
 keyboard and mouse–related properties, 118
 list of events common to most, 123–25
 list of methods common to most, 120–22
 list of properties common to most, 116–19
 locking, 113
 methods for child controls, 121
 resizing several at once, 113
 run time only, 119
 setting properties, 112
 size and position–related methods, 120
 size and position–related properties, 117
 TaxIndex property, 112–13
 text-related properties, 117–18
 in Visual Studio .NET Toolbox, 115–16
 ways to add to forms, 139
 windowless, 116
 Windows Forms.dll library, 115–16
Copy method, 81–83, 236
copying arrays, 78–79
CopyTo method
 ArrayList object, 94
 BitArray object, 89
 IDictionary interface, 88
 IList interface, 87
 SortedList object, 101
Count property
 ArrayList object, 92, 93
 BitArray object, 89
 IDictionary interface, 88
 IList interface, 87
 SortedList object, 100
 Stack object, 90
CreateCommand method, 200
CreateControl method, 122
Created property, 119
CreateGraphics method, 122
CreateInstance method, 77, 79

CreateParameter method, 214
CrystalReportViewer control, 116
CShort keyword, 38
CType keyword, 38
Currency data type, 8–9, 14
Cursor property, 118

D
DAO (Data Access Objects), 27–29
Data Adapter Configuration Wizard, 243–46
Data controls, 116
data grid, 287. *See also* DataGrid control
data providers, 196. *See also* OLE DB .NET data
  provider; SQL Server .NET data provider
data types
 automatic coercions, 18–19
 defining for DataColumns, 238–39
 mapping between Visual Basic and Visual Basic
   .NET, 14
 in .NET Framework, 147
 in Visual Basic .NET, 14
DataAdapter object
 AcceptChangesDuringFill property, 241
 adding to programs, 243–46
 DeleteCommand property, 241
 Fill method, 241
 FillError event, 241
 FillSchema method, 241
 GetFillParameters method, 241
 InsertCommand property, 241
 list of events, 241
 list of methods, 241
 list of properties, 241
 MissingMappingAction property, 241
 overview, 239–41
 RowUpdated event, 241
 RowUpdating event, 241
 SelectCommand property, 241, 242
 TableMappings property, 241
 Update method, 241
 UpdateCommand property, 241
 viewing data, 248–50
Database property, 199
databases
 issuing commands, 216
 multiple queries, 232–33
 opening asynchronously, 205–6
 reading data from, 242

DataGrid control, 116, 247, 282
DataReader object
  closing, 224
  iterating over individual rows, 226
  list of methods, 227–28
  list of properties, 226
  reading column values, 228–31
  reading data, 216, 217
data-related namespaces, 147
DataRelation object, 234
DataSet object
  AcceptChanges method, 236
  CaseSensitive property, 236
  Clear method, 237
  Clone method, 236
  Copy method, 236
  DataSetName property, 236
  DefaultViewManager property, 236
  EnforceConstraints property, 236
  ExtendedProperties property, 236
  GetChanges method, 237
  GetXml method, 237
  HasChanges method, 236
  HasErrors property, 236
  InferXmlSchema method, 237
  list of events, 237
  list of methods, 236–37
  list of properties, 236
  in loan calculator routine, 285
  Locale property, 236
  Merge method, 236
  MergeFailed event, 237
  Namespace property, 236
  object model, 234–39
  overview, 234
  Prefix property, 236
  ReadXml method, 237
  ReadXmlSchema method, 237
  RejectChanges method, 236
  Relations property, 236
  Reset method, 236
  storing objects, 239
  Tables property, 236
  WriteXml method, 237
DataSetName property, 236
DataSource property, 199, 287
DataTable object
  ChildRelations property, 234
  creating, 237–39
  defining relationships between, 234
  ParentRelations property, 234
  PrimaryKey property, 239
DataView object, 287
DateTimePicker control, 115
debugger, 44–45
Decimal data type, 14, 231
Default keyword, 38
DefaultViewManager property, 236
Delegate keyword, 38
DELETE statement, 216
DeleteCommand property, 241
Dequeue method, 91
derived classes
  constructors in, 163–65
  finalizers in, 165–66
  inheritance and, 144, 154–59
  member shadowing, 169–73
DeriveParameters method, 225
determinism, 25–26
dictionary classes, 103
DictionaryBase class, 107–8
DirectCast keyword, 38
Direction property, 222, 225
DirListBox control, 116
Dispose method, 26, 27, 122, 165
Disposed property, 119
Disposing property, 119
Dock property, 117
DoDragDrop method, 122
Domain Name System (DNS), 291
DomainUpDown control, 116
Double data type, 14
DoubleClick event, 123
drag and drop–related events, 124
DragDrop event, 124
DragEnter event, 124
DragLeave event, 124
DragOver event, 124
DriveList control, 116
drop-down list controls, 274, 279–80

E

e-commerce, 289
Enabled property, 118, 130
encapsulation, 150
EnforceConstraints property, 236

Enqueue method, 91
Enter event, 123
error messages, logging, 67–70
ErrorProvider control, 116
errors. *See* programming errors
Errors collection, 204–5
event handling, 40–41
events
  appearance-related, 124–25
  Connection object, 200
  for container controls, 125
  DataAdapter object, 241
  DataSet object, 237
  drag and drop–related, 124
  focus-related, 123
  inheriting, 157
  keyboard-related, 123–24
  list common to most controls, 123–25
  mouse-related, 123–24
  Windows Forms menu, 129
Exception class, 54
exception handling
  central handlers, 64–70
  directives, 70–73
  goals of using, 70
  logging exceptions, 67–70
  overview, 53–54
  Try...Catch...Finally construct, 55–63
  types of handlers, 55–56
  in Visual Basic .NET, 11
exception logs, 67–70
EXEC statement, 224
ExecuteNonQuery method, 214, 216, 221
ExecuteReader method, 214, 216, 217–18, 221
ExecuteScalar method, 214, 216, 218–19
ExecuteXmlReader method, 216, 219
ExtendedProperties property, 236
extender provider controls, 116

F

FieldCount property, 226
File object, 25, 26
FileListBox control, 116
Fill method, 241
FillError event, 241
FillSchema method, 241
Finalize method, 165
finalizers, in derived classes, 165–66

Finally keyword, 39, 57. *See also*
    Try...Catch...Finally construct
FindForm method, 120
fixed-length strings, 42
Focus method, 122
Focused property, 119
focus-related events, 123
focus-related methods, 122
focus-related properties, 118
Font property, 117
FontDialog control, 116
FOR XML queries, 216, 219
ForeColor property, 118
Form class. *See also* forms
  vs. Control class, 114
  features, 112
  in Windows Forms class hierarchy, 114, 146
form designer, Visual Studio .NET
  code generation, 110–12
  Form1 example, 110–12
  new features, 112–13
  overview, 110
forms. *See also* Web Forms; Windows Forms
  as examples of objects, 139–44
  modal vs. modeless, 145
  packages, 36, 37
  resizing, 143
For...Next blocks, 43
Frame control, 115
Framework services–related namespaces, 147
Friend scope qualifier, 178, 182
function overloading, in Visual Basic .NET, 12

G

GarbageCollector class, 18, 24, 25, 27
GDI+, 15
Get method, 89
GetBoolean method, 227
GetByIndex method, 101
GetByte method, 227
GetBytes method, 227
GetChanges method, 237
GetChar method, 227
GetChars method, 227
GetChildAtPoint method, 121
GetContainer method, 120
GetContainerControl method, 120
GetDataTypeName method, 228

GetDateTime method, 227
GetDecimal method, 227
GetDouble method, 227
GetFieldType method, 227
GetFillParameters method, 241
GetFloat method, 227
GetGuid method, 227
GetHashCode method, 96
GetInt16 method, 227, 228
GetInt32 method, 227, 228
GetInt64 method, 227, 228
GetKey method, 101
GetKeyList method, 101
GetLength method, 76
GetLowerBound method, 76, 77
GetName method, 227, 229
GetNextControl method, 122
GetOleDbSchemaTable method, 200
GetOrdinal method, 227
GetSchemaTable method, 228
GetSqlBinary method, 228
GetSqlBoolean method, 228
GetSqlByte method, 228
GetSqlDataTime method, 228
GetSqlDecimal method, 228
GetSqlDouble method, 228
GetSqlGuid method, 228
GetSqlSingle method, 228
GetSqlString method, 228
GetSqlValue method, 228
GetSqlValues method, 228
GetString method, 227
GetTimeSpan method, 227, 231
GetType function, 238, 239
GetType keyword, 38
GetUpperBound method, 76
GetValue method, 227, 229
GetValueList method, 101
GetValues method, 227, 229
GetXml method, 237
GiveFeedback event, 124
Global.asax file, 259
globalization-related namespaces, 147
globally unique identifiers (GUIDs), 30
GotFocus event, 123
graphics-related properties, 118
GroupBox control, 115
GUIDs (globally unique identifiers), 30

H
Handle property, 119
HandleCreated event, 125
HandleDestroyed event, 125
Handles keyword, 38, 40–41
HasChanges method, 236
HasErrors property, 236
hash tables, 96–98
Hashtable class, 95–98
Height property, 117, 142–43
HelpProvider control, 116
HelpRequested event, 124
Hide method, 121
HScrollBar control, 115
HTML code, viewing in Internet Explorer, 268–70
HTML server controls, 260
HTTP GET, 291
HTTP POST, 291
hyperlink controls, 274, 280–81

I
ICloneable interface, 78, 89
ICollection interface, 86–88
IComparable interface, 99
IComparer interface, 97, 98
IDE (integrated development environment), 141, 148–49
IDictionary interface, 86–88, 95
IDisposable interface, 26, 165
IEnumerable interface, 88, 90, 98
If...Then blocks, 43
IList interface, 86–88, 93
Image control, 116
ImageList control, 115
IMEMode property, 118
importing namespaces, 29
Imports keyword, 38, 275–76, 282, 303–4
IndexOf method, 83–85, 87, 95
IndexOfKey method, 101
IndexOfValue method, 101
InferXmlSchema method, 237
InfoMessage event, 200
inheritance
    defined, 151
    by delegation, 152
    early-bound polymorphic code and, 153
    interface-type, 11, 153
    late-bound polymorphic code and, 152–53

inheritance
  overview, 144
  in previous Visual Basic versions, 151–53
  in Visual Basic .NET, 10–11, 154–59
Inherits keyword, 38
Inner classes, 179, 180
Insert method, 87
InsertCommand property, 241
InsertRange method, 94
Integer data type, 14
IntelliSense, 18, 141
interface inheritance, 11, 153
Interface keyword, 38
Internet Engineering Task Force (IETF), 391
Internet Explorer, viewing HTML code, 268–70
Invalidate method, 121
Invalidated event, 125
IsAccessible property, 119
IsClosed property, 226
IsDBNull function, 230
IsDBNull method, 227, 229, 230
IsFixedSize property, 87, 88
IsolationLevel property, 210–11
IsPostBack property, 277
IsReadOnly property, 87, 88
Item property
  DataReader object, 226, 228, 229
  IDictionary interface, 88
  IList interface, 87
  SortedList object, 100

K

keyboard-related events, 123–24
keyboard-related properties, 118
KeyDown event, 124
KeyInfo value, 217
KeyPress event, 124
Keys property
  Hashtable object, 98
  IDictionary interface, 88
  SortedList object, 101
KeyUp event, 124

L

Label control, 115, 273, 274, 282, 302
LastIndexOf method, 84–85, 95
late binding, 18

Layout event, 125
Leave event, 123
Left property, 117
Length property, 76, 89
Line control, 116
LinkLabel control, 116
ListBox control, 115
ListDictionary class, 103
ListItem Collection Editor dialog box, 274
ListView control, 115
loan payment calculator
  adding code to code-behind form, 275–76
  adding controls to form, 273
  adding payment schedule page, 280–82
  building, 273–75
  finished, 271, 272
  how it works, 285–88
  list of control properties, 273–74
  overview, 270–72
  starting project, 273
Locale property, 236
Location property, 117
Locked property, 119
locking controls, 113
logging exceptions, 67–70
Long data type, 14
LostFocus event, 123

M

MagicEightBall project, 294–99
MainMenu control, 115, 126–27
MaxLength property, 238
members. *See also* methods; properties
  defined, 144
  inheriting, 157–58
  overriding in base classes, 159–74
  scope qualifiers, 178, 181–86
  shadowing, 169–73
memory management, in .NET Framework, 24–27
Menu Editor, Visual Studio .NET, 32–33
menus
  adding items at run time, 133
  assigning access keys, 128–29
  assigning shortcut keys, 129
  cloning, 132
  context-type, 129–30
  creating at design time, 126–30
  creating item event handlers, 129

disabling commands, 130
displaying check marks, 131
displaying radio buttons, 131
enabling commands, 130
MainMenu control, 115, 126–27
making items invisible, 131
merging at run time, 132–33
modifying at run time, 130–33
overview, 126
separating items, 128
Merge method, 236
MergeFailed event, 237
message boxes, 142, 145
Message property, 54
MessageBox class, 142
methods
    appearance-related, 121–22
    for child controls, 121
    Command object, 214
    Connection object, 200
    DataAdapter object, 241
    DataReader object, 227–28
    DataSet object, 236–37
    defined, 140, 142
    focus-related, 122
    invoking, 142–44
    list common to most controls, 120–22
    overriding, 160, 161, 162
    position-related, 120
    size-related, 120
    SortedList object, 100–101
Microsoft Intermediate Language (MSIL), 24
MicrosoftJetOLEDB4.0 provider, 200, 202
MinimumCapacity property, 238
MissingMappingAction property, 241
modal forms, 145
modeless forms, 145
ModifierKeys property, 118
Modifiers property, 119
Module keyword, 38
MonthCalendar control, 115
MonthView control, 115
mouse-related events, 123–24
mouse-related properties, 118
MouseButton property, 118
MouseDown event, 123
MouseEnter event, 123
MouseHover event, 123

MouseLeave event, 123
MouseMove event, 123
MousePosition property, 118
MouseUp event, 123
MouseWheel event, 123
Move event, 125
MsgBox function, 145
MsgBox method, 145
MSIL (Microsoft Intermediate Language), 24
multiple database queries, 232–33
multithreading, in Visual Basic .NET, 13, 31
MustInherit keyword, 38, 175–76
MustOverride keyword, 38, 176–78
MyBase keyword, 38, 162–63
MyClass keyword, 38, 166–69

N
Name property, 119
named transactions, 212–13
Namespace keyword, 38
Namespace property, 236
namespaces
    component model–related, 147
    configuration-related, 147
    data-related, 147
    defined, 29
    displaying in Solution Explorer, 148–49
    Framework services–related, 147
    globalization-related, 147
    importing, 29
    list with descriptions, 46–49
    naming syntax, 146–47
    network programming–related, 147
    overview, 146–48
    programming-related, 147
    reflection-related, 148
    rich, client-side GUI–related, 148
    run-time infrastructure services–related, 148
    security services–related, 148
    Web services–related, 148
NameValueCollection class, 103
NASSL (Network Accessible Service Specification
    Language), 290
NativeError property, 205
NavigateURL property, 280–81
nested classes, 178–81
nested scopes, 43
nested transactions, 211–12

.NET CLR Data Performance object, 209
.NET data providers, 196. *See also* OLE DB .NET
    data provider; SQL Server .NET data provider
.NET Framework
    vs. ActiveX, 21–22, 23
    asynchronous operations, 206
    class library, 23, 45–49
    memory management issues, 24–27
    overview, 13
    structures vs. classes, 50–52
    threading model, 30–31
    type identity issues, 27–30
Network Accessible Service Specification
    Language (NASSL), 290
network programming–related namespaces, 147
NextResult method, 227, 232–33
nonzero-based arrays, 77–78
Not method, 89
NotifyIcon control, 116
NotInheritable keyword, 38, 174–75
NotOverridable keyword, 38, 160, 161
NumericUpDown control, 116

O

Object data type, 14
Object Sql data type, 232
object-oriented programming
    classes vs. objects, 138–39
    in Visual Basic .NET, 137–50
objects
    vs. classes, 138–39
    form example, 139–44
    simple example, 139–40
ODBC .NET data provider, 196
OLE DB .NET data provider, 196, 199, 200, 202,
    204, 207, 220, 225, 230
OleDbConnection object, 200, 207
OleDbDataAdapter object, 240
OleDbDataReader object, 217
OleDbException class, 204–5
OleDbTransaction object, 210, 211–12
OleDbType value, 222
On Error statements, 55
OnPageLoad event, 262
Open method, 200, 201, 203
OpenFileDialog control, 116
Option Strict keyword, 38
Or method, 89

OrElse keyword, 38
Outer classes, 178, 179, 180–81
overloaded function, in Visual Basic .NET, 12
Overloads keyword, 38, 161, 170
Overridable keyword, 38, 160, 161, 171, 173
Overrides keyword, 39, 159, 160, 161, 162, 173

P

PacketSize property, 199, 202
@Page directive, 262
Page object, 262, 263
Page organizational behavior, 277
Page_Load event handler, 262, 277
PageSetupDialog control, 116
Paint event, 124
Panel control, 115
parameterized SQL commands, 220–21
Parameters collection, 220–21, 224–25
Parameters property, 214
parent classes, 144
parentheses, when to use, 39
ParentRelations property, 234
Patent property, 117
Peek method, 90, 91
performance counters, checking connection
    pooling, 209
PictureBox control, 115, 116
Pmt function, 278
pointers, 18
PointToClient method, 120
PointToScreen method, 120
polymorphism, 150, 152–53, 158–59
pooling connections, 207–9
Pop method, Stack object, 90
Popup event, 129
position-related methods, 120
position-related properties, 117
PPmt function, 286–87
Prefix property, 236
Prepare method, 214
PrimaryKey property, 239
PrintControl object, 116
PrintDialog control, 116
Printer object, 23
PrintPreviewControl control, 116
PrintPreviewDialog control, 116
Private scope qualifier, 178, 181, 188
ProductName property, 119

ProductVersion property, 119
programming errors. *See also* exception handling
  build vs. run-time, 53
  handling in ADO.NET, 204–5
  handling in Visual Basic .NET, 13
programming languages
  choosing among, 17–19
  cross-language interoperability, 16–17
programming-related namespaces, 147
ProgressBar control, 115
properties
  accessibility-related, 118–19
  color-related, 118
  Command object, 213–14
  Connection object, 199–200
  creation-related, 119
  DataAdapter object, 241
  DataReader object, 226
  DataSet object, 236
  defined, 140, 142
  focus-related, 118
  graphics-related, 118
  keyboard-related, 118
  list common to most controls, 116–19
  mouse-related, 118
  overriding, 160
  position-related, 117
  reading and writing, 142–44
  setting, 112
  size-related, 117
  SortedList object, 100–101
  text-related, 117–18
Property Browser, Visual Studio .NET, 34–35
PropertyChanged event, 125
Protected Friend keyword, 39, 178, 185–86, 188
Protected keyword, 39, 178, 182–85, 188
Provider property, 199
Public scope qualifier, 178, 181, 182, 189
Pubs database, 202, 222
Push method, Stack object, 90

Q
queries, 216, 219, 232–33
QueryContinueDrag event, 124
Queue object, 91–92
queues, 91–92

R
RadioButton control, 115
Range Validator control, 274
Rank property, 76
RDO Data controls, 116
Read method, 227
ReadCommitted isolation level, 211
ReadOnly keyword, 39
ReadOnly property, 160
ReadOnlyCollectionBase class, 103–4
ReadUncommitted isolation level, 210
ReadXml method, 237
ReadXmlSchema method, 237
RecordsAffected property, 226
Recordset type, 27–29, 30
RectangleToClient method, 120
RectangleToScreen method, 120
reflection-related namespaces, 148
Refresh method, 121, 224
Regular Expression Validator control, 274
RejectChanges method, 236
Relations property, 236
ReleaseObjectPool method, 200, 207
Remove method
  ArrayList class, 93
  IDictionary interface, 88
  IList interface, 87
  SortedList object, 101
RemoveAt method
  IList interface, 87
  SortedList object, 101
RemoveHandle keyword, 38
RemoveRange method, 94
Repeat method, 92
RepeatableRead isolation level, 211
RequiredFieldValidator control, 260, 267, 274
Reset method, 236
ResetBackColor method, 121
ResetCommandTimeout method, 214
ResetCursor method, 122
ResetForeColor method, 121
ResetText method, 122
Resize event, 125
resizing
  controls, 113
  forms, 143

resultsets, multiple, 232–33
Return keyword, 39
Reverse method, 80–81, 95
RichTextBox control, 115
Right property, 117
RightToLeft property, 117
Rollback method, 210
RollbackTrans method, 209
RowUpdated event, 241
RowUpdating event, 241
run-time errors, defined, 53. *See also* exception
    handling

S

Save method, 213
SAVE TRAN statement, 212
SaveFileDialog control, 116
Scale method, 121
SchemaOnly value, 218
scope qualifiers
    Friend, 178, 182, 188
    overview, 178, 181–82
    Private, 178, 181, 188
    Protected, 178, 182–85, 188
    Protected Friend, 178, 185–86, 188
    Public, 178, 181, 182, 189
scopes, nested, 43
Screen object, 23
ScrollableControl class, 114
sealed classes, 174–77
Select event, 129
Select method, 122
SelectCommand property, 241, 242
SelectionChanged event handler, 266
SelectNextControl method, 122
SendToBack method, 120
SequentialAccess value, 217–18
Serializable isolation level, 211
server controls, 259, 260, 264
ServerVersion property, 199
Service Description Language (SDL), 290
Service1.asmx file, 295
Set method, 89
SetAll method, 89
SetBounds method, 120

SetByIndex method, 101
SetClientSizeCore method, 120
SetNewControls method, 121
SetSize method, 120
Shadows keyword, 39, 170–73
Shape control, 116
shared members
    inheriting, 157–58
    redefining, 173–74
Short data type, 14, 39
shortcut keys, 129
Show method, 121, 142
ShowFocusCues property, 118
ShowKeyboardCues property, 118
Single data type, 14
SingleResult value, 217
SingleRow value, 217
Size method, 143
Size property, 117
size-related methods, 120
size-related properties, 117
SlideBar control, 115
SOAP (Simple Object Access Protocol), 289, 290
SOAP Contract Language (SCL), 290
Solution Explorer, 148–49, 258–59, 295
Sort method, 79–81, 95
SortedList object
    list of methods, 100–101
    list of properties, 100–101
    overview, 98–100
SortRange method, 95
Source property, Exception object, 54
Splitter control, 116
SQL Server
    DELETE statement, 216
    EXEC statement, 224
    FOR XML queries, 216, 219
    multiple database queries, 232–33
    nested transactions and, 212
    Query Analyzer, 222–23
    SAVE TRAN command, 212
    SELECT statement, 242
    UPDATE SQL statement, 216
SQL Server .NET data provider, 196, 199, 200,
    201, 202, 207–8, 214, 219, 220–21, 225, 231

SqlBinary data type, 232
SqlBoolean data type, 231
SqlByte data type, 231
SqlCommand object, 216, 219
SqlConnection object, 201
SqlDataAdapter object, 240, 243–46
SqlDataReader object, 217
SqlDateTime data type, 231
SqlDbType value, 222, 231–32
SqlDecimal data type, 231
SqlDouble data type, 231
SqlError object, 205
SqlException object, 205
SqlGuid data type, 232
SqlInt16 data type, 231
SqlInt32 data type, 231
SqlInt64 data type, 231
SqlMoney data type, 232
SqlParameter object, 222
SqlSingle data type, 231
SQLState property, 205
SqlString data type, 232
SqlTransaction object, 210, 212–13
Stack object, 90
StackTrace property, 54
State property, 199, 203
StateChange event, 200, 203
StatusBar control, 115
stored procedures, 219, 221–24
String data type, 14
StringBuilder object, 229–30
StringCollection object, 101–3
StringDictionary object, 101–3
strings, fixed-length, 42
Structure keyword, 38
Structure...End Structure blocks, 50–52
structures, 50–52
submenus, 127
subscopes, 43
SyncLock keyword, 39
System namespace
  defined, 46
  list of second-level namespaces, 147–48
System.CodeDom namespace, 46, 147
System.Collections namespace
  ArrayList class, 92–95

BitArray class, 88–90
defined, 46, 86, 147
Hashtable class, 95–98
ICollection interface, 86–88
IDictionary interface, 86–88
IList interface, 86–88
Queue class, 91–92
SortedList class, 98–101
Stack class, 90
StringCollection class, 101
StringDictionary class, 101
System.ComponentModel namespace, 46, 147
System.ComponentModel.Design namespace, 46
System.Configuration namespace, 147
System.Data namespace, 46, 147
System.Data.OleDb namespace, 46
System.Data.SqlClient namespace, 46
System.Data.SqlTypes namespace, 231–32
System.Diagnostics namespace, 46, 147
System.DirectoryServices namespace, 46, 147
System.Drawing namespace, 46, 148
System.Drawing.Drawing2D namespace, 46
System.Drawing.Imaging namespace, 47
System.Drawing.Printing namespace, 47
System.Drawing.Text namespace, 47
System.Globalization namespace, 47, 147
System.IO namespace, 47, 147
System.Management namespace, 147
System.Messaging namespace, 47, 147
System.Net namespace, 47
System.NET namespace, 147
System.Net.Sockets namespace, 47
System.Reflection namespace, 47, 148
System.Reflection.Emit namespace, 47
System.Resources namespace, 47, 147
System.Runtime.CompilerServices namespace, 148
System.Runtime.InteropServices namespace, 47, 148
System.Runtime.Remoting namespace, 48, 148
System.Runtime.Serialization namespace, 148
System.Runtime.Serialization.Formatters.Binary namespace, 48
System.Runtime.Serialization.Formatters.Soap namespace, 48
System.Security namespace, 48, 148

System.Security.Cryptography namespace, 48
System.Security.Permissions namespace, 48
System.ServiceProcess namespace, 48, 147
System.Text namespace, 147
System.Text.RegularExpressions namespace, 48, 147
System.Threading namespace, 48, 147
System.Timers namespace, 48, 147
System.Type object, 238
System.Web namespace, 48, 148
System.Web.Services namespace, 148
System.Web.UI namespace, 49
System.Web.UI.HtmlControls namespace, 49
System.Web.UI.WebControls namespace, 49
System.Web.UI.Web.Services namespace, 49
System.Web.UI.Web.Services.Protocols
    namespace, 49
System.Windows.Forms namespace
  class hierarchy, 113–26
  Control class overview, 114
  defined, 49, 148
  Form class overview, 146
System.Xml namespace, 49, 147
System.Xml.Schema namespace, 49
System.Xml.Serialization namespace, 147
System.Xml.XPath namespace, 49
System.Xml.Xsl namespace, 49

T

Tab Layout Editor, Visual Studio .NET, 35–36
Tab Order command, 112–13
TabControl control, 115
TabIndex property, 112–13, 118
TableMappings property, 241
Tables property, 236
TabStop property, 118
TabStrip control, 115
TargetSite property, 54
Task List, 17
text box controls, 260, 266, 267, 268, 273, 302
Text property, 117, 143
TextBox control, 115, 116, 223
text-related properties, 117–18
threading model, in .NET Framework, 30–31
Throw keyword, 39
Timer control, 115

ToArray method, 94
ToolBar control, 115
Toolbox, Visual Studio .NET
  controls in, 115–16
  overview, 33–34
  Web Forms tab, 259–61
ToolTip control, 116
Top property, 117
ToString method, 285
tracing, enabling, 288
TrackBar control, 115
Transaction object, 210
Transaction property, 214
transactions
  in ADO.NET, 209–13
  creating, 209–10
  enlisting commands, 215–16
  isolation levels, 210–11
  named, 212–13
  nested, 211–12
TreeView control, 115
TrimToSize method, 101
Try keyword, 39, 57. *See also* Try...Catch...Finally
    construct
Try...Catch...Finally construct
  errors in ADO.NET, 204–5
  example, 56–63
  handling anticipated exceptions, 60–61
  handling unexpected exceptions, 70–73
  overview, 55–56
T-SQL, 212
type checking, 13
type identity, in .NET Framework, 27–30

U

UDDI (Universal Discovery, Description, and
    Integration), 291–93
Unicode keyword, 38
Update method, 121, 241
UPDATE SQL statement, 216
UpdateCommand property, 241
UpdateRowSource property, 214
UpDown control, 116
Upgrade Wizard. *See* Visual Basic Upgrade
    Wizard

V

Validated event, 123
Validating event, 123
validation controls, 260, 277–78
Values property
  Hashtable object, 98
  IDictionary interface, 88
  SortedList object, 101
variables, deterministic vs. indeterministic, 24–25
Variant data type, 14, 42–43
VB .NET. *See* Visual Basic .NET
_VIEWSTATE field, 269
virtual classes, 174–77
virtual methods, 159, 162
Visible property, 118, 288
Visual Basic
  changes in Visual Basic .NET, 8–9
  differences in versions, 4–5
  history, 4–6
  modernizing, 8
  and .NET platform, 6
  problems over time, 7
  reasons to upgrade to Visual Basic .NET, 10–19
  upgrading projects automatically, 9–10
  vs. Visual Basic .NET, 3, 4, 21–52
  Visual Basic .NET compatibility issues, 6–8
Visual Basic .NET. *See also* .NET Framework
  arithmetic operators, 11–12
  attributes, 12
  background compiler, 17
  vs. C#, 17–19
  changes from Visual Basic, 8–9
  compatibility issues, 6–8
  creating ASP.NET Web applications, 256–70
  cross-language interoperability, 16–17
  data types, 14
  debugger, 44–45
  event handling, 40–41
  function overloading, 12
  inheritance, 10–11, 154–59
  language differences, 37–43
  list of new keywords, 38–39
  Math library, 278
  memory management issues, 24–27
  multithreading, 13, 31
  new IDE features, 16–17

  new language features, 10–14
  object-oriented programming, 137–50
  overview, 23–24
  reasons to upgrade from Visual Basic, 10–19
  reducing programming errors, 13
  role of structures, 50–52
  structured exception handling, 11
  Task List in, 17
  threading model, 30–31
  type identity issues, 27–30
  vs. Visual Basic, 3, 4, 21–52
Visual Basic Upgrade Wizard, 26, 37, 39, 43
Visual Studio .NET
  form designer, 110–13
  Menu Editor, 32–33
  overview, 31–32
  Property Browser, 34–35
  Tab Layout Editor, 35–36
  Toolbox, 33–34
VScrollBar control, 115
.vsdisco files, 259, 302, 303

W

W3C (World Wide Web Consortium), 391
WaitForPendingFinalizers method, 27
Web Forms
  adding to projects, 280–82
  cleanup stage, 277
  code module, 261
  creating, 256–70
  event handling stage, 277
  HTML-based template, 261–64
  life cycle, 276–77
  list of project files, 259
  page initialization stage, 277
  page load stage, 277
  role of ASP.NET, 262
  running, 267–68
  server controls, 264
  structure, 262–63
  Visual Basic .NET support for, 16, 37
Web Forms Page framework
  base class, 262–63
  WebForm1.aspx file, 263
  WebForm1.aspx.vb file, 263

Web services
  adding proxy classes, 302–3
  vs. ASP.NET, 289
  building client program, 301–2
  building ConsumeEightBall project, 299–301
  building MagicEightBall project, 294–96
  communication standards, 290–91
  finding out what is available, 291–93
  future potential, 293–94
  namespaces, 148
  overview, 289–90
  running, 296–99
  Visual Basic .NET support for, 16
Web Services Description Language (WSDL),
    290–91, 302, 303
Web.config file, 259
WebForm1.aspx file, 259, 262, 263, 279–80, 288
WebForm1.aspx.cs file, 263
WebForm1.aspx.vb file, 263, 264–65, 275–76
When keyword, 39
Width property, 117
windowless controls, 116
Windows 2000 Component Services, 207
Windows Common Controls, 115–16
Windows Forms
  class hierarchy, 113–26
  code generation, 110–12
  controls overview, 115–16
  defined, 15
  designing and modifying menus, 126–33
  events common to controls, 123–25
  faster development, 15
  form designer, 110–13
  methods common to controls, 120–22

  .NET single standard, 36–37
  overview, 109
  properties common to controls, 116–19
  role of GDI+, 15
  support for internationalization, 16
wizards
  Data Adapter Configuration Wizard, 243–46
  Visual Basic Upgrade Wizard, 26, 37, 39, 43
WorkstationId property, 200, 202
WriteOnly keyword, 39
WriteOnly property, 160
WriteXml method, 237
WSDL (Web Services Description Language),
    290–91, 302, 303

X

XML (Extensible Markup Language), Visual Basic
    .NET support, 16
XML schema definition language (XSD), 292
XmlReader object, 216, 219
Xor method, 89

Get the plain facts on
how to upgrade your code
from Visual Basic 6.0 to Visual Basic .NET
efficiently with proven methods
direct from the source—Microsoft.

Microsoft® Visual Basic® .NET offers remarkable power and flexibility, with richer object models for data, forms, transactions, and more. But you must upgrade your applications—sometimes with major modifications—before they'll compile and run in the Microsoft .NET environment. Get the in-depth technical details you need to upgrade code efficiently to the .NET version with this reference, which is dedicated entirely to the upgrade process. Learn about new functionality in Visual Basic .NET such as inheritance, multithreading, drag-and-drop XML Web services, RAD programmability for servers, the new forms package, and more. Examine side-by-side examples of code in Visual Basic 6.0 and Visual Basic .NET. Learn to evaluate projects to determine which ones can benefit most from an upgrade to Visual Basic .NET and which can function best in a mixed-code environment. Along the way, you'll find out everything you need to take full advantage of the epic shift to Visual Basic .NET.

microsoft.com/mspress

Everything you need to know to develop in
Visual Basic .NET

Building on the success of the earlier version of this popular book, this core reference is designed to equip both beginning and veteran developers with the comprehensive instruction and code details they need to get up to speed in the Web-enabled Microsoft® Visual Basic® .NET environment. The book demonstrates best practices for porting and reusing existing Visual Basic code in the .NET environment, as well as exploiting the object-oriented capabilities of the new version. It includes extensive code samples plus the complete text of the previous edition as well as this book on CD-ROM!

U.S.A. **$59.99**
Canada $86.99
ISBN: 0-7356-1375-3

microsoft.com/mspress

Create
killer applications
using best practices for Visual Basic .NET!

**Practical Standards for
Microsoft® Visual Basic® .NET**
U.S.A. $49.99
Canada $72.99
ISBN: 0-7356-1356-7

The same attributes that make Visual Basic .NET exceptionally productive and easy to use can also lead to unexpected problems, especially when you upgrade. Using standardized programming techniques can help you solve those problems so you can exploit all the power of rapid development—without creating hidden land mines in performance and maintainability. This book shows you proven practices to help you eliminate "voodoo variables," create interfaces that make users more productive, write self-documenting code, simplify code modifications, and more. Each chapter illustrates common pitfalls and practical solutions with code samples—many from real-world projects. Whether you're writing just a few lines of code or working with a team to build an enterprise application, you'll learn how to use practical standards to develop better, more reliable code for every process.

Microsoft®
microsoft.com/mspress